Anders Grath

INTERNATIONAL TRADE FINANCE

The complete guide to risk management, international payments, guarantees, credit insurance and trade finance

UK Edition

The Institute of Export

Printed for The Institute of Export by Nordia Publishing Ltd

The Institute of Export
Export House, Minerva Business Park,
Lynch Wood, Peterborough PE2 6FT
e-mail: institute@export.org.uk
www.export.org.uk

First published in the UK in 2005 by Nordia Publishing Ltd, 17 Newstead Way, London SW19 5HR
www.nordia.co.uk

A CIP record of this book is available from the British Library

ISBN 0 9550721 0 7

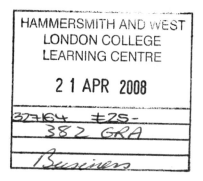
Cover design: Anders Grath and The Institute of Export

Co-edited by Ultimate Proof Publishing Services, Cheltenham:
www.ultimateproof.co.uk

Designed and typeset by
Action Publishing Technology Ltd, Gloucester
www.actiontechnology.co.uk

Printed and bound in Great Britain

Contents

Foreword

The significant growth in world trading and the need to source materials and services between an ever-expanding group of countries around the world brings its own risks. A key issue for many UK suppliers relates to payment and the raising of finance.

There is also clear evidence of a fear in many organisations that payment practices, currencies, exchange rates and the willingness of the general finance market to take risk, makes it all too difficult for many would be international traders – importers or exporters. Such fear is often based on the unknown – and can be countered only by the right knowledge of how to reduce the risks involved in the transaction.

When the author, Anders Grath, first approached The Institute of Export with the idea of creating a new financial handbook for the UK market, based on a concept successfully used for many years in a similar book written for the Swedish Trade Council, we examined what was available on the market. Nowhere could we find a book that was both so comprehensive and easy to use, with a practical approach gained through many years of experience within various European financial institutions.

The ready cooperation of many key players in the UK based international trade finance arena, and the inclusion of their Information Boxes in the book has been particularly pleasing. This cooperation will also facilitate the reader's search for answers to specific questions thus making this book even more beneficial to both the professional and the student.

Jim Sherlock, Director Educational Projects, who has commented on the manuscript throughout its creation and added his knowledgeable advice on both structure and details, has given invaluable support to this project.

I am sure this book will prove an important source of reference and will feature on the required reading list of students of The Institute and other organisations for many years to come. It will also be of significant benefit to all UK international traders, in the daily work of expanding their businesses or entering new global markets.

July 2005   Andy Nemes
                                                 National Chairman,
                                                 The Institute of Export.

Acknowledgement/Disclaimer

The author would like to thank the Institute of Export and the companies, banks and other institutions that have contributed with support, advice and with separate Information Boxes in this book.

However, the author is solely responsible for the views, illustrations, advice and recommendations expressed in this handbook, which are not necessarily those of The Institute of Export or the other institutions contributing with Information Boxes.

While every care has been taken to ensure the accuracy of this work, no responsibility for loss occasioned to any person or company acting or refraining from action as a result of any statement in it can be accepted by the author or publisher.

Introduction

An international trade transaction, no matter how uncomplicated it may seem at the start, is not complete until delivery has taken place, any other obligations have been fulfilled and the seller has received payment. This may seem obvious, however, the fact is that even seemingly simple and straightforward transactions can and sometimes do, go wrong.

These errors usually occur because the buyer is unwilling, or unable, to pay or because the structuring of the financial aspects of the transaction has not been carefully considered prior to agreement. It may be that the seller has agreed to terms that have been used in the past (even if different aspects or risks involved in the transaction have changed) or that the parties have agreed to undefined terms of payment.

Another reason may be that the parties simply have not used the same terminology. This inevitably leads to undefined terms of payment, which are potentially subject to future disputes, something that will perhaps not be revealed until delivery has been made – when the seller is in a weaker bargaining position than the buyer. Even if it is relatively seldom that such errors lead to non-payment, it is more likely that they will lead to delays in payment, possibly with an increased commercial and/or political risk as a consequence.

Another common consequence of unclear or undefined terms of payment is that the seller may have remaining claims on the buyer or that, on the other hand, the buyer feels the same and takes the opportunity to make unilateral payment deductions due to real or alleged faults or deficiencies in the delivery.

IMPORTANT UK TRADE MARKETS, 2004

Country	Export value £ million	Import value £ million
USA	28,467	22,544
Germany	21,501	34,688
France	18,405	19,751
Irish Republic	13,993	10,116
Netherlands	11,947	18,004
Belgium-Luxembourg	10,201	12,701
Spain	9,044	8,764
Italy	8,342	11,992
Sweden	4,326	5,117
Japan	3,784	8,237
Canada	3,335	4,278
Switzerland	2,947	3,574
Hong Kong	2,641	5,894
Australia	2,405	1,897
China	2,378	10,628
India	2,243	2,340
Dubai	2,030	
Denmark	2,020	3,070
Norway	2,011	8,806
South Africa	1,883	3,349

IMPORTANT UK TRADE COMMODITIES, 2004

Commodity	Export value £ million	Import value £ million
Manufacture of electrical, optical, communication & computer equipment.	34,984	49,253
Manufacture of transport equipment.	33,472	43,206
Manufacture of chemicals, chemical products & man-made fibres.	31,710	27,939
Manufacture of machinery & equipment, others	17,312	18,064
Mining & quarrying, incl. crude petroleum and natural gas	14,613	15,241
Manufacture of basic & fabricated metals.	13,159	14,909
Manufacture of food products, beverages & tobacco	9,654	17,674
Manufacture of coke, refined petroleum products and nuclear fuel.	6,993	5,581
Manufacture of textiles & textile products.	5,276	14,786
Manufacture of pulp, paper & paper products; publishing & printing.	5,112	7,394
Agriculture, hunting & forestry	1,187	6,134

Total trade in goods/2004 exports: £189,383 million, imports £250,344 million.

Source:HM Revenue & Customs (HMRC) www.uktradeinfo.com

Each area of international trade requires its own specialised area of expertise, which can include everything from the first contacts between the buyer and the seller to final payment. One specific area of expertise is how to develop professional terms of payment and, if necessary, how to solve the currency and finance-related questions in a competitive way. Both the offer and subsequent contract discussions are areas of vital importance, not only within difficult markets or in larger, more complex deals, but also in quite ordinary transactions.

The choice of currency is of great importance particularly in an increasingly competitive market (not least after the introduction of the Euro), and the ability to extend financing has frequently become a major factor in the negotiations. Even the terms of such credits have changed to the advantage of the buyer and, as a consequence, demand has increased for longer periods and more advantageous terms.

Terms of payment, currency and finance alternatives can in some cases, and/or in similar and repetitive transactions, be developed as standard models but must, in other cases, be adapted to each transaction and its specific preconditions. This is even more obvious if one looks at the chart on the preceding page and evaluates the basic structure of UK international trade.

Regarding UK exports, even if dominated by larger countries in our geographical neighbourhood, there are an additional 100 other countries, including many developing countries and emerging markets, which are not even listed (the same is also applicable to UK imports). The total annual UK export to countries outside OECD amounts to more than £30 billion, with great diversity between countries and commodities (which is not reflected in the chart). In many of these countries the structuring of the terms of payment is the key to more frequent and profitable business.

Every international trade transaction contains many different preconditions, apart from aspects such as the buyer, the country, nature of the goods, size, extent and complexity. This requires the seller to carry out individual assessments and subsequently make decisions that ensure a profitable and secure deal, with a level of risk that is both defined and accepted at the outset and which the seller is prepared to take.

It is thus of great importance, both for the buyer and the seller, to know how to structure practical terms of payment. In practice this often means that during the negotiation process the seller must be willing and able to compromise – even when it comes to specific ques-

Cash management

One important development over recent years has been the demand for capital rationalisation, or 'cash management'. This has affected all aspects of business within the company, not least the sections covered in this handbook. It is especially obvious within the areas of payment, currency and finance, where every decision has direct consequences on the capital required during all phases of the transaction, until payment is received.

This handbook demonstrates primarily how the UK seller can act, within the framework of a defined risk level and with a maintained competitive edge, to optimise the profitability of export transactions. They could then also determine, with a high degree of accuracy, when, where and how payments will be made and, thereby, how to minimize the capital required. The concept of risk is directly connected to the probability for timely payment, the choice of currency related to the exchange rate when paid and the financing connected to the cost of the outstanding credit. Even the UK importer will use the same knowledge, but from their own perspective.

Even if the expression 'cash management' is relatively seldom used in the text, most sections contain comments or advice that, directly or indirectly, has a bearing on the use and latent risk of capital. With this in mind, this handbook could be read as a manual for improved cash management in connection with international trade (this is explained more in the final chapter about the practical structure and design of the terms of payment).

tions related to guarantees, payments, currency and financing. In these situations, and often together with other difficult negotiations, it is important to understand the connections between these parts, what is essential to hold on to and what can be waived.

Any successful negotiation must take reasonable and equal consideration of the demands from both commercial parties in order to avoid unnecessary discussions or misunderstandings. The experienced seller will always try to avoid such situations, thereby also strengthening the potential for future business transactions, providing fundamental demands have been met to safeguard the transaction.

This handbook should be used as a reference manual in the practical day-to-day business of the exporting company, within the sales and shipping departments, administration and back-office. For small and medium-sized companies that do not always have the specialist finance functions in-house this is obvious. But this will also be the case even within the largest companies, where specialisation often means that many employees have detailed knowledge in some, but not all, financial areas. This handbook has been used in countries outside the UK for over 20 years and it has been used in exactly this way.

However, it can also be used within all purchasing departments buying goods or services from abroad. Many comments have also been made about the advantages in describing, in practical detail, the interactive negotiating process between the commercial parties in an international trade transaction, useful knowledge for both the seller and the buyer.

Finally, it is equally important to stress that the subjects within a financial handbook of this nature are constantly changing. It is therefore, important that the reader is aware that some details may change after publication and should ensure they are kept informed about the latest developments by other means. This could for example be done through bank specialists or organisations, institutions and companies participating in this handbook.

INFORMATION BOX

THE INSTITUTE OF

EXPORT

Exporting excellence through education

The Institute of Export was established in 1935 and enjoys the Royal patronage of HRH the Duke of Kent. We are incorporated as a Registered Charity and our mission is to enhance the export performance of the United Kingdom by setting and raising professional standards in international trade management and export practice. We strive to achieve this principally by the provision of education and training programmes.

Primarily comprised of individual members, The Institute also has an increasing Business & Corporate Membership and a growing list of services and benefits designed to meet the various needs of all membership categories.

Dedicated to professionalism and recognising the challenging and often complex trading conditions in international markets, we believe that real competitive advantage lies in competence and that commercial success, especially in the international arena, is underpinned by a sound basis of knowledge.

The Institute of Export is the only professional body in the UK offering recognised, formal qualifications in International Trade. Our professional qualifications, achieved by examination, lead to the award of the Diploma in International Trade, which confers Graduate Membership of The Institute and the entitlement to use the suffix **MIEx (Grad).**

Full membership of The Institute of Export provides an unrivalled and highly relevant portfolio of benefits for today's international trade professionals.

For more details of our programmes, membership or other services, call 01733 404400 or e-mail: institute@export.org.uk

The Institute of Export
Export House, Minerva Business Park, Lynch Wood,
Peterborough PE2 6FT

www.export.org.uk

The main composition of this handbook

This handbook is intended to be a practical reference guide to help in the daily work in the company — mainly seen from the perspective of the UK seller — within sales, shipping and administration. The contents have, therefore, been structured as follows:

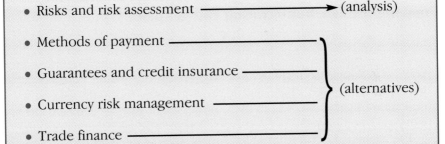

- Risks and risk assessment ⟶ (analysis)

- Methods of payment

- Guarantees and credit insurance

- Currency risk management

- Trade finance

} (alternatives)

- Structure and design of practical
  terms of payment ⟶ (action)

To get a clearer practical picture of the focus of this handbook, please also consider the following statement before browsing through the following two pages.

From the UK seller's perspective ...

Why are some companies doing more frequent and successful export deals than others ...?

... it is because they manage to cover even the most difficult export risks — only then are you in the best position to enter totally new markets.

Sell more — win market shares — enter new markets. Who doesn't want that? ... but the problem is often not making the sale but ensuring you get paid.

Why do things sometimes go wrong in the export chain, from quotation to payment — or in the worst-case non-payment?

The answer is that the seller often underestimates, or simply does not fully understand, the risks involved in the transaction.

Or the seller does not get the terms of payment originally anticipated and, at that stage, does not manage to cover the transaction in some other way — or even abstains from the deal altogether.

Basically it is a matter of learning how to cover the trade risks in a professional way — allowing the seller to manage transactions in most parts of the world.

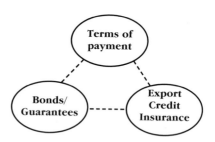

Expanding exports into new markets can be very profitable – if you can control the risks.

This handbook shows how it is done!

... however, the follow-up must also be done professionally at home.

What is needed is an effective handling of the transaction until shipment — and thereafter, effective debt supervision. Time is money — look at the time arrow below.

The follow-up starts immediately after the contract is signed. It can be a forward currency hedge, the issuing of guarantees, communication with the insurance company about an export credit risk policy or the follow-up of the obligations of the buyer, for example, the correct issue of a Letter of Credit.

To end up in the grey area of the time arrow below is always risky, there the seller is more exposed — the goods are shipped but payment is not received in time.

Worst of all, if pre-shipment control is not in place, even the most secure Letter of Credit can be worthless if the seller is not able to fully comply with its terms later on.

It is often the case that the sales person establishes the foundations for a profitable transaction far away from the home organisation. It is always harder to get changes made after agreement — not least regarding the terms of payment.

The follow-up is crucial and will ultimately decide the profitability of the transaction.

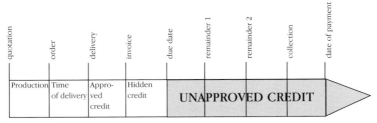

| | quotation | order | delivery | invoice | due date | remainder 1 | remainder 2 | collection | date of payment |

| Production | Time of delivery | Appro-ved credit | Hidden credit | UNAPPROVED CREDIT |

By shortening the time arrow within each segment, the risk situation can be improved – in the same way as liquidity and profitability.

INFORMATION BOX

UK Trade & Investment — Your business partner

UK Trade & Investment is the government organisation that supports both companies in the UK trading internationally and overseas enterprises seeking to locate in the UK. Known previously as Trade Partners UK and Invest UK, our new single identity signifies our continued commitment to meet the needs of companies operating worldwide. Our teams are based in over 200 locations around the world, and across a regional network that provides local knowledge around the UK. Our close links with both the commercial and public sectors enables us to provide fast and authoritative advice to every type of business.

Whether you are exporting for the first time or expanding into new markets, you need to be supported by expert advice, reliable data and professional research. That is where UK Trade & Investment can help, providing specialist, impartial and dependable business assistance, all from a single source.

Our services are concentrated to the following areas:

- **Information**. Our databases give comprehensive and detailed export advice and related services provided by UK Trade & Investment and other Government departments and organisations, but also links to other export related institutions.
- **Business opportunities.** Our UK Suppliers Database for international buyers, our internet-based Sales Leads Services for free export sales enquiries and information on private/public tenders; and our Export Promoter Initiative for expert secondments from private industry are all parts of our efforts to support UK exports (see also Chapter 7, Box 7.4).
- **Market Promotions.** We provide support for participants in overseas exhibitions; sector focused missions and seminars and for business visits through our Outward Missions programmes. Our Events Database provides a searchable list of all our events.
- **Training and support.** 'UK Trade & Investment — your passport to export success' is our flagship assessment and skills-based programme that provides new and inexperienced exporters with the training, planning and ongoing support they need to succeed overseas.

UK Trade & Investment Enquiry Service
Kingsgate House, 66-74 Victoria Street, London SW1E 6SW
Telephone 020 7215 8000   www.uktradeinvest.gov.uk

1
Trade risks and risk assessment

➤ 1.1 International trade practices

All forms of business contain risk elements, but when it comes to international trade, the risk profile gets a new dimension. Internationally, you seldom have common laws that can support the transaction, as would be the case within one country. Instead, established trade practices and conventions are used to settle the undertakings made by the parties. The key to successful trade transactions, therefore, depends on a knowledge of these established practices and ensuring that the undertakings in the individual contract are in line with such practices. This is why it is crucial for the seller to have started with a correct risk assessment before finally entering into the transaction.

The main sources for international trade practices are publications issued by the International Chamber of Commerce (ICC), which will be referred to many times throughout this book.

In every new transaction one has to take for granted that, from the outset, both parties will often have different views about various aspects of the terms of payment. This is quite logical since the most important function of the terms of payment for both the seller and the buyer is to minimise not only the risks involved, but also the cost for payment and for the financing of the transaction.

■ *1.1.1 The negotiation process*

The seller will always try to get the terms that will maximise the outcome and minimise the risk. However, they must also be prepared to accommodate reasonable demands from the buyer in order to match other competitors and reach a deal that is acceptable for both parties, thereby also developing a good long-term business relationship.

Should the seller be inflexible on this point, it could result in an adverse competitive situation with the potential risk of losing the deal. On the other hand, too stringent demands from the buyer can have the same result, or result in a higher price or some other amendment to the final agreement.

The final outcome of these negotiations will be dependent on past knowledge and experience, which is even more important if the buyer bases his request for tender on simplified or standardised terms of payment. In many cases, such terms are adapted to conditions that are not optimal for the seller, compared with what the seller could have reached if they were individually negotiated. In such a case it is important to be able to argue and convince the buyer that there might be other solutions that can satisfy any reasonable demands.

■ *1.1.2 Different forms of trade risk*

Box 1.1 shows the main risk structure in international trade, which will affect both the seller's and the buyer's view on the terms of payment. Obviously the combination of all these risks does not often exist in one and the same transaction. For example, a sale to a Norwegian customer in GBP may only be a matter of a straight commercial risk on the buyer, whereas delivery of a tailor-made machine to Egypt has to be risk assessed in quite another way.

In quite general terms, the risk structure is directly linked to the obligations undertaken by the seller. The assessment can often be made relatively simple as a commercial risk only but, in other cases, for example if the transaction also involves assembly, installation, testing

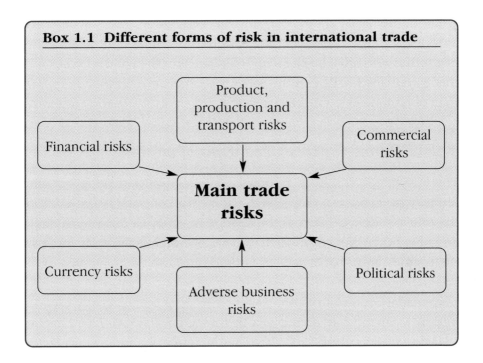

Box 1.1 Different forms of risk in international trade

Product, production and transport risks

Financial risks

Commercial risks

Main trade risks

Currency risks

Adverse business risks

Political risks

or a maintenance responsibility, the assessment has to involve many other aspects as well.

Finally, the question of risk is to a high degree a subjective evaluation, but it is still important for all parties to have good knowledge about these matters in order to be able to do a proper risk assessment. Only thereafter does the question arise for the seller about how to cover these risks through the terms of payment together with other limitations in the contract, if applicable, and together with separate credit insurance or guarantees, as the case may be.

It should also be noted that most export credit insurance, taken by the seller as additional security, could be impaired or even invalid should the seller not have fulfilled – or been able to fulfil – the obligations according to the contract. This is another reason why it is so important that the obligations of the seller according to the contract are always directly related to those of the buyer. Otherwise the seller may end up in a risk situation that is worse than anticipated at the time of entering into the contract.

When all the necessary evaluations have been done, the final decision as to whether the deal is secure enough to be entered into, has to be taken. The worst that can happen is finding after the contract is signed, that it contained risks that the seller was unaware of at that time. It is then often too late to make changes.

■ 1.1.3 Terms of delivery and terms of payment

This handbook describes in detail the structure and design of the terms of payment as an integrated part of the contract. However, also the terms of delivery have to be defined in order to determine when and where the seller has fulfilled the obligations to deliver according to the contract and what is needed in order to do so.

The standard rules of references for delivery of goods mostly used in international trade are *Incoterms 2000*, issued by the ICC. They contain 13 defined terms of delivery with different levels of duties for the seller and the buyer, for example, who should pay the freight, other transport charges and insurance, duties and taxes in the importing country and at what point the risk is transferred from the seller to the buyer.

Some terms of delivery should only be used in connection with sea transport whereas others can be used for all modes of transport. Some are more suited in combination with terms of payment based on 'clean payments' and others in combination with 'documentary payments'. (These expressions are defined in *Chapter 2, Methods of payment*).

When choosing the appropriate terms of delivery, deciding factors include:

- the transportation route and the nature of the goods;
- the buyer and their country;
- the terms of payment.

For a standard delivery within Europe this question may be easily agreed, often with only a small adjustment related to the cost of freight and insurance. When it comes to larger or more complicated transactions, longer transport routes along with increased commercial or

INFORMATION BOX

International Chamber of Commerce

The world business organisation

The International Chamber of Commerce is the world's only truly global business organisation. Based in Paris, its core services/activities are as follows:

- The voice of international business.
- Practical services to business.
- The fight against commercial crime.
- Advocate for international business.
- Spreading business expertise.
- Promoting growth and prosperity.
- Setting rules and standards.
- Promotor of the multilateral trading system.

ICC has direct access to national governments all over the world through its national committees, shaping ICC policies and alerting their governments to international business concerns. ICC United Kingdom is such a national committee, comprising leading companies and business associations and should be contacted by UK companies and business associations interested in joining.

**ICC United Kingdom,
12 Grosvenor Place, London SW1X 7HH
Telephone: 020 7838 9363
www.iccuk.net**

political risks it is often advantageous for the seller to control the various transport and insurance aspects of the transaction, in order to be able to comply with the overall performance obligations.

For guidance only, terms of delivery with the least obligation for the seller, for example:

- Ex Works (EXW)
- Free Carrier (FCA)
- Free on Board (FOB)

are mostly used in connection with clean payments after delivery, often within Europe.

However, the two latter terms (FCA/FOB) are also used in conjunction with documentary payments, even though it is then more common to use delivery terms 'C' (including freight charges) or 'D' (including freight charges, but also with the risk for the seller up to the final destination). These terms are particularly common when the seller wants to have control over the delivery process (which will be explained in more detail in Chapter 2), for example:

- Cost and Freight (CFR)
- Carriage Paid to … (CPT)
- Cost Insurance and Freight (CIF)
- Carriage and Insurance Paid to … (CIP)
- Delivered Duty Unpaid (DDU)
- Delivered Duty Paid (DDP)

DDU and DDP are also used within Europe in connection with terms of payments based on clean payments.

More information about the terms of delivery and its definitions can be found in the present ICC rules, *Incoterms 2000*, which can be ordered directly from ICC United Kingdom.

➢ 1.2 Product risks

Product risks are risks that the seller automatically has to bear as an integral part of their commitment. Firstly, it is a matter of the product itself, or the agreed delivery, for example, specified performance or agreed maintenance or service obligations.

There are many examples of how new and unexpected working conditions in the buyer's country have led to reduced performance of the delivered goods. It can be careless treatment, lack of current maintenance, but also damp, rust or sand damages due to a new climatological environment.

Matters of this nature may inevitably lead to disagreements between the parties after the contract has been signed and to increased cost for the delivery as a whole. It is important for the seller to have the contract, and specifically the terms of payment, worded in such a way that any such changes or modifications, which are directly or indirectly due to actions of the buyer or their country, will automatically include compensation or corresponding changes in the commitments by the seller. This can be either in economic terms or in originally agreed time limits, or both.

It goes without saying that these risks become even more complicated when it comes to whole projects or larger and more complex contracts. These are often completed during longer periods and involve many more possible combinations of inter-related commitments between the commercial parties, not only between the seller and the buyer, but often also involving other parties in the buyer's country, both commercial and political.

■ 1.2.1 Manufacturing risks

The concept of product risk could also include some elements of the manufacturing process itself, even if that in principle falls beyond the scope of this handbook. This risk appears all too frequently when the product is tailor-made or has unique specifications. In these cases there is often no other ready available buyer if the transaction cannot be completed, in which case the seller has to carry the cost for any necessary readjustment.

These manufacturing risks arise from the product planning phase and have to be covered from then – which must be reflected in the terms of payment together with additional coverage, for example credit risk insurance covering this production phase.

■ *1.2.2 Transport risks*

The seller should be very clear as to where the transfer of risk to the buyer takes place according to the agreed terms of delivery. There have been many incidences where the seller has defaulted in the delivery obligations due to unexpected or unknown circumstances or events related to transportation risks.

From a risk point of view it is not only the product but also the physical transportation route that has to be evaluated. The proposed and agreed terms of delivery will at any time during the delivery process determine if it is the seller or the buyer that has to carry the costs and the risks involved. The seller should be observant on where the responsibility for the risks of loss or damage of goods in transit is transferred to the buyer according to the agreed terms of delivery.

The transport risks are almost always possible to insure, even if it may involve additional costs for the seller. Take, for example, the situation where the transport insurance has to be covered by the buyer, but according to the terms of payment the goods are to be paid after shipment. What happens if the buyer does not pay, or even fulfil his duty to insure the goods? But the seller should then also have considered taking additional (subsidiary) transport insurance, to cover the event of non-insurance by the buyer, if it was not possible to get other terms of delivery more suited to the risks involved.

The seller should also bear in mind that cargo insurance is a specialised business. Cover and conditions will vary according to the commodity or goods that are being transported – some will be inherently difficult or dangerous to transport – and the method of transport. Normal risk management procedures will always apply – the policy may, for example, not pay out if the goods have been packaged or transported inappropriately.

The seller should generally try to avoid transport risks and costs for the part of the transportation route, which they cannot safely judge. Apart from neighbouring or well-known countries, the seller should normally try to avoid being involved in transport within the buyer's country,

INFORMATION BOX

SITPRO
Simplifying International Trade

SITPRO Limited was set up in 1970 as the UK's trade facilitation organisation. It is one of the Non-Departmental Public Bodies for which the Department of Trade and Industry has responsibility and is funded by a grant-in-aid from the Department. SITPRO is dedicated to encouraging and helping business trade more effectively and to simplify the international trading process. Its focus is the procedures and documentation associated with international trade.

SITPRO's mission is to use its unique status to improve the competitive position of UK traders by facilitating change through:

- identification and removal of barriers in the international trading process;
- identification and promotion of best trading practices;
- delivering a repository based on internationally agreed standards to facilitate electronic business transactions in international trade
- influencing future trade policy related to international trade.

SITPRO offers a wide range of services including a trade procedures helpline. Its website (www.sitpro.org.uk) includes briefings and checklists covering international trading practices, answers to frequently asked questions and information about SITPRO's policy work. It also publishes a free newsletter, SITPRO News.

SITPRO manages the UK Aligned System of Export Documents, and licenses the printers and software suppliers who sell the forms and export document software. Building on this it has developed UNeDocsUK as a national extension of the standards-based repository, UNeDocs, established in partnership with the UN. This brings together paper, EDI & XML, to facilitate electronic business transactions in international trade.

For further information contact:
SITPRO Ltd
8th Floor, Oxford House, 76 Oxford Street, London W1D 1BS
Tel: 020 7467 7280 Email: info@sitpro.org.uk
www.sitpro.org.uk

unless they can be transferred to a shipping or forwarding agent. It is therefore often wise to use a broker for placing cargo risks for more difficult transport routes or goods involved. A specialist may then also be able to provide additional cover in such cases.

➤ 1.3 Commercial risks (purchaser risks)

Commercial risk, sometimes also called purchaser risk, is often defined as the risk of the buyer going into bankruptcy or being in any other way incapable of fulfilling the contractual obligations. One might firstly think of the buyer's payment obligations but, as seen above, it also covers all other obligations of the buyer according to the contract, necessary for the seller to fulfil their obligations.

How does the seller, therefore, evaluate the buyer's ability to fulfil their obligations? In Western Europe, as in most countries within the Organisation for Economic Co-operation and Development (OECD) area, it is relatively easy to obtain a fair picture about potential buyers, either to study their published accounts or to ask for an independent business credit report, which is a much more reliable way to deal with customer risks. This will also give much broader information about the buyer and their business, and not just some selected economical figures, from which the seller cannot often draw any decisive conclusions.

■ 1.3.1 Credit information

Information about potential foreign counterparts can be obtained from a number of independent providers of business information in the UK, who either have their own offices in different countries or operate through correspondents or affiliated companies around the world. Such credit reports can be provided on a case-by-case basis or be a part of a broader risk management solution, offered by the larger multinational business information companies, who keep huge databases of customers from all over the world.

In one way or another, each seller must have a policy for obtaining up-to-date information about the commercial risk structure, both in

Box 1.2   Global providers of international credit reports

Export trade may be an important factor in the potential growth of business, however, the risks involved in carrying out international business can also be very high. In little more than a decade, the world of commerce has changed dramatically. In this commercial environment, the global suppliers of credit information have become a vital source of knowledge and expertise, based on the great wealth of information that they maintain about consumers and how they behave, about businesses and how they perform, and about different markets and how they are changing.

The more the seller understands its customers, the more they are able to respond to their individual needs and circumstances. Credit information suppliers help the seller use information to reach new customers and to build, nurture and maximise lasting customer relationships. Credit information thus forms a vital part of establishing the structure of a potential export transaction and in particular, the terms of payment to be used, and it is advantageous to compare service and price from some global providers in relation to the seller's needs. Sometimes the information can be provided instantly, inexpensively and standardised on the Internet, where in other cases a more researched profile is required.

Some of the global providers of credit information include:

Coface – the world's largest export insurance group, described in *Chapter 5*. Apart from insurance, Coface also specialises in providing global credit information on companies worldwide, allowing the seller to make informed decisions about trading on credit terms. **www.coface.com**

D&B – (formerly Dun & Bradstreet), one of the largest providers of business information for credit, marketing and purchasing decisions worldwide. Their Business Information Reports help the seller make daily credit decisions, analyse the financial strength of a company, and discover business opportunities. **www.dnb.com**

connection with any new potential buyer or business and with outstanding export receivables. How this is done may differ depending on the volume and structure of the exports, but it is recommended to at least review the business information systems offered by the larger providers and to choose an alternative that is optimal for the individual seller as to the services and costs involved.

The seller should, however, be aware that the contents and accuracy of the business information can vary, dependent on the available registered information about the company. The contents can sometimes also be difficult to evaluate and questions always arise about how up-to-date it really is, particularly when dealing with customers outside the most advanced industrialised countries.

Regarding buyers from non-OECD countries the matter becomes even more complicated. The information will be much more difficult to evaluate and it will be harder to assess how it has been produced and how it should be analysed. In these cases, the information probably has a limited value anyway, because other risk factors, such as the political risk, may also be greater – and terms of payment have to be chosen that reflect this combined risk.

The seller may also be able to get assistance abroad through UK Trade & Investment (see separate Information Box in the Introduction,) and the commercial sections of our embassies abroad, which can assist with market surveys and other studies in that country. Even banks can participate by issuing introductory letters to their branches or correspondents, enabling the seller to get more up-to-date information from that bank about the local business conditions and form an opinion about the buyer and their business in connection with the contract negotiations.

➤ 1.4 Adverse business risks

Adverse business risks include all business practices of a negative nature, which are not only common but also almost endemic in some parts of the world. This could have serious consequences on the individual transaction, but also on the general business and the financial standing of the seller, as well as their moral reputation.

Having said that we are, of course, referring to all sorts of corrupt practices that flourish in many countries, particularly in connection with larger contracts or projects; bribery, money laundering and a variety of facilitation payments.

'Bribery in general can broadly be defined as the receiving or offering of an undue reward by or to any holder of public office or a private employee designed to influence them in the exercise of their duty, and thus to incline them to act contrary to the known rules of honesty and integrity.'

The above quotation is taken from UK Trade and Investment, the government trade-supporting organisation, even if it is not a legal definition.

If bribery in general is a technique to press the seller for undue rewards, money laundering often has the opposite purpose, that is to invite the seller to do a deal that may on the face of it seem very advantageous, but where the true intention is to disguise or conceal the actual origin of the money involved.

Money laundering is a process through which the proceeds of criminal activity are disguised to conceal their actual origins. It covers criminal activities, corruption and breaches of financial sanctions. It includes the handling, or aiding the handling of assets, knowing that they are the result of crime, terrorism or illegal drug activities.

Criminal and terrorist organisations generate a lot of physical cash, which they need to channel into the banking, corporate and trade financial systems, and both banks and traders can innocently fall victim of such activity if not exercising due diligence.

An often used technique is over-invoicing or inflated transactions with or without payment to a third party, where the seller may be completely unaware that they could be part of a ruse to launder money. The seller should also be particularly observant in case of cash payments. If cash payments of EUR15,000 (about £10,000), or more for any single transaction are involved, irrespective of currency, new anti-money laundering regulations must be complied with.

A reputable business adds respectability to any organisation being used for laundering operations, and money launderers will try to use any business, directly through ownership, or indirectly by deceit. A British government report in 2000 stated that almost all big money-laundering operations in Britain involved shell companies, and new rules are now in place in most countries where among others those companies whose shares are not publicly traded must identify their beneficial owners. Developing nations are particularly vulnerable to money launderers because they usually have less well regulated financial systems. These provide the greatest opportunities to criminals.

In general terms, a suspicious transaction is one that is outside of the normal range of transactions from the seller's point of view, in particular in relation to new customers or where an old customer changes transaction structure in an unusual way. It can include:

- unusual payment settlement;
- unusual transfer instructions;
- secretiveness;
- rapid movements in and out of accounts;
- numerous transfers;
- complicated accounts structures.

Any and all of the above should be considered suspicious.

Bribery, money laundering and any other form of corrupt behaviour is bad for business; it distorts the normal trade patterns and gives unfair advantages to those involved in it. It is also extremely harmful for the countries themselves, due to the damage it causes to the often fragile social fabric; it destroys the economy and is strongly counterproductive on trade and all forms of foreign investments into the country.

In the long run, such practices also prevent social and economic stability and development, and it has an especially negative impact on the most disadvantaged parts of the population. Even within the countries where these practices are frequent among individual public and private employees, it is almost always illegal, even if the countries lack the means and the resources to tackle these problems effectively.

■ 1.4.1 The need for a strong policy

The World Bank and the OECD have put a lot of resources into combating corruption worldwide, and in all industrialized countries corruption is now illegal. That is, of course, particularly the case for the UK, and today both UK registered companies as well as nationals can be prosecuted under the Anti-terrorism, Crime and Security Act and under special UK money laundering regulations for bribery, money laundering and other corrupt behaviour committed overseas. The companies also have full responsibility for the wrongdoings of their employees in their act of duty for the company.

As a consequence of the inclusion of anti-corruption laws in the UK, it is incorporated in the procedures of all government departments, for example, in the rules for the Export Credits Guarantee Department (ECGD), the UK's official export credit agency, which will be described in length later in this book. Any violation of the anti-corruption state-ment that the seller has to give when applying for export credit risk insurance could have serious implications on its validity.

It is often not even the threat of prosecution that should most worry the seller. There have been a number of cases in which companies were allegedly involved in corrupt behaviour, but where the true circum-stances were not fully disclosed. The allegation could be bad enough, sometimes based only on rumours emanating from economic groups or political factions within the society (a frequently used method) to stop or postpone a project or give favour to another bidder.

Such rumours, true or false, or involving either smaller facilitation payments or large scale bribery to senior private or public officials, can drag on for years, with economic and detrimental consequences for the company, both overseas and at home.

Every UK company involved in overseas trade or investments should have a clear anti-corruption policy that is implemented and clearly understood by all its employees, and supervised by the management in an appropriate way. Such a policy is also supported by new UK laws, which give both the companies and its employees a much stronger moral and legal defence against every attempt to extort bribes from them or attempt to induce them in any other form of corrupt practice.

➢ 1.5 Political risks

Political risk or country risk is often defined as:

'The risk of a separate commercial transaction not being realized in a contractual way due to measures emanating from the government or authority of the buyer's own or any other foreign country.'

No matter how reliable the buyer may be in fulfilling their obligations and paying in local currency, their obligations towards the seller (according to the contract) is nevertheless dependent on the current situation in their own country – or along the route of transport to that country.

However, in practice, it may be difficult to separate what is a commercial or political risk because political decisions or other similar acts by local authorities also affect the local company and its capabilities of honouring the contract. For example, some countries may change taxes, import duties or currency regulations often with immediate effect, which could undermine the basis for contracts already signed.

Other common measures include import restrictions or other regulations intended to promote local industry and to save foreign currency. Even with just the risks of such actions, they all have the same negative implications on the transaction and the buyer's possibility of fulfilling their part of the contract.

Seen from a broader perspective, political risk could be divided into different underlying causes, such as:

- political stability;
- social stability; and
- economic stability.

Political stability (ie, local political structures and ideology combined with external relations to other countries) is often seen as important criteria of the real political risk. This stability indicates, in general terms, the likelihood or the probability of a country's involvement in, or being affected by acts of terror, war or internal violence from groupings within the country or sanctions or blockades from other nations.

The constant risk of rapid and unexpected change in the economic policy or in the form of nationalisations or similar measures as a consequence of this political instability will also have the same effect; they are all extremely damaging for any private commercial economic activity in the country. Unfortunately, there are presently numerous examples of this political instability in many parts of the world.

The **social stability** of a country is also of great importance, mainly on a long-term basis. However, the development in many counties, not only developing countries, show all too well how unexpectedly and rapidly a social instability (uneven income distribution and ethnic or religious antagonism) can turn into violence or terror activity that can paralyse the country or its economy.

Economic stability is equally important to maintain the confidence of a country and its economy. A weak infrastructure, dependence on single export or import commodities, a high debt burden and lack of raw materials are critical factors that, together with other developments, can easily change the economic stability in a short time. Even currency restrictions and other more indirect currency regulations such as 'pegging' against other currencies, often USD, could have long-term disastrous economic consequences – as seen in some South American countries.

The turbulent situation in many developing countries is a constant reminder of the fragility of economic stability in many countries around the world.

■ *1.5.1 Other forms of political or similar risk*

Apart from the real political risks already discussed, there are other measures taken by authorities in the buyer's home country that can affect the buyer and their possibility or willingness to fulfil the transaction. For example, demands for product standards, new or changed energy, or environment requirements – measures that could have a genuine purpose or be put in place partly to act as trade barriers to promote sectors or important industries within the country. Irrespective of the purpose, such actions, often called 'Non-tariff barriers', could have a negative impact on the signed transaction.

The risks covered so far have been related to the buyer's country, but even countries involved in transit of the goods have to be considered as well as counties related to sub-contractors or suppliers of crucial components. In these cases, perhaps it is not the political risk as defined, but other measures that are more important. For example, the risk of labour market conflicts in the form of strikes or lockout that could interrupt delivery of components needed for the timely execution of the agreed sales contract.

Not least the risk involved in ordinary *force-majeure* clauses should be mentioned, even if the background need not be political but is caused by many other different factors, outside the control of the commercial parties themselves. When used by other parties, such clauses could for example release a sub-contractor from their delivery obligations during the periods they are applicable, with corresponding effects for the seller. And even bank guarantees and other obligations could be of limited value during such periods if, as is normally the case, they only cover commitments according to the contract.

However, when used by the seller, such clauses could protect them against actions for breach of contract, where performance of their contractual obligations is prevented by incidents outside their control. In English law this is described as 'frustration of contract' and a typical clause might say:

'The Company shall have no liability in respect of any failure or delay

in fulfilling any of the Company's obligations to the extent that fulfilment thereof is prevented, frustrated, impeded and/or delayed or
rendered uneconomic as a consequence of any fire, flood, earthquake,
other natural disaster or Act of God, industrial dispute or other circumstances or event beyond the Company's reasonable control ('*force
majeure* conditions').'

■ 1.5.2 Information about political risks

The development of political risks has been rather gloomy during past
years, not least in some Asian, Middle East and African countries. In
fact, in many countries outside the OECD-area, the political instability
and/or the currency situation has been so uncertain that political risks
are a major problem for most sellers exporting to these countries or
regions.

The seller is always advised to use the expertise and knowledge that is
available, for example, within the major banks, UK Trade & Investment
(*see* Chapter 8, Box 8.2) or ECGD, but also from some of the main
private credit insurers, for example, Coface with their country rating
experience on the website www.trading-safely.com (for more info
about Coface, see Information Box in Chapter 5). Country information
can also be bought from specialised agencies whose core business is to
analyse and evaluate political risks in different countries.

Such agency information often contains a more commercially oriented
business analyses on countries or regions (ie, evaluations that the individual seller or investor can use for the business area or in connection
with establishing local subsidiaries, project or investments).

➢ 1.6 Currency risks

If payment is going to be made in a currency other than that in which the
seller has their costs, a new currency risk will arise. In most cases in the
UK, the seller's costs will be in GBP, which automatically creates such a
risk if invoicing in another currency. The size of that risk will mainly
depend upon the currency and the outstanding period until payment.

Since the introduction of the Euro, invoicing in that currency has become increasingly common in European trade with sellers outside the Euro-zone. This development is likely to accelerate with additional EU-countries.

Traditionally, GBP has also been used in sales outside Europe, not only to the Commonwealth countries but the USD is now dominantly the preferred third party currency. That applies particularly for raw materials and certain commodities in general, and for many other services such as freight and insurance. It is also commonly used in countries where the US maintains a strong economic or political influence.

UK statistics do not show currency distribution for international trade of goods and services, but it can generally be expected that exports invoiced in GBP are diminishing, and will probably continue to do so. UK suppliers will therefore have to get increasingly used to invoicing in other currencies and in the management of currency risk exposure.

■ 1.6.1 Assessment of currencies

Traditionally, currencies have been divided into groups of 'strong' or 'weak', and this view has affected the general conception of strong or weak trade currencies, even though the highest preference is often for the currency of the home country. GBP, EUR and CHF and maybe some others would probably be regarded as strong currencies, while others would be seen as weak, neutral or unstable.

An evaluation such as this may perhaps have its justification in a longer perspective for currencies where the home countries have maintained economical and political stability over the years, together with a strong economy, low inflation and a stable confidence in the future maintenance of this policy.

It could, on the other hand, be enough to look at the development of the USD, which has changed its value towards other large currencies dramatically during the lasts years (and often quite rapidly), to realise that such sweeping statements can have its risks.

Box 1.3   Currency abbreviations

The International Organization for Standardization (ISO) has established official abbreviations for all currencies, which are now commonly used. The abbreviations for some of the most common currencies are as follows:

Pound Sterling	**GBP**
Euro	**EUR**
US Dollar	**USD**
Swiss Franc	**CHF**
Canadian Dollar	**CAD**
Japanese Yen	**JPY**
Chinese Yuan-Renminby	**CNY**
Swedish Krona	**SEK**
Danish Krona	**DKK**

The abbreviations of other currencies can be obtained from the banks but can also be found on ISO's website **www.iso.org**

For most parties it is not the long-term currency development that is most interesting, but rather the shorter perspective, limited to the time-span during which current deals shall be paid. In which case, the situation can be reversed, for in that shorter perspective, a currency can have a development in complete contrast to its long-term trend.

In the shorter perspective, other factors, real or expected, may be more important, such as interest rates development, political news and larger price changes in base commodities, central bank currency interventions, statements and statistics. All these factors, combined with subjective evaluations by millions of participants in the currency markets, will together create constantly new short-term trends. This disparity between long and short currency trends is well illustrated in *Figure 1.1*.

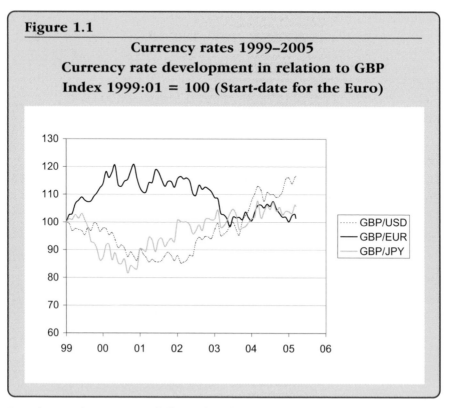

Figure 1.1

Currency rates 1999–2005

Currency rate development in relation to GBP

Index 1999:01 = 100 (Start-date for the Euro)

For those who want to follow the short-term currency development, most banks publicise information via the Internet or e-mail – both retrospectively and with analysis and evaluations about future trends.

➢ 1.7 Financial risks

In practice, every international trade transaction contains at least a certain element of financial risk. Purchasing, production and shipment also contain a financial burden on the transaction that forces the seller to determine how alternative terms of payment would affect the liquidity during its different phases until payment – and how this should be financed. And if the deal is not settled as intended, an additional financial risk has occurred. In the case of sub-contractors, who do not share the risks of the transaction and are paid according to separate agreements, the risk increases accordingly and even more so in case the seller has to offer a supplier credit for a shorter or longer period.

In particular, when it comes to larger and more complex transactions, this financial risk aspect can be seen more clearly. One of the major problems for the seller could be to obtain bankable collateral for the increased need of finance and guarantees. Even after production and delivery, the seller could still be financially exposed in case of unforeseen events and delays until final payment.

Sometimes the interaction between the seller and the buyer can make it difficult to establish the exact cause for the delay in payment and there are then fewer chances for the seller to refer to a specific breach of contract on behalf of the buyer. On the other hand, if the seller has given enough attention when drafting the contract, including the terms of payment, then it is more likely that any reason for delays will be possible to determine according to the clauses of the contract. There could be numerous reasons for such delays, for example, issuing a Letter of Credit too late; late changes in specification of the goods; late arrival of the vessel; congestion in port; changes in the route of transport, etc.

The real risk also tends to increase with longer and consequently more costly transport distances. Even systematic bureaucratic delays in many countries, as well as delays in the banking system, will have the same results – the final payment to the seller will not be made as anticipated according to the contract.

Apart from ordinary overdrafts during the time of production and delivery, the need for finance is also determined by the supplier credit the seller may have to offer as part of the deal. If so, the financial risk is increased in line with the prolonged commercial and/or political risks.

■ *1.7.1 Financial risk and cash management*

Other forms of financial risk are more obvious but have to be underlined in this context, for example, if the seller misjudges the risks involved in the transaction and becomes exposed through terms of payment that do not cover the real risk situation. Or, mistakenly entering into the deal without proper risk protection – it goes without

saying that such miscalculations can have serious financial consequences, from delays in payment to loss of capital.

The financial risks are generally intimately connected to the structure
of the terms of payment. The safer they can be made, the more the
financial risk will automatically be reduced, the timing of the payments
can be more accurate and the liquidity aspect of the transaction better
assessed – in fact, the very essence of cash management.

The safer the terms of payment the parties have agreed upon, the more
costly they will normally be. And, if they also contain bank security,
such as a Letter of Credit or a bank guarantee, that will also reduce
available credit limits within the buyer's own bank.

However, the buyer is often not prepared to take the higher costs and
the use of their own credit limits in order to satisfy what might be seen
as excessive demands from the seller, involving methods of payments,
which in their opinion, are not normal practice in their country or
normally accepted by the company. It is then up to the seller to evaluate the transaction, including the potential competition from other
suppliers.

Eventually, the seller may have to accept the offered terms of payment
and try to cover the remaining risks in some other way or to find a
compromise by offering compensation to the buyer for the increased
bank charges and/or the additional costs incurred by the use of the
buyer's existing credit limits.

Box 1.4 Risk assessment — a summary

A careful risk assessment is the first important step to a successfully completed transaction because it is the basis for the seller's own strategy, and for the final decision of what is acceptable in the negotiations with the buyer in order to minimise the risks involved.

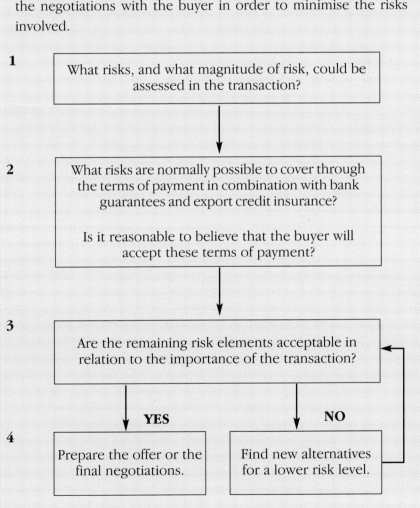

1   What risks, and what magnitude of risk, could be assessed in the transaction?

2   What risks are normally possible to cover through the terms of payment in combination with bank guarantees and export credit insurance?

Is it reasonable to believe that the buyer will accept these terms of payment?

3   Are the remaining risk elements acceptable in relation to the importance of the transaction?

YES   NO

4   Prepare the offer or the final negotiations.   Find new alternatives for a lower risk level.

2
Methods of payment

➤ 2.1 Different methods of payment

Primarily the method of payment determines *how* payment is going to be made ie, the obligations that rest with both the buyer and the seller in relation to the monetary settlement. However, the method of payment also decides – directly or indirectly – the role the banks will have in that settlement.

Box 2.1 Methods of payment and terms of payment

These two expressions are sometimes used synonymously, but in this book they have been kept separate.

'Methods of payment' represents the defined form of how the payment shall be made ie, through a bank transfer, documentary collection or Letter of Credit.

'Terms of payment' defines the obligations of both commercial parties in relation to the payment, detailing not only the form of payment and when and where this payment shall be made by the buyer, but also the obligations of the seller; not only to deliver according to the contract, but also, for example, to arrange stipulated guarantees or other undertakings prior to or after the delivery.

As this chapter deals with the different methods of payment, this distinction should be kept in mind — terms of payment will be discussed in *Chapter 8, Terms of Payment.*

Box 2.2   Summary of the different payment methods

The role of the commercial parties			The role of the banks		
Method of payment	Seller's obligations	Buyer's obligations	Money transfer	Document handling	Payment guarantee
Bank transfer[1]	Sending an invoice to the buyer after delivery	Arranging for payment according to the invoice	X		
Payment by cheque[1]	Same as above	Arranging for a cheque to be sent to the seller	X		
Documentary collection	After delivery, having the agreed documents sent to the buyer's bank	Pay/accept at the bank against the documents presented	X	X	
Letter of Credit	After delivery, presenting conforming documents to the bank	To have the Letter of Credit issued according to contract	X	X	X

[1]Bank transfers and bank cheques are often referred to as 'clean payments', in comparison with documentary payments (collections and Letters of Credit).

There are, in principle, only four basic methods of payment that are used today in connection with monetary settlement of international trade (barter and counter trade transactions are described at the end of this chapter), one of these methods is, therefore, always the basis for the terms of payment:

- Bank transfer (also often called bank remittance);
- Cheque payment;
- Documentary collection (also called bank collection); and
- Letter of Credit (also called documentary credit).

Box 2.2 illustrates the most important aspects of the obligations that the buyer and seller have to fulfil in each case. In reality, things are of course more diversified and complex, particularly when it comes to the documentary methods of payments, which have many alternatives. For example, complexity in handling, speed in execution and level of costs and fees, but the most important factor is the difference in security they offer. This aspect is thoroughly dealt with in this chapter.

■ 2.1.1 Bank charges and other costs

The costs for the alternatives are mainly governed by what function the banks will have in connection with the execution of the payment. Other forms of fees do sometimes arise, which can have an indirect connection to the payment, such as different charges related to the creation of the underlying documents, for example, consular fees and stamp duties. However, such fees are more related to the delivery than the payment and are, therefore, normally born by the party that has to produce these documents according to the terms of delivery. Other costs, such as payment of duties and taxes are also governed by the agreed terms of delivery.

Bank charges will arise not only in the UK but also abroad, where they can vary between countries, both in size but also, more importantly, in structure. In some cases they are charged at a fixed rate, in others as a percentage of the transferred amount. Sometimes they are negotiable, sometimes not and these differences not only occur between countries but also between banks.

The best solution for both parties is often to agree to pay the bank charges in their respective country, but whatever the agreement, that should be included in the contract. However, such a deal would probably minimise the total costs for the transaction since each party would get a direct interest to negotiate these costs with the local bank. Bank charges in the UK are also more easily calculated and, even if the difference between the UK banks is relatively small, they are often negotiable for larger amounts.

Bank charges are often divided into the following groups:

- **fees** – normally charged at a flat rate;

- **handling charges**, ie, for checking of documents – normally charged as a percentage on the underlying value of the transaction;
- **risk commissions**, ie, issuing of guarantees and confirmation of Letters of Credit – normally charged as a percentage of the amount at a rate according to the estimated risk and the period of time.

Box 2.3 shows the fees and commission normally charged by UK banks. It is, however, only an indicative illustration to show the relative figures and not all details have been included. More accurate information can always be obtained from the bank and, as pointed out earlier, for larger transactions, fees and commissions are often negotiable.

➤ 2.2 Bank transfer (bank remittance)

Most trade transactions, both to and from the UK, are based on so-called 'open account' payment terms, meaning that the seller delivers goods or services to the buyer without receiving cash, a Bill of Exchange or any other legally binding and enforceable undertaking at the time of delivery, and the buyer is expected to pay according to the terms of the agreement and the seller's invoice.

Therefore, the open account is a form of short, but agreed, credit extended to the buyer, in most cases only verified by the invoice, and the specified date of payment therein, together with copies of the relevant shipping or delivery document, verifying shipment and shipment date.

When the terms of payment are based on open account terms and the buyer offers no additional security for the payment obligations, the normal bank transfer is by far the simplest and most common form of payment. The buyer, having received the seller's invoice, simply instructs the bank to transfer the amount a few days before the due date to a bank chosen by the seller. This can either be done directly to the seller's account at a bank in their country (which is the most common case) or to a separate collection account that the seller may have at a bank in the buyer's country.

Box 2.3 UK banks approximate payment charges (payments related to exports of goods and services)

Method of payment	Bank transfer/ cheque	Documentary collection	Letter of Credit
Payment fee ❶	£0–10		
Collection charges ❸		0.25–0.3%	
Advising fee			£40–50
Payment commission ❸			0.1–0.3%
Confirmation/ ❷ ❸ acceptance commission			0.5–3% p.a.

1) Inward EU-payments (see *section 2.2.2*) are often free of charge.

2) The commission is dependent on the banks perception of risk involved and could, therefore, in some cases even be higher than indicated above. These commissions are normally calculated and chargeable quarterly.

3) Most charges/commissions have minimum tariffs of £40–60.

The banks will charge separately according to specified tariffs for additional services such as extensions, amendments and cancellations as well as for other services related to the payment or the documents involved. These tariffs, including the detailed payment charges applicable, could be ordered directly from the bank.

■ 2.2.1 Payment structure follows the trade pattern

Bank transfers are a method of 'clean payments' (as compared with the documentary payments, to be described later), which are dominating both in size and number; more than 80 per cent of all commercial payments to and from the UK are in this form. The main reason is not only that it is a simple method of payment, cheap and flexible for both buyer and seller, but it is also an indication of the underlying UK trade pattern.

The majority of UK trade is with West European and certain other countries (mainly the US and some commonwealth countries) where the commercial risk is generally regarded as low and open account terms traditionally used. That is the case with European trade in particular, with its short shipping distances and its often regular business patterns between well-known companies, even between companies belonging to the same group, or companies that can be properly evaluated from a risk point of view. In these cases it is also quite normal that a practice is established on the market, where a bank transfer is the most common form of payment.

Even in individual cases when the seller should have preferred a safer method of payment, this can often be difficult to achieve due to competition or established practice. Instead many sellers use export credit insurance covering the risk on different customers or even their whole export and, with this cover, the bank transfer may be the best payment alternative even in these cases.

■ 2.2.2 EU payments

In order to achieve uniformity in the handling of bank transfers between the European EES counties, there is a maximum limit established by the EU of five banking days from the time the buyer has given instructions to the bank until the payment must be available with the receiving bank which, thereafter, must make the amount available at the seller's account according to local practice, normally one day later. However, as described above, most transfers are done much more rapidly.

There is also another EU rule in force, which stipulates that banks under certain conditions are only allowed to charge payments within the EU in the same way as domestic payments, as long as they are in a currency of the remitting or receiving country, so-called 'EU payments'.

Box 2.4 Bank transfer

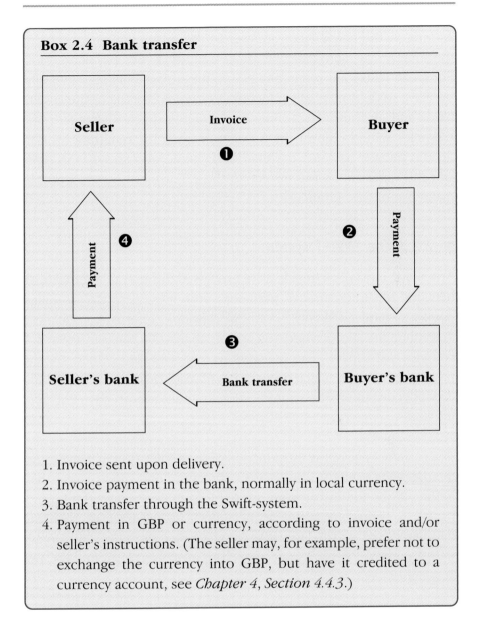

1. Invoice sent upon delivery.
2. Invoice payment in the bank, normally in local currency.
3. Bank transfer through the Swift-system.
4. Payment in GBP or currency, according to invoice and/or seller's instructions. (The seller may, for example, prefer not to exchange the currency into GBP, but have it credited to a currency account, see *Chapter 4, Section 4.4.3.*)

There are, however, certain restrictions in order for a transfer to classify as a EU payment; the maximum amount is EUR 12,500 or the counter-value thereof, and the receiver's account must be stated in IBAN standard (International Bank Account Number), containing also country and bank code according to a standardised structure. The receiving bank must also be identified with a correct BIC code (Bank Identifier Code), which is the same as the SWIFT-address (explained below).

As long as the above rules are met in the instructions to the bank, the transfer is automatically processed as a EU payment. Most European banks are today processing these payments automatically, but have to do it manually if incorrect or not according to these standards and, in these cases, they will charge a much higher fee. The UK seller should request the buyer to instruct the remitting bank to do the transfer as a EU payment and should also specify the IBAN and BIC numbers on the invoice to those European buyers who can make use of this advantage.

■ 2.2.3 The SWIFT system

Nowadays, most bank transfers are processed through an internal bank network for international payments and messages, the so-called 'SWIFT-system' (Society for Worldwide Interbank Financial Telecommunication), where today more than 4,000 banks in about 200 counties participate. This network is cooperatively owned by the participating banks, which thereby, have created a low-cost, secure and very effective internal communication system for both payments and messages.

As a consequence of the introduction of the SWIFT-system, bank transfers between countries and banks are now done much faster than before. When the instructions are fed into the system by the buyer's bank it is normally available at the seller's chosen bank two banking days later, and usually available for the seller the next day. Urgent SWIFT-messages (express payments) are processed even quicker, but at a higher fee.

However, it should be stressed that even if the speed of processing has increased through the SWIFT-system, this is only when the payment instruction has been brought into the network. The seller is, as before, dependent on the buyer giving correct instructions in time to their bank and it is still up to the seller to maintain a high standard of their own systems and routines for a close monitoring of outstanding and over-due payments.

■ 2.2.4 Collection accounts abroad

The bank transfer has, so far, been described as a payment between two countries, arriving directly from the buyer's bank to that of the seller, and that is usually also the case. But it is also more and more common that the seller instead chooses to open an account in local currency in the larger OECD-countries, where they already have or can expect larger flows of payments within one and the same country.

The buyer will then do a domestic and not an international payment to this account, which for them is both easier and mostly also cheaper – and the seller will have direct access to the payment when it has reached that account.

These accounts are often established with branches abroad of the UK banks or in cooperation with one of their banking partners. The structure can vary depending of how these accounts are integrated in the seller's cash-management system, and the cost will be dependent of the set-up and the service level required.

The use of collection accounts has also been accelerated by other developments within the banking system, for example a quicker or even online reporting of transactions and balances, whereby it is possible for the seller to monitor individual transactions on a daily basis, even integrated into their own bank-connected terminal. The balance of these collection accounts can then also be used for local payments within that country, for intra-company transfers or for direct transfer back to the UK Head-office account.

■ 2.2.5 Payment delays in connection with bank transfers

Since the main role of the banks in connection with bank transfers is an intermediary function, the responsibility for a correct and timely payment rests with the commercial parties. It is the buyer who has to give correct payment instructions to their bank, but the obligations do not normally arise until the seller has fulfilled the delivery obligations according to contract.

However, delays in payment are common, not only with regards to different countries but also with individual buyers. Sometimes the reason may be non-acceptance of delivery, or other related claims, but in these cases an on-going dialog should already have been established between the parties and the seller can be expected to be fully aware of the situation and the reason for the delay in payment.

Box 2.5   Payments via the Internet

International payments between banks are done through the SWIFT-system and work is also continuously going on to find new solutions for electronic invoicing and automatic payments between companies.

Focus has also been increasing on the Internet trade as a base for developing new business, both for companies looking for new markets and for individuals hoping to gain access to a worldwide range of products.

The problem with Internet payments has always been the security aspect and the risk for unauthorized use of customer and account information, spread over an open system — not least for international payments. Many payments related to Internet trades are still made as invoice payments, but payments through debit/credit cards are increasing rapidly in line with new technology for increased security, in particular within areas where Internet trade is widely used, such as leisure or travel business and most segments of the retail market; but more seldom as business to business payments.

New techniques are constantly introduced to increase security when using debit/credit cards, however, for the foreseeable future international trade payments between companies will continue to be based mainly on the established SWIFT-system used by the banks.

However, in some cases the seller may not be aware of any such open payment disputes with the buyer, but still has not received payment in time – this may be for many different reasons:

- In some countries or companies it may be an established practice to delay local payments, and international payments are then treated in the same way.
- The interest level in local currency could make it advantageous to delay all payments, including payments to suppliers.
- Supplier payments are often based on open account payment terms i.e., without a Bill of Exchange or similar instruments. Such payments could then have a low priority among other debts.
- The buyer may want a self-liquidated deal in order to improve liquidity, and may prefer to delay the payment until being paid by their customer.
- The buyer may see currency advantages in delaying the exchange from local currency into the currency to be transferred to the seller.
- Larger corporations often have internal payment systems with batch payments only at certain intervals during the month.
- In the worst case, the delay may depend on liquidity or solvency problems on behalf of the buyer, or if applicable, the buyer's country.

■ 2.2.6 Reducing payment delays

Even if it is not possible to establish the exact cause for the delay in payment, there are always some steps the seller can take to reduce such delays.

Firstly, the seller must have an agreement or contract with clear terms of payment. This should also include detailed instructions on how to pay and the invoice to be issued after delivery should specify the same information, a fixed due date, full bank name and address, IBAN and BIC references.

It could also prove advantageous to stress the right, according to the contract, for a late payment interest charge and to specify the applicable rate. Even if it is difficult to collect interest afterwards, the mere indication could have a positive effect on the speed of payment.

Box 2.6 Be vigilant about the problem of delays in payment

Intrum Justitia, a leading European provider of Credit Management services, carries out a written survey in more than 20 European countries on a biannual basis involving several thousand companies. The results of the survey are published in their European Payment Index Reports. This half-yearly interval survey (Sept. 2004 below), calculated from differently weighted sub-indices, is intended to capture and compare international trends and provide companies with a reliable basis for decision making and effective benchmarks. Further information could be obtained directly from the company, **www.intrum.com**

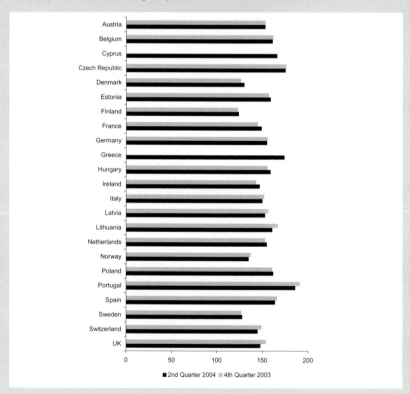

Payment Index – Implications for Credit Policy

100 no payment risks, i.e., payments are made in cash, on time (or in advance) without credit.

101 – 124 preventive actions - measures to secure the current situation are recommended.

125 – 149 need to take action.

150 – 174 strong need to take action.

175 – 199 major need to take action.

Over 200 urgent need to take action.

Perhaps the most important and effective way to speed up payments lies within the structure and efficiency of the internal system implemented within the company in order to treat outstanding and over-due payments. The seller must have clear internal rules and guidelines with a limit for amounts, timing and frequency of individual over-due payments, together with instructions on reporting and how to deal with such matters.

It is equally important to have a working internal communication between the sales and administrative departments within the company so that the sales person responsible for that particular buyer becomes aware of any late payments. This person might have additional information and can contact and get support from their opposite number at the buyer, who is not normally the one responsible for payments and is probably also unaware of the delay.

Box 2.7   Supervision and follow-up

All companies should have a strict but sensitive credit control to enable the buyer to clearly see that whatever is agreed should be honoured. However, many sellers are reluctant to fulfil the direct or indirect threat of further action for fear that it will undermine the prospects for future businesses.

This fear is almost always unfounded; if the terms of payment are clearly defined from the beginning and the invoice correctly issued, then further reminders or actions will perhaps not be appreciated but they will be respected as part of the agreement.

Experience has shown that if no agreement can be made with the buyer as how to settle overdue payments, it is important for the seller to involve a reputable collection company early in the process. Such a company can help the seller with a clearer understanding of the cause of the delay and can also act swiftly in consultation with the seller.

> Tight supervision after delivery is a key element of the transaction — a lot of money can often be made.

Above all, the seller should not let the matter take too long. If the buyer has economic problems, then the seller will often learn about that after it is known among local business partners, who will then be the first to press for payment. The buyer might also be more dependent on them than on a foreign supplier for on-going business, and might act accordingly in their payment priorities.

➢ 2.3 Cheque payments

To pay by cheque was once a common form of payment, but following the introduction of more cost effective and faster ways of processing international bank transfers, this is no longer the case. Perhaps not more than a few per cent of all international payments are now processed by cheque, often when it is enclosed with the order, as is the case with smaller orders or subscriptions.

Box 2.8 shows that the handling of cheques is different from bank transfers. However, as a form of clean payment with no direct connection to the underlying trade documents, the level of security for the seller is almost identical. What was said earlier regarding the disadvantages related to bank transfers is therefore, also valid for cheque payments.

It has become increasingly common for buyers to pay with their own cheques for cash-management purposes, as opposed to banker's cheques or 'drafts'. The corporate cheque (usually post-dated and mailed at due-date by the buyer) will not be paid to the seller until it is received and presented to the seller's bank, often with a delayed value date, thereby delaying liquidity for the seller and often incurring additional fees; and also subject to being honoured later on by the buyer's bank. The cheque will then be sent back to that bank for reimbursement by the seller's bank and only at that time will it be charged to the buyer's account – with a profit for the buyer of many interest-free days. The whole procedure will have the corresponding disadvantages for the seller, both from a liquidity and cost perspective.

The seller should, therefore, be aware that if payment by cheque is agreed, and no other stipulation is made, then it is likely that they will

Box 2.8 Cheque payment (corporate cheque)*

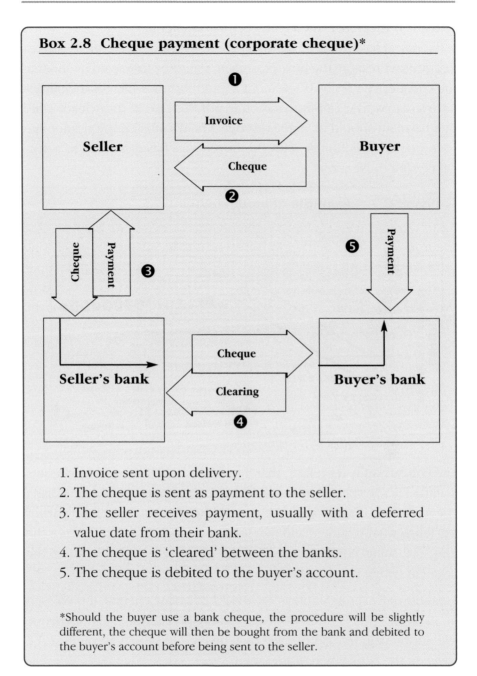

1. Invoice sent upon delivery.
2. The cheque is sent as payment to the seller.
3. The seller receives payment, usually with a deferred value date from their bank.
4. The cheque is 'cleared' between the banks.
5. The cheque is debited to the buyer's account.

*Should the buyer use a bank cheque, the procedure will be slightly different, the cheque will then be bought from the bank and debited to the buyer's account before being sent to the seller.

receive a corporate cheque, with the liquidity disadvantage mentioned above. However, larger companies in particular, may have this payment procedure as a policy, which the seller then may have to accept – but in such cases, this may be of minor importance compared to other aspects of the transaction.

There is one further risk aspect relating to cheques in general, which is the postal risk. If lost in transit to the seller, or delayed due to strikes or any other reason, the buyer can claim that they have paid by sending the cheque. The terms of payment should decide which of the parties have to carry this risk but this is often not the case. If they clearly state that payment should be made through a bank transfer, the risk for late presentation is definitely with the buyer who has not acted in accordance with these terms.

Figure 2.1 Example of bank cheque

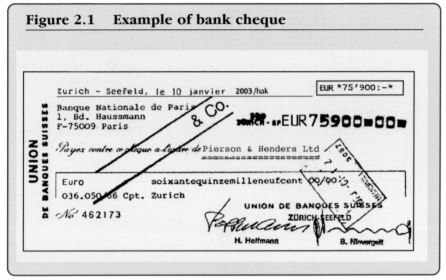

The conclusion is therefore, that if payment shall be made by cheque, it must clearly state if this should be a corporate cheque or a bank cheque that is issued by a bank and not by a buyer. Then both parties will know what is agreed and that is what is important. If that is not the case, the seller could expect that the buyer will probably make the payment with a corporate cheque.

As is shown by the example in *Figure 2.1* of a bank cheque, it is crossed on its front. This is often done as a safety precaution; such a cheque will not be paid in cash but will only be credited to an account of the payee in the bank where it is cashed.

'Where a cheque is crossed and bears across its face the words 'account payee' or 'a/c payee', either with or without the word 'only', the cheque shall not be transferable, but shall only be valid as between the parties thereto.'

(Cheques Act 1992)

➤ 2.4 Documentary collection

Documentary collection, also sometimes referred to as 'bank collection', is a method of payment where the seller's and buyer's banks assist by forwarding documents to the buyer against payment or some other obligation, often acceptance of a Bill of Exchange. The basis for this form of payment is that the buyer should either pay or accept the Bill, before they gain control over the goods or at least over the documents that represent the goods.

The role of the banks in a documentary collection is purely to present the documents to the buyer, but without responsibility that they will be honoured by them. The collection contains no guarantee on behalf of the banks, which only act upon the instruction of the seller, but it is nevertheless a demand against the buyer, performed by a Collection Bank at their domicile, often their own bank. It is, however, in most cases, a more secure alternative for the seller, compared to trading on open account payment terms.

The collections are often divided into two main groups:

- documents against payment and
- documents against acceptance.

Document against payment (D/P) – when the bank notifies the buyer that the documents have arrived and requests them to pay the amount as instructed by the seller's bank.

Documents against acceptance (D/A) – when the buyer is requested to accept a Bill of Exchange that accompanies the documents instead of payment. The seller's risk position deteriorates by handing over the documents against a Bill of Exchange instead of receiving payment and is dependent on the buyer's ability to pay the bill at a later stage, but the seller has lost the advantage of having control of the documents related to the goods.

■ *2.4.1 Documentary collection and control of goods*

The general advantage with this method of payment is that the buyer knows that the goods have been shipped and can examine the related documents before payment or acceptance. From the seller's perspective, the documents are not placed at the disposal of the buyer until they have paid or accepted the Bill of Exchange. The practical value for the seller of this control of the documents is however dependent on the documents involved (in most cases the transport documents). For example, compare the two scenarios below:

Scenario 1
The goods are being sent by air to a European buyer, who will be able to get hold of them at arrival, without presentation of the relevant Air Waybill. Besides, the goods have then normally arrived at the buyer's destination long before the documents have arrived at the bank

Scenario 2
The goods are sent by sea to the buyer who, in this case, cannot get hold of them until the corresponding shipping documents ie, the Bill of Lading can be presented, which are part of the documents under collection at the bank.

The main difference between the two cases is the mode of transport and the related documents. The Air Waybill is simply a receipt of goods for shipment, issued by the airline company, similar to a Rail Waybill or a forwarding agents receipt. Sometimes a Multimodal Transport Document is used, providing for combined transport by at least two different types of transport. This document is also a receipt of goods but *not* a document of title to the goods.

A Bill of Lading is, however, not only an acknowledgement that the goods are loaded on-board the ship, but also a separate contract with the shipping company, which includes the title to the goods. The buyer cannot get access to the goods under a Bill of Lading without possession of this document. If other transport documents are used and the seller is anxious to have control of the goods until the buyer honours the presented documents, then this has to be arranged in some other way. For example, that the goods are addressed to a consignee other than the buyer, perhaps the collecting bank (if they agree), or alternatively to the forwarding agent.

To address freight bills or forwarding agent receipts to someone other that the buyer or to insert clauses about the release of the goods could cause problems or even be prohibited in some countries. Before taking such action, the seller should get prior approval from the bank or shipping agent.

■ 2.4.2 Inspection of the goods

So far, the description has mainly been made from the seller's viewpoint; however, the use of documentary collection could also have certain disadvantages for the buyer. Perhaps the most important being that there are no opportunities to examine the goods before payment, the buyer has to rely solely on what can be seen from the documents presented. There are, however, some actions the buyer can take to help deal with this drawback. The buyer or the buyer's agent may have the opportunity to inspect the goods before shipment or may use a company specialised in such inspections to do the same, as part of the agreement. Such a certificate could then be included in the set of documents sent for collection. This is described in detail later in this chapter.

Other ways for the buyer to increase security in connection with documentary collections could be to have the contractual right to postpone payment/acceptance until the goods have arrived and then have the right to inspect them or to take samples. However, measures like this have to be approved by the seller who might see other disadvantages or practical obstacles with such procedures.

Another solution could be to avoid collections altogether and instead agree on a bank guarantee or a Standby Letter of Credit (both terms described in the next chapter, Bonds and Guarantees) in favour of the seller, thus covering the buyer's payment obligations. The parties can then agree on open account payment terms and use bank transfer instead of collection and the buyer can inspect the goods upon arrival before payment, knowing that the seller can only use the guarantee if and when they have fulfilled their delivery obligations. The buyer is then obliged to pay anyway under the terms of the contract. The disadvantage for the buyer is of course the costs involved and that such a guarantee has to be issued under available credit limits with their bank.

If the buyer does not accept the documentary collection but only open account terms without any guarantee, one alternative for the seller could be to agree to such terms, but in combination with a separate credit risk insurance covering the payment obligations of the buyer. However, if no such insurance can be obtained, then the seller should probably anyway opt for a safer method than the documentary collection, for example a Letter of Credit.

■ 2.4.3 Documentary collection documents

It is important that the documents required under a collection are specified in the terms of payment in order to avoid disputes later with the buyer, which will only delay the collection procedure. Documents often used include:

- Bill of Exchange, issued at sight or as a term bill (usance bill)
- invoice, sometimes also separate consular invoices;
- specifications and separate packing or weight lists;
- the relevant transport document;
- certificate of origin;
- other certificates, such as health test or performance certificates;
- inspection certificates, verifying quality or quantity of the goods;
- insurance documents.

If import or currency licences are required in connection with a documentary collection, this must always be part of the contract, together with a statement of the buyer's responsibility to produce these documents prior to shipment. However, if this is the case, the seller really should consider if collection is the most suitable form of payment in that particular transaction or if a Letter of Credit or a bank guarantee would be more appropriate.

Box 2.9 Documentary collection (bank collection)

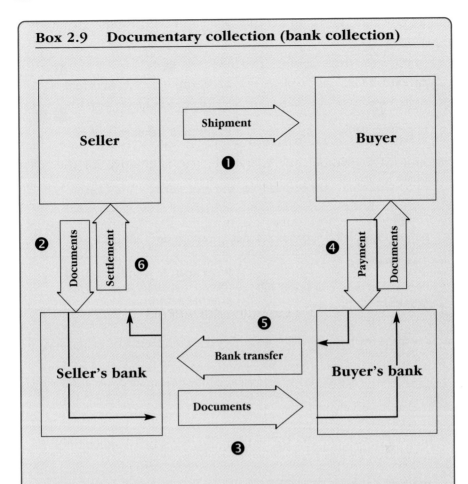

(1-2) The first step in the collection procedure normally comes after shipment, when the seller is preparing the documents, which together with the instructions for the collection, are sent to their bank.

(3) The bank checks the seller's instructions to ensure they conform with the enclosed documents. They are then sent to the collection bank chosen by the buyer together with the instructions to that bank.

(4) The buyer is advised about the collection. Before payment/acceptance, the buyer has the right to inspect the documents — that they are all included and appear to conform to the agreed terms. If so, the buyer is expected to pay/accept the amount due and receives the documents.

(5-6) Payment is transferred to the seller's bank and thereafter to the seller as per instructions. In the case of acceptance, the accepted Bill of Exchange is often kept at the buyer's bank until maturity and is then presented for payment as a 'clean collection'.

Figure 2.2   Example of a trade-related Bill of Exchange

Drawer's reference number: EA 2891-83	Date of issue **2** 12/02/05	Maturity **3** At sight
Payable at: **5** Dresdner Bank, Bahnhofstrasse 23, Dortmι nd 23001	Pay against this Bill of Exchange to: **1** **4** Pierson & Henders Ltd	

Amount in words and currency: Five-thousand, three-hundred and six Euro	Currency and amount in figures: €5,306.00

For: **6** Value received in goods as per invoice no. 2891-83 of February 12ᵗʰ, 2005	
Accepted by Drawee: [Signature of Drawee along with full name and address]	Drawers Signature: **Pierson & Henders Ltd** [Drawer's signature along with full name and address]

(1) A Bill of Exchange is defined in the Bills of Exchange Act 1882 as 'an unconditional order in writing, addressed by one person to another, signed by the person giving it, requiring the person to whom it is addressed to pay on demand, or at a fixed or determinable future time, a sum certain in money, to or to the order of a specified person, or to bearer. A cheque is a special form of a Bill of Exchange'.

Documents to distant countries are sometimes sent as duplicates in two different mails, one bill marked 'First Bill of Exchange (second not paid)' and the other marked 'Second Bill of Exchange (first not paid)'. But otherwise only one Bill of Exchange is issued, as in this case.

(2) The date of issue should normally be the same as invoice date, shipment date or any other specified date related to the underlying contract or agreement.

(3) The example is due at sight, which means that this Bill of Exchange is not supposed to be accepted but paid by the buyer at first presentation. If it is to be accepted as a term bill, the maturity date could be a fixed future date or at a certain date after presentation to the buyer, for example, 90 days sight, or from the date of issue of the Bill of Exchange, ie, 90 days date.

(4) The bill is normally payable to the drawer, as in this case but, as a term bill, could also be endorsed on the back in order to transfer its title and its rights, either in blank (to the bearer) or to a specific order, the collecting bank or a refinancing institution.

(5) The place of payment specifies the obligations of the drawee (see more in *Chapter 8, Section 8.2.2, Place of payment*). If not specified in some other way, a bill should be presented at sight or at maturity either at the debtor's bank or to the debtor personally, which is normally executed as a part of the original instructions in the documentary collection.

(6) Commercial trade bills should have the statement that value has been received, referring to the invoice and/or the underlying contract, in order to specify the background of the bill.

Box 2.10 International rules for documentary collection

ICC has issued a set of standardised rules and guidelines, *Uniform Rules for Collection (URC 522)* along with a separate commentary *(No. 550)* and guide *(No. 561)* to minimise the difficulties that banks and their customers may face due to differences in terminology and bank practice in connection with documentary collections through banks. They contain common standards and definitions, rules for the banks, obligations and responsibilities, guidelines for presentation of documents and for payment or acceptance. They also contain guidelines for protesting Bills of Exchange and the banks responsibilities after payment/acceptance.

The publications have successively been updated and are now used by all international, and most local banks around the world. They can be obtained from the banks or directly from ICC **(www.iccuk.net).**

If the documents are to be released against acceptance, a term Bill of Exchange issued by the seller should also be included. (At a later stage, this bill will be presented for payment under a so-called 'clean collection', where no other documents are included.). But even if the documents are to be released against payment it is still common that an 'at sight' or 'on demand' bill (often called 'draft') is included for the following reasons:

- The bill will show the total amount due for collection, which will avoid misunderstandings where several invoices and credit notes are included.
- The bill will show the name of the company to whom the presentation should be made, which is not always the same as in the documents.
- The bill is in itself a request for payment, with a reference to the underlying contractual obligation.

➤ 2.5 Letter of Credit

The Letter of Credit (L/C) is a combination of a **bank guarantee** issued by a bank upon the request of the buyer in favour of the seller (normally through an Advising Bank) and a **payment/acceptance/ negotiation** against documents in conformity with specified terms and conditions. This is defined in ICC *Uniform Customs and Practice for Documentary Credits (UCP 500)*:

'[The Letter of Credit] means any arrangement, however named or described, whereby a bank (the Issuing Bank) acting at the request and on the instructions of a customer (the Applicant) or on its own behalf:

I.   is to make a payment to the order of a third party (the Beneficiary), or is to accept and pay Bills of Exchange (Draft(s)) drawn by the Beneficiary; or

II. authorises another bank to effect such payment, or to accept and pay such Bills of Exchange (Draft(s)); or

III. authorises another bank to negotiate against document(s), provided that the terms and conditions of the Credit are complied with.'

The L/C is normally advised to the seller through another bank (the Advising Bank) but without engagement for that bank. The Advising Bank is usually located in the seller's country and its role is to take reasonable care to check the authenticity of the L/C and to advise the seller according to its instructions. This authentication fulfils a very important role as can be seen from the extract in *Box 2.11*.

The L/C has many advantages for the seller. Payment is guaranteed and there are fewer concerns about the buyer's ability to pay, or about other restrictions or difficulties that may exist or arise in the buyer's country – but only if the seller can meet all the terms and conditions stipulated in the L/ C.

Box 2.11   Fraud warning

'The importance of knowing your customer cannot be over-emphasised; it is the best protection against fraud. Unfortunately there have been instances where forged documents or documents relating to non-existent goods have been presented to banks under Documentary Credits (Letters of Credit).

Since the documents appeared prima facie to comply with the terms and conditions of the Documentary Credit, banks have been obliged to pay and debit the importer's account. This arises because all parties, including banks, deal with documents — not with the underlying goods. Exporters should be extremely cautious about shipping goods against the receipt of an unsolicited Documentary Credit. From time to time, forgeries of Documentary Credits come to light and there have been instances where exporters have shipped and presented documents against a completely false instrument. If in any doubt, check its authenticity with your UK bank.

Importers and exporters should be particularly careful about proposals to transact international trade business, which is markedly different from their normal line of business or for unusually large amounts. There have been cases where fraudsters have obtained advance payments from UK traders in the expectation of the award of a contract, which never really existed."

Extract from *Understanding International Trade: an information guide for importers and exporters published* by HSBC.

There are also advantages for the buyer when using a L/C. While it is considerably more expensive than other forms of payment and has to be issued under existing credit limits with the buyer's own bank, the buyer is assured that the stipulated documents will not be paid unless they conform to the terms of the L/C. This may be very important for the buyer, particularly in connection with goods where fulfilment of special shipping arrangements are essential or in the case of seasonal deliveries, where the timing of the delivery may be the crucial factor.

Box 2.12   Terminology

The Documentary Credit is the formal name used by ICC, often abbreviated to D/C or simply Credit, but **in this book we will use the expression Letter of Credit and its abbreviated form L/C,** terms that are recognised and still widely used throughout the world.

The correct terminology used in connection with a L/C is 'applicant', 'Issuing Bank', 'Advising Bank' and 'beneficiary'. However, when dealing with commercial trade only, and for the sake of simplicity, this book sometimes uses the term 'buyer' instead of 'applicant' and 'seller' instead of 'beneficiary'. 'Issuing Bank' is also known as 'Opening Bank', but only the former expression is used here.

With regard to cost, a L/C is sometimes of such importance to the seller that the buyer may be able to obtain fair compensation or even a better deal overall, if able to offer a form of payment that, in principle, eliminates the seller's commercial and political risks.

The L/C can be issued in many ways, depending on how it is going to be used, and the design will vary in each case. However, a L/C has certain general features that have to be included in each case, particularly with regard to:

- period of validity;
- time for payment;
- place of presentation of documents;
- level of security; and
- documents to be presented.

These areas will be covered in detail below.

■ *2.5.1 Period of validity*

A L/C can be either **irrevocable** or **revocable**. An irrevocable L/C is a binding undertaking on behalf of the Issuing Bank to pay or accept a

term draft against presentation of correct documents, within the stipulated period of validity. This undertaking cannot be withdrawn or
amended during that time without the consent of the Issuing Bank, the
Confirming Bank (if any) and the seller. The Issuing Bank, however,
can withdraw a revocable L/C at any time until presentation of documents and without prior notice or consent of the seller.

Revocable L/Cs are, therefore, for obvious reasons rarely used in international trade, unless they are to be used only as a matter of formality
or within a group of companies where this distinction is of no material
importance. In most other cases, only the irrevocable L/C will give the
seller the desired level of security and, in the following text this is what
is referred to, unless stated otherwise.

■ 2.5.2 Time for payment

A L/C must stipulate when payment is to be made to the seller. It can
be payable either **at sight** or at a specified time thereafter, by
deferred payment or **by acceptance**.

A L/C at sight will be paid on presentation of documents, either at
the Issuing Bank, the Advising Bank or any other Nominated Bank.
If payment is to be effected at a later stage, normally a specified time
after shipment or after presentation of documents as specified in the
L/C, this can be done either through presentation of a Bill of Exchange
(to be accepted by one of the banks) or by a stipulated deferred
payment, which allows that bank to effect payment at a later specified date.

In both cases (acceptance and deferred payment), the Issuing Bank is
guaranteeing payment on due date and based on that guarantee, the
seller may generate instant liquidity through discounting or advance
payment while finance is provided to the buyer during the same
period. Apart from the extended period of risk on the Issuing Bank (if
that is at all an issue) the difference for the seller between an at sight
and a term L/C is mainly a question of interest for the credit period
until due date.

■ *2.5.3 Place of presentation of documents*

When referring to the place of presentation of documents under a L/C, this is a question of at which place **the documents are to be available for payment, acceptance, deferred payment or negotiation.** Unless the L/C is made available only with the Issuing Bank, (in which case it is payable in that country only), this bank must authorise another bank (the Nominating Bank, which is often the same as the Advising Bank) to pay, negotiate, incur a deferred payment or to accept drafts – if all terms and conditions have been complied with. In the case of a freely negotiable L/C, any bank is the Nominated Bank. Presentation of the documents can be made to any of these banks, but from the seller's perspective, the best place to present the documents is at the Advising Bank in their country, for reasons explained below.

It is important to stress that, unless it has also confirmed the L/C, the Advising or Nominated Bank is under no obligation to take up the documents when presented by the seller, if at that time this bank – at its own discretion – is uncertain whether the Issuing Bank is able to fulfil its corresponding reimbursement obligations.

On the other hand, if the L/C is available only with the Issuing Bank, usually but not always domiciled in the country of the buyer, that bank will make payment or accept the term Bill of Exchange if the terms and conditions are complied with. But, even in this case, the Advising Bank, or any Nominated Bank, may still negotiate the documents at presentation and 'give value' to the seller at that earlier stage, with deduction of interest until reimbursement. Such negotiation is normally made with recourse to the seller until such reimbursement, unless the negotiating bank also has confirmed (guaranteed) the L/C.

It is usually more advantageous for the seller to have the documents under the L/C available with the Advising Bank because:

- The payment/acceptance will take place at the earlier stage when the documents are delivered to and approved by the Advising Bank.
- In case of discrepancies or other faults in the documentation, it may be much easier and quicker to remedy these directly with the

Box 2.13 Key aspects of a Letter of Credit

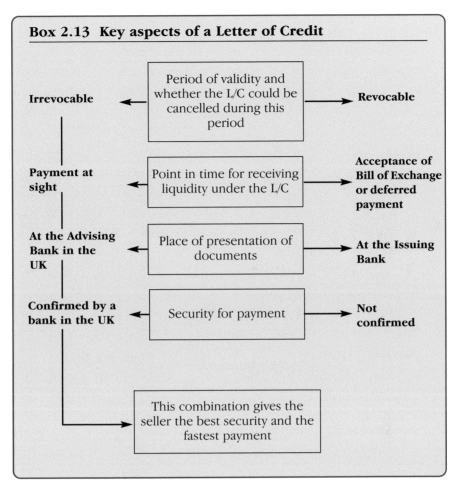

Irrevocable ← Period of validity and whether the L/C could be cancelled during this period →	**Revocable**
Payment at sight ← Point in time for receiving liquidity under the L/C →	**Acceptance of Bill of Exchange or deferred payment**
At the Advising Bank in the UK ← Place of presentation of documents →	**At the Issuing Bank**
Confirmed by a bank in the UK ← Security for payment →	**Not confirmed**

This combination gives the seller the best security and the fastest payment

Advising Bank before the documents are forwarded to the Issuing Bank

- The seller avoids any postal risk and other delays from the Issuing Bank until payment is made and effectively transferred to the seller.

What is an advantage for the seller could however also be a disadvantage for the buyer, who normally, for the same reasons as above, often prefers the L/C to be available/payable with the Issuing Bank only. This question has to be decided in each case but, in many countries, local practice will influence this outcome. In some countries this matter may be subject to specific rules or regulations, mostly working in the buyer's favour.

Box 2.14   Letter of Credit

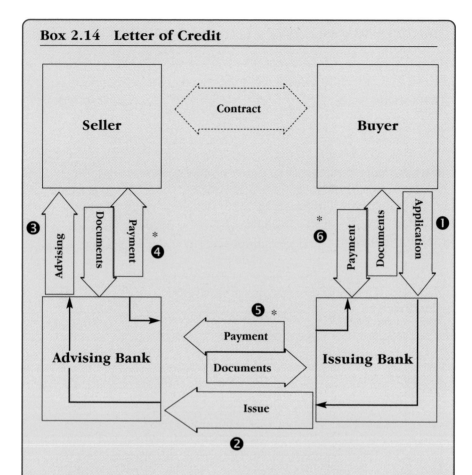

*Payment could also alternatively be acceptance, deferred payment or negotiation depending on the stipulation in the L/C.

(1) After signing the contract, it is up to the buyer to take the first step by applying to their bank (the bank referred to as the Issuing Bank in the terms of payment) to issue the agreed L/C.

(2) The Issuing Bank must process a formal credit approval of the application and check if local permissions, import licences or currency approvals, if needed, have been granted. When all formalities and procedures are dealt with (this may take time) the L/C is issued, hopefully as stipulated in the terms of payment, and forwarded to the selected Advising Bank.

Continued ...

(3) Upon arrival of the L/C from the Issuing Bank – by letter, fax or more often nowadays by SWIFT message — the Advising Bank will assess its contents and determine where it should be made available (payable). If the Advising Bank is instructed to add its confirmation, this also involves a separate credit decision in this bank, after which the seller is notified of the L/C and its details, including information of where it is available for payment or acceptance, and if the Advising Bank has confirmed it or not.

Already at this point, it is vital that the seller checks the terms of the L/C against the agreed terms of payment to make sure that all the details and instructions can be met at a later stage when the documents are to be produced and delivered. If not, the seller must immediately communicate directly with the buyer so that the necessary amendments are made and confirmed to the seller through the banks. Only then does the seller have the security on which the whole transaction is based.

(4) After shipment the seller receives the transport documents and prepares the other documents required. Checks are also made to ensure that they conform with the terms of the L/C, but equally important, that the contents of the documents presented are consistent between themselves.

The documents are then forwarded to the Advising Bank, which checks their conformity with the terms of the L/C. The seller is contacted about any discrepancies. Discrepancies that cannot be corrected at this late stage, for example, wrong shipping details or late presentation, will be subject to later approval by the buyer, and any payment made by the Advising Bank will be with recourse, subject to this approval.

(5) The Issuing Bank will also check the documents and the buyer has to consider any discrepancies. When approved, or if the documents are compliant, the buyer has to pay. If unapproved, the documents will be held at the disposal of the Advising Bank, pending any new negotiation between the buyer and the seller of the terms for such an approval, or ultimately returned to the Advising Bank (and the seller) against repayment of any earlier payment made with recourse to the seller.

(6) The documents are released to the buyer against payment at sight or at any later date as stipulated in the L/C.

If it is agreed in the terms of payment that the L/C should be available (for payment, acceptance, deferred payment or negotiation) at the Advising Bank, that should also be openly stated in its terms and appear from its reimbursement instructions to the Advising Bank, to enable this bank to make it available at its counters. But, if nothing is stated to that effect, the L/C will probably be made available at the Issuing Bank only. The seller's own bank will know what local practices, if any, are applicable in different countries.

■ 2.5.4 Level of security

The Issuing Bank always guarantees an irrevocable L/C under the entire period of its validity without exception. However, many countries have such economic and/or political problems that the seller may be uncertain if the Issuing Bank can fulfil its obligations and/or is able to transfer the amount out of the country in a freely convertible currency. New and deteriorating events may also take place in the country during the validity of the L/C and, in such cases, the Advising Bank may refuse to take up the documents until reimbursement is first received from the Issuing Bank.

To cover the payment obligations of the Issuing Bank, the seller can also have the L/C **confirmed** (that is guaranteed) by the Advising Bank. This is usually made upon request from the Issuing Bank based upon instructions from the buyer, according to the agreed terms of payment in the contract. Such confirmation may occasionally, although more as an exception, also be made directly by the Advising Bank upon request of the seller, without the Issuing Bank being aware of it. This **silent confirmation** is also sometimes given by separate forfaiting institutions in the form of a payment guarantee in competition with the banks – or where the Advising Bank is not willing to add its confirmation due to the perceived risks involved.

Only irrevocable L/Cs can be confirmed, since they have to be based on the undertaking of the Issuing Bank for the whole period of validity. The cost for a confirmation is normally calculated per quarter and varies dependent on the assessed risk involved and the length of such confirmation. Confirmation of a L/C involves a risk for the confirming bank and, if doubtful, the seller must always get approval in advance from that bank, together with a price indication, should the transaction materialise later on. In some countries L/Cs are more or less always confirmed in principle, whereas in other countries that is not normally the case. However, between these two categories there are also many other countries where both alternatives are used.

The buyer and the seller have to agree whether the Advising Bank should confirm the L/C or not. In some cases, agreeing on a more internationally recognised bank as the Issuing Bank might be enough additional security for the seller without the need for a confirmation. In some cases an international bank may even be necessary for the willingness of the Advising Bank to add its confirmation. Regarding more 'problematic' countries this is something the seller should discuss with their bank prior to the negotiations with the buyer, and if needed, get the commitment from this bank to confirm any L/C that may be the outcome of the negotiations. Such commitments are often issued by the banks against a commitment fee.

■ 2.5.5 Other common forms of Letters of Credit

It is relatively common that someone other than the seller makes the actual delivery, for example, when acting as agent, using independent suppliers or having an intermediary function in the transaction. In these cases it can be a big advantage to have the L/C expressly stated as being **transferable**, which permits the seller to transfer the rights and obligations under the L/C to another beneficiary, a business partner or some other supplier who will make the actual delivery. (If the master L/C allows partial shipment, parts of this credit can be transferred to different beneficiaries).

The transferable L/C can be transferred only when it relates to identical goods and the same terms and conditions as in the master L/C, with the exception of amount, unit price, shipping period and expiry date – or any earlier date of presentation – which may be reduced or curtailed. When later presenting the documents under the master L/C, the seller is also allowed to exchange the suppliers' invoices for their own.

However, if the goods to be delivered by other suppliers need to be changed, upgraded or altered before delivery to the ultimate buyer, then the goods may not any longer be identical and the L/C may not be used as transferable. In such cases it can nevertheless often be used as supplementary security against which one or more new L/Cs, so called **'Back-to-Back Credits',** can be issued by the Advising Bank on the seller's behalf in favour of suppliers and with payment out of documents to be presented under the original L/C.

Sometimes the expression **'Red clause Letter of Credit'** is used, referring to a special clause that can be inserted in the L/C (earlier written in red ink, the reason for its name). Through such a clause the seller can receive an advance with a certain part of the value of the L/C before presentation of shipping documents, enabling them to purchase raw material or to meet other costs prior to receiving full payment upon presentation of conforming documents. However, such a clause creates an additional risk for the buyer and is, therefore, seldom used. The buyer cannot be sure that final documents will be presented under the L/C and a Red Clause arrangement has to be part of the overall agreement between the parties when forming the sales contract.

If the L/C is to be used for repeated shipments under a long-term contract or for similar shipments to the same buyer over longer periods, it could be practical to have it issued as a **'Revolving Letter of Credit',** which is automatically reinstated to its original value after each presentation of documents or when reaching a certain lower level. This L/C must, however, have a final due date and/or limits for the number of times it can be revolved.

■ 2.5.6 Issuing and advising Letters of Credit electronically

Nowadays, it is common practice that L/Cs are issued as SWIFT-messages in a standardised format to be used only for L/Cs. This procedure facilitates both the issue of the L/C and the authentication at the Advising Bank, which will then be able to immediately advise it to the seller. *Box 2.16* shows such a SWIFT-format example, which is easy to read and understand due to its standardised format. In this example, we have an irrevocable, freely negotiable L/C, available at sight with the Issuing Bank, and advised to the seller without the Advising Bank's confirmation. Many UK banks can also advise the L/Cs to the seller through their Internet-based advising services, which means that the seller can expect to receive the L/C the banking day after the bank receives it. In this form the L/C can easily be distributed in an exact format to and within the company, so increasing the effectiveness and reducing possible errors in transmission.

The next phase in the chain, the presentation of documents, can also be made electronically in some cases. ICC has issued a *'Supplement for Electronic Presentation' (eUCP)* to the general rules and guidelines for Documentary Credits (described in more detail later in this chapter). This supplementary documentation must be seen more as guidance for how electronic presentation of documents should take place because many obstacles still remain to be solved before that is a practical reality. The main limitation seems to be documentation from third parties, mainly the transport documents, which are not always available in an electronic format.

■ 2.5.7 Presentation of documents

The characteristic feature of the L/C in international trade is that the undertaking of the Issuing Bank is only valid if the specified terms and conditions are fully complied with within the period of its validity. If this is not the case then the Issuing Bank and the buyer have the right to refuse payment. From the seller's perspective, not complying with all the terms of the L/C could reduce what was originally a bank guaranteed payment, to a documentary collection without any such guarantee. This is the main reason why the due fulfilment of all terms and conditions specified in the L/C is so important, and why this subject is discussed in such a detail below.

As stated earlier, when the seller receives the L/C it is up to them to decide if it is in accordance with the contract and its terms of payment. However, the seller must also ensure that all details specified in the L/C can be complied with when the documents are prepared for presentation at the bank. This requires both experience and caution for if not

Box 2.15 Example of a Letter of Credit

Overseas Chinese Banking Corporation Ltd

High Street, Singapore

Date 14 September 2005 Irrevocable Documentary Credit No. 53368

Beneficiary

ABC Exporters Ltd.
Shady Lane, Bolton, England

Applicant

Tan Chee Eng Ltd.
1 East Coast Avenue, Singapore

Advising Bank

UK Commercial Bank,
Manchester, England

Amount

UK £50,000 (fifty thousand
pounds Sterling)

Available by your draft(s) in duplicate at **sight** drawn on the Advising Bank for the full invoice value, accompanied by the following documents:

1. Full set of clean on board bills of lading made out to our order showing the applicant as notify party marked 'Freight Paid'.
2. Signed commercial invoices in triplicate.
3. Insurance Policy/Certificate in assignable form for 10% above the invoice value with claims payable in Singapore covering Institute Cargo Clauses 'A', including War and Strikes.
4. Certificate of Origin showing goods of UK origin.

Evidence shipment of Diesel Engine Spare Parts CIF Singapore

Partial shipments ~~permitted~~/**prohibited** **Transhipment** ~~permitted~~/**prohibited**

Shipment from UK Port to Singapore no later than 24 Oct. 2005

All documents must be presented within 10 days from date of shipment

This credit is IRREVOCABLE and valid until 4 November 2005

This credit is subject to the 'Uniform Customs & Practice for Documentary Credits (1993) International Chamber of Commerce Publications No. 500

Authorised signatures

Box 2.16 Example of a L/C issued through SWIFT

Today, most L/Cs are issued in a standardised SWIFT-format, as shown below.

```
ITD-REF ASNA1415744  0090  DMO  0     MSG-REF 490DM95140300042
OVERSEAS CHINESE BANKING CORPORATION LTD.

RECEIVED BY BB AT 09.59 HRS ON 14TH

DOC CR ISSUE RECEIVED VIA SWIFT          14 SEPTEMBER 2005
S700 09/03  GROUP  REF LCUK53368
INPUT TIME    1559                       INPUT REF    04BEIIIDJAA003093813
OUTPUT TIME  0950                        OUTPUT REF 04BBKGB2LBXX313753

MESSAGE AUTHENTICATED

40A        FORM OF DOC CR             IRREVOCABLE
20         DO CR NO.                  LCUK53368
31C        DATE OF ISSUE             050914
31D        EXPIRY ON/AT              051104 ENGLAND
50         APPLICANT                 TAN CHEE ENG LTD. 1 EAST COAST
                                      AVENUE, SINGAPORE
59         BENEFICIARY               ABC EXPORTERS LTD. SHADY LANE
                                      BOLTON, ENGLAND
32B        AMOUNT                    UK POUNDS (£) 50,000.00
41D        AVAIL WITH/BY             ANY BANK BY NEGOTIATION
42C        DRAFTS AT                 SIGHT (IN DUPLICATE)
42D        DRAWEE                    UK COMMERCIAL BANK, MANCHESTER
43P        PART SHIPMENT             NOT ALLOWED
43T        TRANSHIPMENT              NOT ALLOWED
44A        LOAD/DISP/TID             SEAPORT ENGLAND
44B        FOR TRANSP. TO            SINGAPORE
44D        LAST DAY SHIP.            051024
45B        SHPMT OF GOODS            DIESEL ENGINE SPARE PARTS
46A        DOCUMENTS REQD            1. SIGNED COMM INVOICE IN TRIPLICATE
                                     2. FULL SET OF CLEAN ON BOARD B/L MADE
                                     OUT OF ORDER, MARKED FREIGHT PAID AND
                                     NOTIFY THE
                                     APPLICANT
                                     3. INSURANCE POLICY/CERTIFICATE (INSTITUTE
                                     CARGO CLAUSES 'A' INCLUDING WAR AND
                                     STRIKES) IN ASSIGNABLE FORM FOR 10% ABOVE
                                     THE INVOICE VALUE WITH CLAIMS PAYABLE IN
                                     SINGAPORE.
                                     4. CERTIFICATE OF ORIGIN SHOWING GOODS
                                     OF  UK ORIGIN.
47B        ADDNL CONDITIONS          1. ALL DOCS MUST BE PRESENTED WITHIN 10
                                     DAYS FROM DATE OF SHIPMENT.
                                     2. CONTRACT MATERIALS MUST BE PACKED IN
                                     GOOD SEA/AIR WORTHY EXPORT PACKING.
                                     3. INVOICED FREIGHT NOT TO EXCEED
                                     AMOUNT OF FREIGHT DUE ACCORDING TO
                                     B/L/AWB.
71B        CHARGES                   ALL BANKING CHARGES OUTSIDE SINGAPORE
                                     INCLUDING REIMBURSEMENT CHARGES ARE
                                     FOR BENEF'S ACCOUNT.
79         NARRATIVE                 BOTH PARTIES ALREADY UNDERSTAND WiTH
                                     THE L/C  SO THAT YOU COULD JUST ADV IT
                                     TO BEN WITHOUT YR RESPONSIBILITY AS PER
                                     UCP ART 12. UPON RECEIPT OF CONFORM
                                     DOCS WE WILL EFFECT PYT SOONEST.
49         CONF. INSTRCTS            WITHOUT
```

accurately scrutinised and, if necessary, amended when the L/C is first received, it may be difficult to make corrections later.

On the other hand, having an uncomplicated L/C and including only the essential documents and specifications, together with a reference to the underlying contract, is normally advantageous for both parties. The documents most commonly used in connection with L/Cs are basically the same as were mentioned earlier in connection with documentary collections (*Chapter 2, Section 2.4.3*), even if the stipulations in the L/C are usually more detailed as to how, and by whom they should be issued.

As can be seen in the examples in *Chapter 8, Terms of payment*, wording may also be inserted in the terms of payment to the effect that the L/C should be issued 'in form and substance acceptable to the seller according to contract'. This wording is suggested in order for the

---

Box 2.17 Dealing in documents and not in goods

As pointed out earlier in this chapter, both directly and indirectly, documentary payments through banks is a matter of dealing in documents and not in goods or services. That is particularly important to have in mind when using L/Cs, where the approval of the documents will be made by the banks, as stated in the ICC rules: 'Banks must examine all documents stipulated in the Credit with reasonable care, to ascertain whether or not they appear, on the face, to be in compliance with the terms of Credit'.

This documentary aspect may be seen as a risk mainly for the buyer, but it is equally important for the seller to be careful with even the smallest print in the documents, so they in all aspects, appear, on the face, to be in compliance with the terms of the L/C.

Also see *Box 2.11* where the same message is put forward, but from another perspective.

Box 2.18 International rules covering L/Cs

In order to reduce the difficulties that the users of L/Cs may face through differences in bank terminology and practice, ICC has issued a number of uniform rules as guidance (*Uniform Customs and Practice for Documentary Credits (UCP 500)*). These include different forms of credit, obligations and responsibility of the participating banks, documents, presentation and validity. These rules are constantly updated and are now used by most banks around the world. The seller using L/Cs must be familiar with these rules and some general aspects should be stressed:

* All L/Cs must clearly indicate how they are available, if revocable or irrevocable and where documents are to be presented, however, the rules also specify what will be applicable should these aspects not be indicated by the L/C.
* All L/Cs must stipulate an expiry date, however, the rules also specify situations when both limitations and extensions to such an expiry date may apply.
* The rules contain a number of articles about ambiguity as to the issuers of documents as well as their contents, particularly regarding the freight and insurance documents, including detailed interpretations.
* The rules also contain articles about definitions of specific words, dates, expressions, terminology and tolerances.
* The rules specify the detailed definition of transferable L/Cs, what rules apply to them and what obligations apply to the banks.
* The rules also deal with the responsibility and the liability of the banks in dealing with L/Cs, including '*force majeure*'.

To bring about a more common approach and uniformity to the examination of the documents as performed by the participating banks, ICC has also published an additional paper, named *International Standard Banking Practice (ISBP)*, establishing an international standard for examination of documents presented under Letters of Credit in relation to the *UCP 500*.

The above rules and other documents and guidelines related to L/Cs can be obtained from most banks or directly from ICC **(www.iccuk.net).**

seller to have a stronger case when arguing for amendments, should the L/C technically be issued according to the contract but, at the same time, contain additional details or stipulations that will restrict or potentially prevent the seller from fulfilling all conditions at a later stage when the documents are presented to the bank.

■ 2.5.8 Third party documents

One general aspect that must be commented on at this stage, is the importance for the seller to be particularly observant with regard to documents that are to be produced, verified, stamped or signed by a third party, and also on other terms and conditions in the L/C over which the seller may not have full control.

When it comes to the documents, some of them, often the invoice, may have to be certified or legalised by a third party, often a Chamber of Commerce and/or the embassy of the importing country. If so, the seller has to make absolutely certain that such a procedure can not only take place, but that it can be done in time to comply with the dates of the L/C, primarily with regard to the due date of shipment or presentation of documents. The same check has to be done for any other third party documentation, such as test certificates and inspection records.

The seller should also be aware of the interaction between the terms of delivery and the documents related to the L/C (see *Chapter 1, Export risk and risk assessment*). Some terms of delivery stipulate that it is up to the buyer to arrange the transportation, after which the transportation documents, for example the Bill of Lading can be released.

Some buyers, particularly those from developing countries, often try to arrange transportation themselves, in some cases with ships from their own country. The reason could be established contacts with the local shipping company, but also import regulations in order to support the country's shipping industry or simply because it is cheaper and payment may be made in local currency. For these reasons, the buyer might prefer FOB as their choice of terms of delivery, however, the buyer does not have control of the shipping schedules, which might be changed or the designated ship may have been rerouted with short notice.

Should this happen, the seller will not be able to load as planned and will consequently not be able to produce the Bill of Lading stipulated in the L/C – or will receive them too late to comply with the stipulated timeframes. There are ways for the seller to eliminate such risks if the parties cannot agree on some other more suitable term of delivery, but they have to be agreed on beforehand as part of the terms of payment. For example, to stipulate an alternative to the Bill of Lading in the L/C, such as a warehouse or other certificate, which the seller knows can be arranged.

Finally, not only must each document be issued as stipulated, but they also have to be consistent between themselves with regard to goods description, markings, etc. In practice, however, it is relatively common that this is not the case, due to carelessness, last minute changes or lack of documentary knowledge, but it should always be possible to avoid such potential discrepancies. ICC rules (*UCP 500*) contain detailed information about the more commonly used documents in international trade and what they generally should contain in order to be approved under the L/C.

■ 2.5.9 Inspection of the goods in conjunction with documentary payments

With regard to both documentary collections and L/Cs, the buyer has to honour the documents as presented, but normally without having seen the actual delivery. The documents may be scrutinized when presented for collection and the banks check their correctness under the L/C, but they have no responsibility for the genuineness or correctness of the information contained therein.

In many cases this may not be important, the parties may know each other through earlier transactions, the goods delivered can be standardised or well-known to the buyer, and they can always claim compensation after delivery, whatever value that may have. But, in

INFORMATION BOX

WHEN YOU NEED TO BE SURE   **SGS**

SGS is the world's leading inspection, verification, testing and certification company, registered in Geneva as Société Générale de Surveillance in 1919. SGS is recognised as the global benchmark for quality and integrity. With 37,000 employees, SGS operates a network of about 1,000 offices and laboratories around the world, of which several are located in the UK.

The core services offered by SGS can be divided into three categories:

- **Inspection services.** SGS inspects and verifies the quantity, weight and quality of traded goods. Inspection typically takes place at transhipment.
- **Testing services.** SGS tests product quality and performance against various health, safety and regulatory standards. SGS operates state of the art laboratories on or close to customers' premises.
- **Certification services.** SGS certifies that systems or services meet the requirements of standards set by governments, standardisation bodies (eg, SO 9000) or by SGS customers. SGS also develops and certifies its own standards.

SGS United Kingdom Ltd
Rossmore Business Park, Ellesmere Port CH65 3EN
Telephone: 0151 350 6666
www.uk.sgs.com

other cases, this question may be of greater importance to the buyer and the parties involved. In particular, the seller must then find other ways to satisfy the buyer in order for them to agree to a L/C. This is often done through the inclusion of a separate Certificate of Inspection in the documentation, issued by an independent surveyor who verifies the goods before delivery through samples or production surveys. Such arrangements must form part of the contract and the certificate should be included in the required documents in the terms of payment.

■ 2.5.10 Frequent discrepancies in documentation

Apart from genuine mistakes in preparing the documentation, some of the more frequent discrepancies include:

- The expiry date of the L/C has passed.
- Late presentation, ie, the specified period of time after the date of shipment during which presentation should be made, has expired.
- Late shipment, ie, the shipping document is signed too late or indicates shipment after the stipulated time of shipment.
- A document has not been presented or, if presented, not issued by a correct company or authority.
- Stipulated tolerances in credit amount, quantity, unit price or other variables have not been met.
- The shipping documents are not in accordance with the terms, for example, loading/unloading in the wrong port or not on the specified ship, issued to the wrong order or wrongly endorsed.
- The Bill of Lading does not indicate that the goods are loaded on-board or loaded on deck, if that is not explicitly allowed, or not correctly endorsed.
- The insurance documents are incorrect, for example, not endorsed correctly, not covering the risks required or showing incorrect insurance value – or not explicitly indicating additional statements as required in the L/C.
- Shipping details are incorrect, eg, showing part shipments or transhipment, if not allowed, or the packing/marking is not in accordance with the terms.

One general and very common reason for documents not being approved is, as stated above, that the documents do not match each other, for example, that late changes in the marking of the goods as they appear on the Bill of Lading has not been changed in other documents, or that changes in the shipping route has not been included in the insurance policy.

■ 2.5.11 How to avoid discrepancies in the Letter of Credit

L/Cs that do not totally comply with the term of the credit are dependent on the approval of the buyer and will, therefore, in such cases contain an additional risk that the seller did not anticipate when entering into the deal – if this risk had been known beforehand, the seller might not even have entered into the transaction at all.

As pointed out earlier, the bank guarantee incorporated in the L/C will then disappear and the L/C will, in practice, be transformed into a documentary collection (dependent on the willingness of the buyer to pay). In smaller trading companies, with high volumes of export sales with small margins, such an added risk is unacceptable and one single such default could lead to bankruptcy. It is also among these trading companies that you often see real professionalism in dealing with L/Cs and the banks very seldom find discrepancies in their documents.

Based on that experience, which can be achieved by all companies, there are at least some measures that can be taken to avoid such discrepancies:

- Make use of the experience of the UK international banks, they have professionals that will help you in this matter.
- SITPRO (see *Information Box* in *Chapter 1*) has issued a *Letter of Credit Checklist and Guide for Exporters*, which contains valuable information on how to check the L/C and its required terms and conditions, both when the L/C is received and later on at presentation of documents. Visit **www.sitpro.org.uk/trade/lettcredexport** for this checklist.
- The rules and guidelines on L/Cs (ICC's publication, *UCP 500*) contain the detailed information that the seller must know. They can be ordered directly from the ICC together with the booklets *International Standard Banking Practices (ISBP, No. 645)* dealing with the documents, and the ICC *Guide to Documentary Credit Operations (No. 515)*. This is the necessary theoretical background when dealing with L/Cs.
- The seller must be particularly observant on the details of the terms of payment in the contract. They will automatically become the basis for the L/C that the seller will receive.
- It is at the time of receipt that the L/C can be amended (if not issued correctly). Someone in the company must have the direct responsibility for such internal approval so at that time no obstacle exists

or will reasonably not appear later on, which will prevent the seller from delivering documents without discrepancies.

- The L/C should be available at the Advising Bank if possible and the documents should be sent to that bank directly after shipment. This bank will then advise on any discrepancies and the seller will have time to amend the documents when it is possible to do so. Should that not be the case, this is usually an indication that the seller's own approval of the L/C when it was issued was incorrect; it should have been amended in order to accommodate what was later not possible to correct.

- Timing is essential, always allow for a longer period than expected for issuing the L/C and for shipment, presentation and expiry dates. Deliver the documents in good time before expiry in order to be able to do the correcting amendments, or deliver completely new documents, if necessary.

- Finally, some banks also offer additional services which could help the seller avoid discrepancies in the documents altogether. (For example, freight management and even export document preparation, as offered by HSBC, see the Information Box below.)

■ 2.5.12 The Letter of Credit as a tool in the business process

One big advantage when using a L/C is not only the security it gives to the seller, but also the flexibility and adaptability in helping solve complicated business problems and, thereby, also creating the base for additional business. This enables the seller to give reasonable advantages to the buyer in return for acceptance of a L/C, for example, with an extended credit on favourable terms, or sharing the bank charges.

It is true that when a contract is signed, any later amendment will demand the corresponding amendments also in the L/C, and that may take time and involve additional costs for the transaction as a whole. But before signing, almost any transaction can be structured in a way which allows the L/C to function as a glue to hold the deal together and to protect the interest of both parties. When the L/C is thereafter correctly issued, both the seller and the buyer will know in advance that they are safeguarded in a way that can be controlled by one and the same payment instrument and guaranteed by at least one of the

INFORMATION BOX

participating banks. Some examples are given below on how the L/C can be used as part of a more complicated business transaction:

- Advance payment or 'red clauses' can be included, payable against an advance payment guarantee or other obligation from the seller or the parent company.
- Separate procedures can be arranged for tests or samples to be received by the buyer before main delivery.
- If required by the buyer, both the process of production as well as the final delivery of the goods can be monitored or verified by using independent inspection certificates under the L/C.
- The transferability of a L/C makes it possible for the seller to arrange for multiple or combined deliveries without added security or liquidity.
- Arrangements of different supplier or buyer credits with repayment with or without coverage under the L/C can be arranged, at the same time giving credit to the buyer and cash payment to the seller.
- Arrangements of different types of barter trade transactions can also be connected to the underlying contract (see example below).
- Increased business opportunities are generally available to the seller when using the L/C as supplementary security for pre-financing during the period of purchase, production and delivery (see below).

■ 2.5.13 The Letter of Credit as a pre-delivery finance instrument

As a guaranteed payment, subject to fixed and known terms and conditions in the individual case, the L/C can also be used as part of the pre-financing needed, in order to produce and deliver the goods. This may be particularly important in cases of longer production and delivery periods or in single large transactions, when the most difficult period to finance is often up to delivery, after which a clear claim on the buyer can be obtained. Many such transactions may also require pre-financing of a scale that could exceed the seller's ordinary credit limits, even without regard for any supplier credit given to the buyer after delivery, and the L/C may be the tool to close this gap.

The financial consequences of each transaction are directly connected to its size, structure and time of payment, combined with additional demand on the seller for credits and guarantees, perhaps starting several months before delivery and payment, for example:

- demand for performance and/or advance payment guarantees;
- acquisition of raw material or additional/changed production facilities;
- additional contracts with suppliers or sub-contractors with a payment structure independent of the underlying contract;
- additional bonds or guarantees covering shipment obligations or insurance;
- additional running costs covering production and delivery.

These additional expenditures, including the costs for insurance cover and necessary reserves for unforeseen events, have to be taken out of the seller's own resources and existing credit limits, but often the financial advantages that the L/C in itself can generate may be needed as well as these facilities. When that is the case, it is particularly important to get the buyer to accept the L/C as the method of payment, in order for the seller to be able to arrange the supplementary financing that the transaction will require – even if the seller has to compensate the buyer by taking part of the bank charges involved or giving concessions in other areas of the contract.

With this in mind, the advantage of having the L/C transferable is obvious; the possibility of transferring it on to other suppliers will relieve cash-flow pressures from the seller and these suppliers will get the same pre-delivery advantages of knowing what terms and conditions will apply in order to receive payment. Even if the L/C is not made transferable, it could be used as a master L/C and supplementary security for new back-to-back L/Cs in favour of the suppliers, with the same advantage to them as a transferable L/C would have had.

Many banks, acting as Advising Banks, also offer special Export loans (or similar facilities), with a percentage of the value of the L/C as additional working capital, to be repaid from the proceeds upon presentation of documents. Such loans are often backed by a pledge on the underlying L/C.

Even without the explicit use of the L/C in a back-to-back arrangement, or if it is already used for additional finance through Export loans or Red Clauses, its mere existence may also indirectly help the seller in obtaining new or extended credits from the suppliers involved in the transaction. In short, apart from its other advantages to the seller, the L/C may also be used as an important tool in arranging many different forms of pre-delivery finance.

➤ 2.6 Barter and counter trade

So far, the assumption has been that goods are delivered against payment, at sight or at a later date. But there are also other forms of transactions, even if they are not so common today as they have been in the past, where payment or settlement, wholly or partially, is made in some other way.

The most common of these alternative forms of trade transactions are:

- **Barter trades** – with payment in other goods.
- **Compensation trades** – with payment partly in money but also in other goods, agreed between the parties.
- **Repurchase agreements** – in which payment is made through products, generated by the equipment or goods delivered by the seller.
- **Counter trades** – with settlement in money, but with the transaction being dependent on a corresponding sales/purchase transaction to balance the payment stream.

There are probably many reasons why these alternative trade transactions are used, but at least four main reasons are often referred to, namely:

- to enable trade to take place in markets which are unable to pay for imports. This can occur as a result of a non-convertible currency, a lack of commercial credit or a shortage of foreign exchange;
- to protect or stimulate the output of domestic industries and to help find new export markets;

- as a reflection of political and economic policies which seek to plan and balance overseas trade;
- to gain a competitive advantage over competing suppliers.

Barter trade, the oldest form of trade, had its recent peak during the 1980s, when it was very common amongst the East European and other countries with a state-regulated economy. But today, with some Asian, African and Latin American currencies in a state of destabilisation, leaving the countries unable to pay for their import needs in the usual way, barter or counter trade may once again be more frequently used.

Apart from extremely large or complex transactions, particularly within the areas of defence, nuclear installations and complete production plants, large aircraft deals or similar transactions, most other barter and counter trade transactions are made with developing countries – or other countries with a non-competitive or regulated trade system or a destabilized currency. Sometimes it is also more the character of the deal itself, its size and complexity, rather than the importing country, that necessitate these transactions, often structured through specialised trading houses that have the overall knowledge and expertise for creating new trading combinations that would otherwise probably not have made the export deal possible.

The terms of payment in these transactions are dependent of the structure of the deal, and the participation of the banks may be totally different compared to ordinary transactions with payment in currency. In real barter trade situations, only a designated clearing account may be needed in order to register the value of the transactions and the net balance of the flow of goods. When it comes to other forms of counter trade, the banks often have a more central role, often through the use of L/Cs, each being structured to come into force simultaneously, when all other arrangements are in place and approved by the individual trading partners. But thereafter, they could often be handled as individual transactions with each L/C being settled separately.

■ 2.6.1 Example of a simple counter trade transaction

As an example of how the mechanism of a simple counter trade could work, a UK seller of machine equipment has made a deal with a buyer in Honduras. In order to finance the deal, a UK trading house has arranged with a Danish company to buy raw sugar from another company in Honduras for the equivalent amount, which the Danish company is going to sell to an African buyer.

In this example, the Danish company has to take the first step by instructing their bank to issue a L/C in favour of their seller in Honduras, but its validity has to be conditional upon a second L/C being issued by a bank in Honduras in favour of the UK seller. Such a clause could have the following wording in the L/C first to be issued, in order to create the security for the combination of transactions that form the counter trade:

'This Letter of Credit is not operational until:

1. Banco Central, Honduras, has issued through UK Commercial Bank, London as Advising Bank, an irrevocable Letter of Credit for the amount of USD 1,000,000, covering shipment of coffee grinding equipment, in favour of UK Grinding Machinery Ltd, London. The Letter of Credit should be payable at sight with the Advising Bank and contain instructions to this bank to add its confirmation.
2. The Advising Bank has confirmed that UK Grinding Machinery Ltd has approved the terms and conditions of the Letter of Credit above.'

When both L/Cs are issued, they will become operative at the same time, but can thereafter, be settled as separate transactions, or alternatively be structured in such a way that payments received under one L/C should be used as outgoing payments under the other. It is then advantageous if both L/Cs are payable at the same bank, which, in this case, will use the payments from the Danish buyer to pay the UK seller upon due fulfilment of the terms and conditions under the L/C. In the same way, the payments between the companies in Honduras are settled between their banks, often in local currency.

3

Bonds and guarantees

➤ 3.1 The use of bonds and guarantees

In international trade it is very common for either or both parties to demand separate undertakings – usually in the form of written bonds or guarantees, covering the obligations assumed by the other party.

It could be the seller's delivery obligations that have to be secured by a guarantee issued by the seller's bank, or the seller receiving a guarantee covering the payment obligations of the buyer. In any case, the guarantee is often 'the glue' that holds a deal together, a deal that might not otherwise materialise due to the inherent latent risks that must be covered. This is most common for transactions that, apart from delivery, also cover installation, future performance, warranty periods or similar undertakings, when the parties are mutually dependent on each other – often for a long period.

In certain cases, particularly with more straightforward deals or in combination with a simple service and/or performance undertaking, it is often enough that the seller, or the parent or group/company, issues these bonds/guarantees – particularly if the seller is part of a larger or well-known group. However, in most cases, bonds/guarantees are issued by a separate party, normally in the form of a bank guarantee or an insurance bond (from an insurance company).

Bank guarantees are most commonly used in connection with ordinary transactions in international trade and can be defined as:

'... any arrangement, by which a bank, upon the request of the Principal, irrevocably commits itself to pay a sum of money to the Beneficiary in accordance with the terms of the guarantee'.

Regardless of the obligations covered by it, a bank guarantee is always a commitment to pay (wholly or partly) the amount stated, but does not guarantee fulfilment of the actual delivery or any other obligation, which the Principal may have towards the Beneficiary.

Internationally, so-called 'surety bonds' may also be issued by insurance or surety companies, particularly in connection with whole projects, with an alternative obligation to fulfil or arrange for the completion of the underlying contract. This could be to appoint another supplier to complete the project if, for any reason, the Principal is not capable of doing so. Such surety bonds are mainly designed for building and engineering firms and suppliers of large industrial equipment.

Most guarantees are related to an underlying commercial contract between the buyer and the seller. In such cases, and if and when disagreement occurs between the commercial parties whether the claim is justified or not, payment may be suspended until such a dispute is settled, either by later agreement, arbitration or through the courts.

The risk of disputed claims is also one of the main reasons behind the introduction, in recent years, of so-called 'demand guarantees', with an unlimited right for the Beneficiary to claim under the guarantee, irrespective of any objections from the Principal or the Issuing Bank. This type of guarantee is described in *Section 3.3* below.

■ 3.1.1 Terminology

Bonds, surety bonds, guarantees, indemnity or similar expressions are all used to describe undertakings by a third party but, regardless of the title, it is the wording of the document that is important.

Unless otherwise dictated by the context or by common practice, this book will only use the term 'guarantee' in accordance with ICC terminology, particularly when dealing with undertakings from banks for payment in money only.

The text will, however, not deal with the more complex subject of the nature of the guarantee, but simply describe the main differences between:

a) a primary and independent obligation separated from the contractual obligations of the Principal; and
b) a secondary and accessory obligation, connected to the underlying trade contract.

The following expressions will therefore be used in the text in order to separate the main categories of guarantees:

- **demand guarantees** (primary and independent undertakings);
- **conditional guarantees** (secondary and accessory undertakings);
- **standby letters of credit** (often used as an alternative to demand guarantees).

Furthermore, the expressions 'Principal' and 'Beneficiary' are the correct terms in connection with guarantees, but in this book the words 'seller' and 'buyer' are sometimes also used in order to focus on the trade aspect and facilitate the reading.

■ 3.1.2 Parties involved in the guarantee

The general question of who should issue the guarantee is determined mainly by the Beneficiary, but could also be dependent on rules or local conditions in that country. In industrialised countries, the guarantees are often issued directly to the Beneficiary, either by the Principal themselves or, more frequently, by an Issuing Bank.

Guarantees can also be issued through an Advising Bank at the Beneficiary's location, but without any responsibility for that bank under the guarantee. The role of the Advising Bank is to forward the guarantee to the Beneficiary, verifying the authenticity of the Issuing Bank.

There are also situations when a local bank in the country of the Beneficiary has to issue the guarantee (which is the standard procedure in many countries) particularly if the Beneficiary is a local authority or similar body. In some countries it may even be stipulated by law that they should be issued by a local bank. In these cases the Principal's bank (the Instructing Bank) will issue a counter guarantee as an indemnity to the local bank (the Issuing Bank). This would be accompanied by instructions to issue a guarantee in favour of the Beneficiary – either in a specified form (if that is possible) or otherwise according to local law and practice.

The instructions between the banks involved in the guarantee are nowadays often processed in a structured format through the banks internal Swift-system, with the same speed and accuracy as for international payments.

When issued by a local bank in the country of the Beneficiary, it is important for the Principal to know in advance what rules apply in that country and, if possible, to have the wording of the guarantee agreed in advance and inserted as an appendix to the contract. This will help to avoid the many surprises that may appear later on when the guarantee is to be issued, for example, if the guarantee is issued without a fixed expiry date or subject to other rules according to local customs and practices. Moreover, it is up to the local Issuing Bank, and not to the Instructing Bank, to decide whether a later demand for payment is correct and if the payment itself should be made under the guarantee in accordance with the Issuing Bank's interpretation of the terms and conditions.

■ 3.1.3 Costs for issuing guarantees

A guarantee is normally charged with a flat fee covering handling costs plus a commission fee, usually ranging from 0.5–2 per cent per annum on the outstanding amount. For larger transactions and companies, the commission fee may be even lower. The actual cost is determined

---

Box 3.1 Example of a performance guarantee issued by a UK bank, related to the underlying contract (conditional guarantee)

Messers ATV Radiocommunications Spa
18 Vie Rosle, Cassina di Spati
1081 PADOVA, Italy

Guarantee No. G-32768/34

Between you as 'buyer' and Highland Communications Ltd, 31 Dover House Road, Wokingham RG41 8HX, as 'supplier', an agreement has been signed according to contract GHTY 376 dated 25.02.05, regarding the supply of 1075 Satellite Adaptors, model A-346, for a total contract amount of EUR 47,437.00.

At the request of the 'supplier', we, the undersigned bank, hereby guarantee as for our own debt, the due fulfilment of the obligations assumed by the 'supplier' under the above-mentioned contract.

However, we shall not by reason of this undertaking be liable to disburse more than 4,743.00 in total (four-thousand, seven-hundred and fourty-three Euros).

This guarantee, issued under English law and jurisdiction and to be governed by the ICC rules URCG, ICC 325, is valid until November 25th, 2005 by which date (at the latest) all claims must have reached us in writing in order to be taken into consideration. After expiry, this guarantee shall be returned to us for cancellation.

London, March 15th, 2005

UK Commercial Bank Plc

Signature _____ Signature _____

---

by factors such as customer relations, commercial background, form of guarantee (demand or conditional), guarantee amount, the competitive situation and also the potential for additional business for the issuing institution, such as advising Letters of Credit or the possibility of arranging finance.

The costs of other banks involved also have to be taken into account if the guarantee is either to be issued by a local bank (based on a counter guarantee), or forwarded by an Advising Bank at the Beneficiary's location. When more than one bank is involved in the guarantee, either in an issuing, counter-guaranteeing or advising capacity, the costs could vary considerably, which is one good reason for not accepting guarantee costs outside the UK if possible. This is particularly the case with

Box 3.2   Different structures of bank guarantees

Direct Guarantees (Alt A) or guarantees forwarded via an Advising Bank (Alt B)

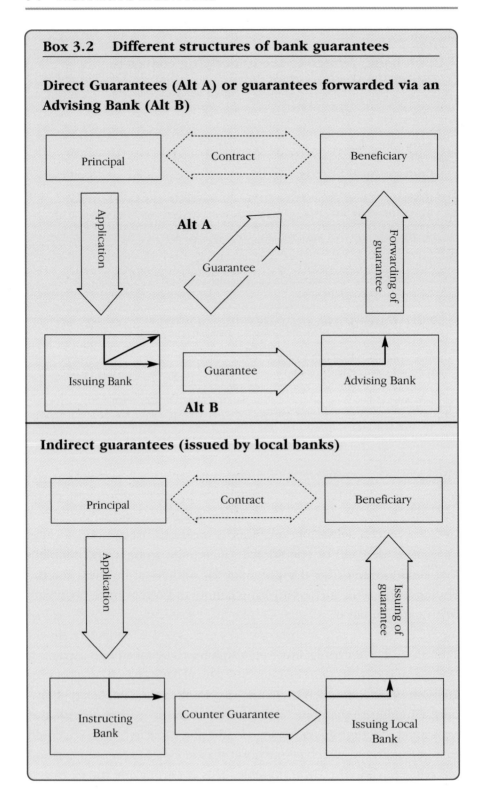

Indirect guarantees (issued by local banks)

'demand guarantees' since these can be prolonged for a considerable time at the sole discretion of the Beneficiary (extend or pay). However, whatever is finally agreed upon regarding guarantee charges and other conditions, should also be included in the contract.

➤ 3.2 Common forms of guarantee

The forms of guarantee described in *Section 3.2.1* below are often grouped together as contract guarantees due to their direct link with the course of events in a commercial contract consisting of offer, contract, shipment, acceptance of delivery, warranty period and final payment. Other commonly used guarantees are described in *Section 3.2.2*.

■ 3.2.1 Contract guarantees

Tender Guarantee or Bid Bond

This guarantee is delivered in conjunction with the offer or tender for contract, and guarantees the obligation of the seller to stand by the undertaking, including the issuing of additional guarantees, should the bid be successful.

The guarantee is sometimes substituted by an **undertaking to provide a guarantee**, often issued by the seller or its parent or group company covering the obligation of the seller to sign the contract if awarded, and to deliver the promised guarantees.

Advance Payment Guarantee

This guarantee has to be in place before or along with the advance payment from the buyer and should cover the obligation on behalf of the seller to repay the amount (wholly or in part) should the delivery and/or some other contractual undertaking not be fulfilled.

Advance payments normally range between 10–25 per cent of the contract value depending on size, complexity and time span of the contract until completion.

Box 3.3 Summery of the use of contract bonds/guarantees

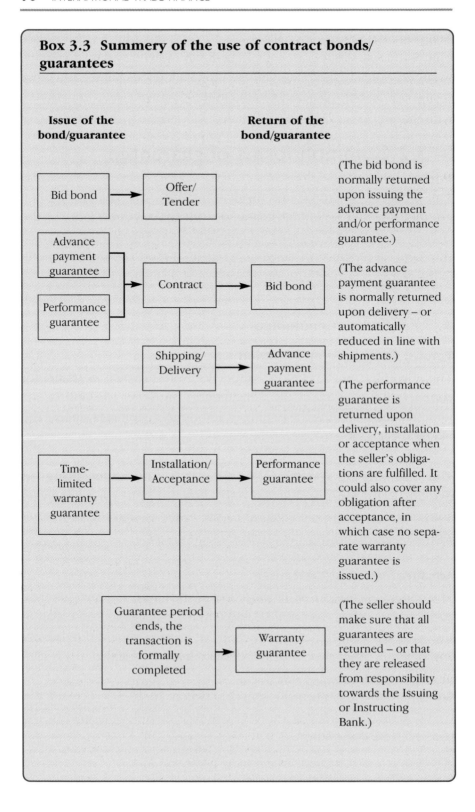

Issue of the bond/guarantee

Return of the bond/guarantee

Bid bond → Offer/Tender

Advance payment guarantee

Performance guarantee

→ Contract → Bid bond

Shipping/Delivery → Advance payment guarantee

Time-limited warranty guarantee → Installation/Acceptance → Performance guarantee

Guarantee period ends, the transaction is formally completed → Warranty guarantee

(The bid bond is normally returned upon issuing the advance payment and/or performance guarantee.)

(The advance payment guarantee is normally returned upon delivery – or automatically reduced in line with shipments.)

(The performance guarantee is returned upon delivery, installation or acceptance when the seller's obligations are fulfilled. It could also cover any obligation after acceptance, in which case no separate warranty guarantee is issued.)

(The seller should make sure that all guarantees are returned – or that they are released from responsibility towards the Issuing or Instructing Bank.)

Progress Payment Guarantee

This form of guarantee is issued when the buyer cannot effectively make use of the seller's delivery or other obligations until these are finally completed but, nevertheless, has agreed to pay in connection with the progress of such work or delivery. The amount of this type of guarantee is dependent on the nature of the commitment.

Performance Guarantee

This guarantee is perhaps the most commonly used contract guarantee. It should be issued and delivered on behalf of the seller at the signing of the contract or before the start of delivery – guaranteeing the seller's obligations to deliver and perform according to the contract. For ordinary commercial transactions, the amount of a performance guarantee normally ranges between 10–15 per cent of the contract value.

Retention Money Guarantee

The purpose of this guarantee is to safeguard the final installation or start-up phase of machinery, equipment or other delivered goods, and to allow the buyer to recover payments already made under the contract should the seller not fulfil these obligations.

Such guarantees are mainly used as an alternative to terms of payment where the buyer would otherwise withhold part of the payment, often 10–15 per cent, until completion. Against this guarantee the seller will instead receive this part payment at an earlier stage.

Warranty Guarantee

Many contracts include maintenance or performance obligations of the delivered goods for a certain period of time after delivery or installation. Instead of retaining part of the payment until such period has expired, the buyer will release it earlier against this guarantee. The amount could be in the range of 10–15 per cent depending of the warranty commitments.

■ 3.2.2 Other common guarantees in international trade or finance

Payment Guarantee

Payment guarantees are issued on the instruction of the buyer in favour of the seller, in order to cover the buyer's payment obligations for goods or services to be delivered according to contract. This form of guarantee is often used to cover either single or recurring deliveries under a long-term contract, with a total amount covering outstanding and anticipated deliveries. The guarantee covers the buyer's solvency and ability to pay, but not their will to do so if the claim is contested, unless the guarantee is 'on demand'.

The terms of payment, in connection with payment guarantees, are often arranged on an 'open account' basis (see also *Section 3.4.1* and definition in the *Glossary*). The handling of delivery and documentation could then be made more flexible with a payment guarantee compared to a Letter of Credit, but the security for the seller is dependent on the nature of the guarantee.

Guaranteed acceptance (Aval)

Sometimes the acceptance by the buyer of a Bill of Exchange is not adequate security for the seller to cover the commercial risk. In such cases a bank may strengthen the security by adding its guarantee directly to the Bill of Exchange by signing and adding the statement 'good per aval' or 'per aval for the account of the drawee', thereby guaranteeing the due payment obligations of the drawee (the buyer).

In many developing countries, where guaranteed acceptances are most common, such a guarantee, if issued by a larger domestic bank, could automatically include the approval of transferring foreign currency out of the country. Whereas in other cases, such approvals have to be executed separately in the form of a **Transfer guarantee**, issued by the Central Bank.

Credit Guarantee

This guarantee covers the contractual obligations of the borrower towards the lender. In many countries, the seller may have local subsidiaries or affiliates without credit capacity of their own, and the credit guarantee will then support credits from local banks to finance general activities or a specific transaction.

The credit guarantee could also apply to other facilities from local banks, such as overdrafts or credit lines for issuing of guarantees or Letters of Credit. But the support could also cover business obligations against parties other than banks, for example, the obligations of subsidiaries towards local main contractors or insurance companies.

The guarantee could in fact cover any other third party in that country, for example, in connection with a request to a court to issue an injunction. In all these cases, the guarantee will cover the obligations which the subsidiary cannot cope with on its own merits.

In some cases, the credit guarantee may be substituted with more indirect support towards the lender or a third party, in the form of a **Letter of Support, Letter of Comfort** or **Letter of Awareness**. These documents do not impose any formal or legal obligations but are rather a form of assurance on behalf of the issuer (often a parent or group company) declaring its knowledge of the undertaking, and that it will monitor the borrower to ensure that they should be able to repay the loan or fulfil other obligations.

Banks or other recipients of such letters will of course be aware of the limited legal value of these documents and will accept them as an alternative to guarantees only in cases where the supported party has a standing of its own but needs additional security, and where the issuer is a company of such a high rating that its reputation and moral standing would be severely affected by a default.

Duty-exempt Guarantee

This form of guarantee is often used at exhibitions, fairs or in connection with installations or projects when machinery or equipment must be temporarily brought into the country. By issuing this guarantee in favour of the local customs authorities, the customs duties are guaranteed should the equipment not be brought out of the country within the specified period.

Letter of Indemnity

This guarantee is issued upon request of the buyer and in favour of the shipping company when the goods have arrived at port but without the buyer having access to the necessary Bill of Lading. The guarantee thus safeguards the shipping company from the risks and costs involved by delivering the goods to the buyer without presentation of this title document.

➢ 3.3 Demand guarantees

The most usual interpretation of a guarantee is that it becomes payable when the Issuing Bank has verified that the Principal has defaulted or is in breach of the contractual obligations, but also that the Beneficiary, as a result of that breach, has suffered a loss or damages as specified in a Claim Document, submitted together with the demand for payment. This is the principle of a conditional guarantee, related to the underlying commercial contract.

In most cases, it is probably quite clear if the Principal has fulfilled the obligations or not, and if payment should therefore be made under the guarantee. However, sometimes this is not that easily established – the parties may have different versions of the events and the Principal may simply refuse payment by the Issuing Bank under the guarantee.

If the Principal is of the opinion that the claim is incorrect, an instruction will be sent to the Issuing Bank accordingly and, unless such an instruction is obviously wrong, the Issuing Bank will refuse to pay. Such a claim could finally be settled in arbitration or end up in court if not agreed earlier by the parties. This procedure can take time, which further acts to the disadvantage of the Beneficiary since it may delay the final outcome of the deal and thereby the entire value of the contract, despite payments or other commitments having already been made.

This lack of perceived equality between the commercial parties has contributed to the introduction of a relatively new form of guarantee with a much stronger position for the Beneficiary. In many countries, even within the OECD-area, the Beneficiary often requests the guarantee to be issued 'on demand' or on 'first demand'. This guarantee is then payable on the first demand from the Beneficiary and without the approval of the Principal or without having to prove to the Issuing Bank that a default has occurred. It is in that respect similar to a bank cheque, which the Beneficiary can cash in at any time during the validity of the guarantee. This form of guarantee (also called Simple Demand Guarantee or Unconditional Guarantee) gives the Beneficiary (mostly the buyer in the case of UK exports) a much stronger position. The risk of improper use, or Unfair or Unwarranted Calling as it is often known, will of course be higher, even if such events are relatively few.

A major disadvantage of a demand guarantee, (from the seller's perspective) is not just the risk for unfair calling, but also that such a guarantee will automatically put the buyer in a stronger contractual bargaining position than what might originally have been intended. During the lifespan of the contract, and if and when disputes or other discussions arise between the parties, the buyer always has the option to call on the guarantee – and even without ever doing it, the seller will be aware of the threat and the advantage that gives to the buyer.

Finally, it should be noted that once payment has been made under a demand guarantee, it can be difficult for the seller to get such payment repaid, if not agreed with the buyer and then on their terms. The buyer is perhaps not willing to take part in any arbitration or court proceedings, even if stipulated in the contract – and even if the seller is proven right at the end, that does not in itself guarantee repayment.

■ *3.3.1 Reducing the risks with Demand Guarantees*

In situations where the Principal is unable to avoid issuing a Demand Guarantee, there are some measures that can be taken to help reduce the real risk of unfair callings. In most cases, the best approach may be to take a separate insurance against any 'unfair callings', and both the Export Credits Guarantee Department (ECGD) and private insurance companies are issuing such insurance (see *Chapter 5, Export risk insurance)*, even though with different preconditions.

Box 3.4 Example of an advance payment guarantee issued by a bank, not related to the underlying contract (demand guarantee)

Messrs ATV Radiocommunications Spa
18 Via Rosle, Cassina di Spati
1081 PADOVA, Italy

Guarantee No. X-32799/34

Between you as 'buyer' and Highland Communications Ltd, 31 Dover House Road, Wokingham RG41 8HX as 'supplier', an agreement has been signed according to contract GHTY 376 dated 25.02.05, regarding the supply of 1075 Satellite Adaptors, model A-346, for a total contract amount of EUR 474, 370.

The 'supplier' is entitled to receive an advance payment of EUR 71.155, according to the contract. We the undersigned bank, therefore, hereby guarantees the repayment of the above advance payment on the first written demand, supported by your written statement, stating that the 'supplier' is in breach of their obligations under the above contract and specifying the details of such breach.

It is, however, a condition for claims and payments under this guarantee that the above advance payment has been received in full on an account with us in favour of the 'supplier'.

However, we shall not by reason of this undertaking be liable to disburse more than in total EUR 71.155 (seventy-one-thousand, one-hundred and fifty-five Euro). This guarantee, <u>issued under English law and jurisdiction and to be governed by ICC Uniform Rules for Demand Guarntees, *URDG, ICC 458*</u>* remains in force until November 25th 2005, by which date (at the latest) your claims, if any, must have reached us in writing in order to be valid against us. After expiry, this guarantee will become null and void whether returned to us or not.

London March 15th 2005

UK Regional Commercial Bank

Signature   Signature

This text is to be included, if acceptable to the buyer, also see Section 3.3.1

Box 3.5   Standby Letters of Credit — an alternative to Demand Guarantees

---

Apart from the different ways (shown below) of reducing the risk for the Principal in connection with the use of demand guarantees, there is another (and often more advantageous) alternative for the seller to accommodate the request from the buyer for an unconditional undertaking. That is to have the buyer accept a Standby Letter of Credit, which, in essence, will give them the same advantages of a Demand Guarantee but within the framework of more internationally accepted rules. The Standby Letter of Credit will be described later in this chapter.

The Principal could also try to find a compromise between the two basic forms of guarantee, for example, by agreeing in principle to a Demand Guarantee, but only together with some form of descriptive documentation to support any claim, according to ICC rules. Even if the Beneficiary would not accept a direct reference to these rules, an alternative clause could be worded as follows:

'The demand for payment must be accompanied by your statement that the Principal is in breach of its contractual obligations and specify in which respect/s such breaches have occurred.'

Even though such wording does not change the general nature of the Demand Guarantee and the right for the Beneficiary to claim under it, it could act as a certain deterrent against unfair claims. It could also somewhat strengthen the position of the Principal not only during the period of the contract, but also later on, when trying to recover any amount unduly paid under the guarantee. Such a solution would also be relatively similar to the use of a Standby Letter of Credit as an alternative to a Demand Guarantee, as described in *3.4 Standby Letters of Credit*.

Box 3.6 An example of a performance bond issued on the back of a counter-guarantee, made on-demand by the local Issuing Bank

ARAB ORIENTAL BANK S.A.E

①

PERFORMANCE BOND NO BA 38769/C

Whereas our Bank stands as joint and several surety for the debtor and as joint and several co-debtor, for the definite guarantee fund of USD 150,000 (one-hundred and fifty-thousand US dollars) which the below mentioned contractor is obliged in order to ensure full performance of the contract 347 of February 20th, 2005 between Shirat Shipyard Co, PO Box 29031, 02451 Istambul (the 'buyer') and the 'contractor' Majestic Lift Machinery, PO Box 3465, Birmingham BM2 6YA, concerning delivery and installation of three heavy lift transportation systems.

We hereby undertake and state, on behalf of the Bank, and as responsible representatives with full power to affix our signature that, in the event our Bank is notified in writing by the 'buyer' that the contractor has violated the provisions of the contract and/or has failed to perform his undertakings completely or partially, the amount under surety will be paid in cash and in full, immediately and without delay to the 'buyer' or their order, upon their first written request, without the need to resort to any legal

② procedure or to issue a protest or to obtain a court order or the 'contractor's' consent.

This bond has been issued upon the counter guarantee of UK Trade Bank Ltd, London, (NO 18346), dated March 19th, 2005.

③

Ankara, March 28th, 2005

ARAB ORIENTAL BANK S.A.E

Abdul Mohar   Akram R. Salidi

Comments

1 The wording is set by the standards of the local Issuing Bank, which has used the word 'bond' for what in reality is a guarantee.
2 The on-demand character of the bond is only too obvious, even underlining the rights of the buyer and the lack of rights for the contractor.
3 The text contains no reference to validity or other limitation in time, and the bond may, therefore, continue to be in force under local law until it has been returned to the Issuing Bank. There is also no reference to applicable law, jurisdiction or any of the ICC rules.

Box 3.7 International rules for guarantees

ICC has, for some time, tried to create a recognised and accepted standard for trade-related guarantees in international trade, and has issued common rules for both contract guarantees and on-demand guarantees.

The rules for contract guarantees (*Uniform Rules for Contract Guarantees, URCG, ICC 325*) issued in 1978, do not deal with the nature of the guarantees, but more with the prerequisite for payment under the guarantee, based on a third party, ie, arbitration, deciding the right to make a payment. As these rules do not fully reflect international practice, they are however not yet commonly used today as a reference in contract guarantees.

The rules for on-demand guarantees (*Uniform Rules for Demand Guarantees, URDG, ICC 458*) were introduced in 1992 as a consequence of the increased use of this form of guarantee. These rules are, even though still not widely known and practically used, adapted to the prevailing practice with the main purpose to strengthen the rules and guidelines around these guarantees and reducing the risk for unfair calling, through stipulations that claims should be made in writing and supported by documentation showing the circumstances motivating the claim.

The rules can be obtained from banks or from the ICC, **www.iccuk.net**

➢ 3.4 Standby Letters of Credit

As previously discussed, there are many uncertainties for the Principal in having Demand Guarantees issued without support of internationally accepted ICC rules. The use of Standby Letters of Credit, governed by established ICC rules could reduce some of these uncertainties.

Standby Letters of Credit have been used for many years to support payments, both when due and after default, in cases of repayments of

> ### Box 3.8 International rules for Standby Letters of Credit
>
> One of the main advantages of using a Standby Letter of Credit is that it is supported by an internationally recognised set of rules issued by ICC (*International Standby Practices, ISP 98*, in force from 1999) with similarities to the *Uniform Customs and Practice for Documentary Credits UCP* and to the *Uniform Rules for Demand Guarantees URDG*. These rules can be ordered directly from ICC.

money loaned and advanced, or upon the occurrence or non-occurrence of an event in relation to financial or commercial transactions. This document originated and has been widely used outside Europe for many years, but is now recognised worldwide.

The Standby Letter of Credit is an irrevocable, independent, documentary and binding undertaking, which means:

- it is **irrevocable** and cannot be amended or cancelled without the approval of the Beneficiary;
- it is **independent** and does not depend on the commercial parties' obligations against each other or any other information related to the transaction;
- it is **documentary** and dependent on the presentation of stipulated documents to be examined by the Issuing Bank;
- it is **binding** and enforceable against the Issuing Bank irrespective of other events or developments.

The Standby Letter of Credit is commonly described according to its purpose, often in the same terms as, for example, a contract guarantee, with the wording 'Performance Standby', 'Advance Payment Standby' or 'Bid Bond/Tender Bond Standby'. It could also be referred to as a 'Commercial Standby' and be an alternative to a payment guarantee in favour of the seller, covering the obligations of the buyer to pay for goods or services.

The structure of the Standby Letter of Credit is relatively similar to that of ordinary Letters of Credit. This is also why the corresponding ICC rules are more known and accepted internationally than the more unknown rules for Demand Guarantees. This will make it easier for the Principal, often the seller, to be able to agree with the buyer to have a Standby Letter of Credit issued instead of a Demand Guarantee.

The general advantages for the Principal, but often also for the Beneficiary, with having the undertaking governed by the rules of the Standby Letter of Credit are as follows:

- It has a defined terminology, but also gives examples of undesirable expressions that should be disregarded.
- It contains strict obligations for the Issuing Bank as to how to issue the standby and amendments, if any.
- It contains rules for presentation and examination of documents, partial drawing and multiple presentations.
- It contains rules on termination and cancellation, among others the Issuer's discretion regarding a decision to cancel.
- It has a defined duration and must either have a fixed expiry date or permit the Issuing Bank to terminate the standby upon reasonable prior notice or payment.

The Standby Letter of Credit also requires some form of statement or certificate as evidence of a default, and such documentation should at least contain:

a) a representation to the effect that payment is due because of an event described in the standby has occurred;
b) a date indicating when the statement was issued; and
c) the Beneficiary's signature.

The Standby Letter of Credit is often made irrevocable at sight as an ordinary commercial Letter of Credit (see *Chapter 2, Section 2.5.1*), mostly payable at the Advising Bank in the buyer's (Beneficiary's) country, against the document(s) that the parties have agreed upon, and subject to the rules *ISP98*. Even if they cannot agree on any other documents, payment will only be made against at least the presentation of the above documentation.

■ *3.4.1 The Standby L/C underpinning open account trading*

The general advantage to both parties from using open account payment terms based on clean payments (bank transfers and cheques) instead of documentary payments, is that they are cheaper and more flexible. Changes in the delivery can also be made with short notice and they are often used, or would often be preferred in trading on an ongoing basis – as long as the credit risk involved is acceptable to both parties, and then primarily to the seller.

In terms of frequency, UK overseas trade is largely based on open account payment terms, due to its widespread use in trade with neighbouring countries where these terms are most commonly used. But even in these cases, the seller might have taken supplementary measures to cover the perceived risk, often in the form of export credit insurance, covering total exports or just single transactions.

But open account payment terms could also be used in other situations when the risk is greater, and/or a separate insurance is not available. The open account trading must then be supported by some form of bank guarantee, covering the obligations of the buyer. However, of the different forms of trade related guarantees, only some can be used in combination with open account trading, as is shown below:

- A Letter of Credit. This is the more commonly used bank guaranteed instrument in overseas trading, due to its strict adherence to the principle of payment to the seller against specified and correct documents representing the goods. But payment is determined not by the buyer but by the banks.
- An ordinary conditional payment guarantee, issued by a bank. Such a guarantee is commonly used in conjunction with open account terms, but its potential drawback, seen from the seller's perspective, is that it covers the buyer's obligations to pay, but not their willingness to do so, if not accepting the claim due to alleged deficiencies in the delivery or some other reason.
- An unconditional payment guarantee, issued by a bank. Such a guarantee is however seldom used when covering the buyer's

commercial payment obligations, when instead a Standby L/C fulfils the same purpose, also covered by more widely used ICC-rules.

- A commercial Standby L/C. AS shown in the previous point, this instrument has many similarities with an ordinary L/C, but is often used as a guarantee in conjunction with open account terms, however, giving the seller better protection than a conditional bank guarantee.

When used as a guarantee in conjunction with open account terms, the commercial Standby L/C is more similar to an unconditional than a conditional bank guarantee, dependent only on the document(s) to be presented by the seller, showing the event of default on the part of the buyer. When so presented, the seller will receive payment, irrespective of any objections from the buyer.

The decision of whether to use an ordinary L/C or open account trading terms in combination with a Standby L/C has to be decided in each case, and is dependent on the parties internal relationship, the goods and the frequency of the transactions involved as well as the importance of the flexibility needed for short-term changes in the contract or the delivery. The security for the seller is almost the same in both cases, whereas it is up to the buyer to evaluate the advantages of the open account trading and the flexibility therein, compared with potential disadvantage by giving the seller the right to draw under the Standby L/C simply against their own certificate, indicating an event of default.

➢ 3.5 The structure and design of guarantees

The practical structure and design of the guarantee should be governed by the underlying commercial contract, its character, size and the structure of its terms of payment in general, but also with necessary regard to local practices. All these factors combined will determine the final structure and wording, but all guarantees, demand, conditional or Standby Letters of Credit, issued directly or through an Advising or Instructing Bank, should contain at least the following information:

Box 3.9 Checklist of details in a guarantee application

☐ **Full name and address of Beneficiary**

Full name and address of Beneficiary's bank as:

☐ Advising Bank ☐ Local Issuing Bank ☐ No Beneficiary Bank to be used

Basic form of guarantee:

☐ Conditional Guarantee ☐ Demand Guarantee ☐ Standby L/C

Type of guarantee:

☐ Bid Bond ☐ Warranty Guarantee ☐ Performance Guarantee
☐ Payment Guarantee ☐ Advance Payment Guarantee ☐ Other

Guarantee details:

☐ Reference of tender/contract ☐ Currency and amount of tender/contract

☐ Short description of tender/contract ☐ Validity (expiry date) of the guarantee

☐ Currency and amount of guarantee ☐ Other

Guarantee text:

☐ Bank standard ☐ As enclosed guarantee text
☐ To be structured according to the enclosed tender/contract ☐ Other

Additional information:

☐ The guarantee must/must not specify being issued subject to relevant ICC rules.

☐ The guarantee must/must not specify being issued subject to English law and jurisdiction.

☐ What supporting documentation should accompany any claim.

☐ At what time and under what circumstances, if any, should the guarantee come into effect.

☐ Any reduction clauses of the guarantee amount during the validity.

Distribution of guarantee:

☐ To be sent to applicant as draft for approval.

☐ To be send directly to applicant for further distribution.

☐ To be sent directly to Beneficiary/Advising Bank/or as instructions to the local Issuing Bank.

Commission and charges (as agreed between the parties):

☐ Applicant to take all guarantee costs.

☐ Applicant to take guarantee costs in the UK.

☐ Any other agreement.

- contract parties and the underlying commercial contract;
- the purpose of the guarantee and what it should cover;
- currency and maximum amount;
- time of validity and expiry date, if possible;
- last date when claims, if any, are to be presented;
- if and when supporting documentation should be presented;
- the reference to some of the relevant ICC-rules, whenever possible;
- the applicable law governing the guarantee.

Some of these points are of special importance and are commented on below.

■ 3.5.1 Jurisdiction and applicable law

Commercial parties have the freedom to choose the applicable law for both the contract and for the guarantees related to it. The governing law does not necessarily have to be the same for both the commercial contract and the guarantee, even if it is to the advantage of both parties to use the same legal framework, and that is almost always also the case.

The UK party, often the seller, should do their utmost to get the buyer to accept English law and the jurisdiction of English courts. The problem is often that no such agreement is made, or is only made for the commercial contract but not for the guarantees, either because the parties have not thought about it or because the seller prefers not to raise the question due to fear of ending up with the law and jurisdiction of the buyer's country.

If nothing is stated about governing law, the rules of the Rome Convention (as introduced by the European Commission in 1980) should be applicable, which states that in such cases, the law of the provider should apply.

This would also be the case for a guarantee issued by a local Issuing Bank upon the request of an Instructing Bank, in which case the Instructing Bank would also be regarded as the provider. But the matter of governing law is a difficult one; in some countries the guarantee has to be governed by local law by tradition or by the law of the country, irrespective of what is stated by the Instructing Bank. The starting point for a UK supplier should, however, always be English law and jurisdiction, because it would offer protection from many uncertain interpretations in the buyer's country.

■ 3.5.2 Commencement and expiry dates

An important factor to consider is at what time the guarantee comes into effect. A performance guarantee, for example, should not be operative until the buyer has fulfilled their corresponding obligations, (ie, to have a Letter of Credit not only issued but also its details approved by the seller) or that the advance payment is paid and all legal requirements and approvals are met.

Other stipulations could be that the guarantee should come into effect simultaneously with some other contractual event, for example, a warranty guarantee that only becomes valid upon the return of a performance guarantee. The expiry date is equally important. Whenever possible a guarantee should expire on a specific calendar date, but it is worth noting that the rules governing expiry of a guarantee may differ depending on laws and practices in different countries. This is another reason why the seller, as Principal, should try to have the guarantee governed by English law.

However, sometimes the parties cannot agree on a specific expiry date, perhaps due to uncertainty about the date of delivery or completion. In such cases, the guarantee could be limited in time in relation to some other document, for example, the shipping document, an approved test certificate or simply by the issuing of another guarantee that is time limited (eg, a performance guarantee to be replaced by a 180-day warranty guarantee).

In some countries law prohibits time restrictions for guarantees but other rules may also apply, for example, that the guarantee will continue to be valid until it is returned to the Issuing Bank, regardless of any specified time of validity. Many local Issuing Banks do not accept time limitations on a counter- guarantee, and to make it even more complicated, in some countries it is possible under local law to present a valid claim even after expiry if it could be argued that the event causing the claim took place within the period of its validity. In such cases, the only way to release the Instructing Bank and the Principal is through a confirmation to that effect from the Issuing Bank.

Regarding both Conditional and, in particular, Demand Guarantees, where the Beneficiary has a stronger position, it is quite common that a demand for an extension of the guarantee (extend or pay) is forwarded to the Issuing Bank. If the guarantee is of a conditional type, that has to be part of a negotiation with the Principal, but with a Demand Guarantee, such a request is at the sole discretion of the Beneficiary.

The risk for the Principal (usually the seller) could also be lessened through some form of reduction of the outstanding amount during the period of its validity. For instance, the guarantee could contain reduction clauses, which automatically reduces the maximum amount of the guarantee in line with specified events of due fulfilment of the contract, or against presentation of copies of the shipping documents. A reduction clause could read as follows:

'Our liability under this undertaking shall not exceed in aggregate GBP... and shall be automatically reduced by X% of the contract price of each delivery performed under the Contract and the production to us by the Company of a copy of a signed Certificate of Acceptance (or copy of the shipping documents) shall be conclusive evidence of this for this purpose.'

The general conclusion is that the seller, as Principal, should try to have all undertakings issued according to English law and/or according to any of the relevant ICC rules, particularly with Demand Guarantees or guarantees issued by local Issuing Banks. This would also make it easier to obtain cover against the risk of 'unfair calling' through a separate insurance policy.

■ 3.5.3 Some final comments about trade-related guarantees (from the seller's perspective)

- Banks normally request collateral for issuing guarantees as well as for extending credits, either under existing limits or under separate credit approvals, and the seller should know at an early stage what demands the bank may have to issue the guarantee. Additional collateral may be requested for a Demand Guarantee since the Beneficiary may extend the expiry date (extend or pay), also resulting in higher bank charges.
- Insurance bonds/guarantees covering the undertaking of the seller are sometimes used as an alternative to guarantees issued by banks. Such guarantees have the additional advantage of normally being issued only on the strength of the balance sheet of the seller, therefore not affecting existing bank lines, improving the cash flow and contributing to a more effective use of the working capital.
- The guarantees should, as far as possible, be related to the underlying contract or have a reference to the contract (even if the guarantee is on- demand). If the guarantee is to be issued by a local bank in the buyer's country, the exact wording should be agreed in advance and be included in the contract.
- Whenever the buyer is requesting a Demand Guarantee, the seller should try to make such approval conditional upon using ICC rules for Demand Guarantees or alternatively, try to get the buyer to agree on a Standby Letter of Credit with reference to its ICC rules.
- Finally, if the guarantee is to be issued in favour of the seller, they should themselves make a proper evaluation of the commercial and political risk on the Issuing Bank or any other issuing party. This also includes the wording, which may be interpreted according to the law and practice in the buyer's country if nothing else is specified, however, the seller should insist on English law and jurisdiction wherever possible.

4

Currency risk management

➤ 4.1 Currency risk

Since the early 1970s, when the system of fixed currency rates finally collapsed, exchange rates between industrialised countries have more or less floated. The possibility of coordinating alternative exchange systems along with the political ambition to do so has decreased over time, based on the realisation that currency cooperation, in any meaningful sense, is dependent on close economic cooperation.

The real exception to this is of course the introduction of the Euro but, apart from that, other countries have dealt with the currency exchange mechanism in their own way. The most common ways include:

- Allowing the currency to float freely on the currency market. Examples of such currencies are GBP, EUR, USD, CHF and JPY, even though free-floating is sometimes limited through Central Banks market interventions or changes of interest rates, with or without the intention of moving the exchange rate in a certain direction.
- Allowing various exchange rates for different types of transactions, often a fixed or controlled rate for commercial transactions and a floating rate for financial transactions. This system was occasionally used in the past in order to create stable conditions for the country's international trade, but it is not used today for any of the major currencies.

- A close cooperation with some specific currency but allowing a free-float against others. The most obvious example is the Danish krona (DKK), which presently moves within a certain interval against the Euro, but freely against other currencies.
- Pegging the currency to internally constructed trade-weighted currency baskets, but nowadays this system is not used for any major currency.
- Pegging the currency, officially or unofficially, to a base currency, often USD, which is done for many currencies in the Middle East, Asia and South America.

Pegging to other currencies may be a risky business if the underlying economic development is different between the countries, and could trigger sudden and often violent currency disturbances. Such events could be dramatic, not only as a potential currency risk, but also because they can disturb the trade system and the whole economy of the country, as was shown recently by the developments in some South-American countries.

Another example is the Chinese currency (CNY), which is (presently) unofficially pegged to USD, even if the problem in this case seems to be the opposite to that of many other countries, with the market expecting a substantial appreciation against the dollar, which would immediately affect the existing trade pattern in both the short and the long term. Finally, the Danish krona's present pegging to EUR seems to be an example of how such currency cooperation can work smoothly and without friction even over longer periods, if based on similar economic development and a strong commercial integration between the countries involved.

The currencies mentioned so far, are mainly so-called convertible currencies, which means that they can easily be exchanged into other 'hard currencies', (eg, USD, GBP, CHF and EUR) in an existing and effective currency market – all currencies in the industrialised countries, but also some from the Emerging Markets, are convertible in this sense.

Other currencies (not least from the developing countries) are generally perceived as politically or economically unstable or under such constant convertibility risk, subject to change of law, restrictions and/or exchange controls within the country, that they are, in practice, non-convertible and not traded in an open market. If they are traded (often unofficially or in local currency trade only), or exchanged in single transactions, such trades are always subject to discounts, high volatility or other draw-backs. However, many of these currencies are frequently used in regional trade, but they have a very small share of the world market, in particular in trade with the industrialised countries.

Box 4.1   The Euro (EUR)

The Euro has been a currency since the beginning of 1999 and, during 2004 it was introduced in additional 10 countries. It is also floating freely against most other currencies (eg, GBP) which, from a UK company's perspective, makes the risk similar to that of any other currency.

However, even if the UK does not join the Euro zone in the fore-seeable future, the Euro will nevertheless affect the commercial aspects of many UK companies. The structure of UK trade makes the Euro an even more important invoicing currency for many importing and exporting companies, particularly following the addition of new countries. It makes price comparisons easier and increases the competition, which will affect both the choice of currency in offers and tenders and will, in the long-term, also have repercussions on investment and production decisions. Even business between UK companies may take place in EUR as part of larger European trade contracts or as a method to balance outstanding currency risks and minimising transaction costs.

Please state your offered price in euro [EUR].

Dublin, February 2005

➤ 4.2 The currency markets

The currency market does not operate at any single exchange as it is dominated by inter-bank trading. Trading in foreign exchange occurs 24 hours a day – as the day progresses, different banks come and go off-line. For example, as the London trading day comes to a close (around 5pm), trading in the US is already underway. Likewise at the end of the US trading day, banks in Asia-Pacific are already open and trading. Hence large multinational banks simply pass their FX orders around the globe to be executed as and when required.

These banks provide liquidity for anyone wishing to trade in foreign exchange (the bank's clients will typically include the corporate sector, central banks, brokers, hedge funds, other banks, but also private individuals).

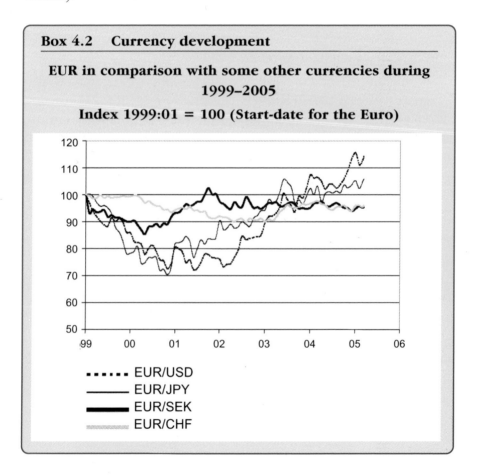

Box 4.2   Currency development

EUR in comparison with some other currencies during 1999–2005

Index 1999:01 = 100 (Start-date for the Euro)

- ······ EUR/USD
- ——— EUR/JPY
- ▬▬▬ EUR/SEK
- ~~~~~ EUR/CHF

◼ *4.2.1 The spot market*

The spot rate is the rate at which a foreign exchange trade can be immediately transacted. Most currency pairs exchanged will then settle two business days later (T+2). The major exception to this rule is USD/CAD which settles T+1 (ie, one business day later). If required, trades can also be settled on a different and later date – however a forward rate is now agreed, described in *Section 4.2.2*.

The reasons for transactions in the spot market could be:

- to settle a commercial transaction through buying or selling local currency;
- to settle a financial operation (eg, transferring a loan in foreign currency to local currency or buying foreign currency for interest payments and amortizations);
- to balance or hedge an unwanted position in foreign currency; or
- to increase/decrease a currency position as a speculative move due to expected future currency movements.

❑ 4.2.1.1 The spot trade

Currencies are normally quoted against the USD in the inter-bank market, even if nowadays most non-Eur European currencies are traded directly against the EUR rather than the USD. Whilst major currencies can be traded directly (i.e. a direct quote for EUR/GBP can be readily obtained as the currency pair is directly traded), smaller currencies are always traded indirectly, via the USD. Hence there are two portions to the trade.

A currency table in April 2005 could look as follows (*see* page 121) for some larger currencies, however some currencies, including GBP, are sometimes seen expressed both ways, for example either EUR/GBP or GBP/EUR or GBP/USD or USD/GBP. In this chapter we have tried to use the alternative that is mostly traded in the inter-bank markets, but the reader should generally be aware of that both alternatives are sometimes used, when evaluating or comparing currency data.

Box 4.3 Sterling Exchange Rate Index (ERI)

Movements in GBP against other currencies affect the UK economy as well as individual companies. The value of GBP against any other single currency is measured as a bilateral exchange rate, which is the relevant measurement used when for example the seller determines the currency risk in any given export transaction to be invoiced in a foreign currency. As can be seen from other currency charts in this chapter, such bilateral exchange rates have fluctuated widely over the years.

The Bank of England also publishes the long-term movements of the GBP against a basket of different currencies (ERI) in order to focus on the general trend of the currency. The basis for such an index is presently based on the trade pattern for traded goods; however, the ERI will probably be readjusted during 2005 in order to take account of services that are a growing part of total trade. Other variations, such as constantly updated changes in the UK trade pattern and price competitiveness, will probably also be included in the new ERI.

The chart below shows the calculated new ERI, with relatively large currency fluctuations over short and longer periods, seen from the perspective of a currency basket (as a comparison with the development of bilateral exchange rates).

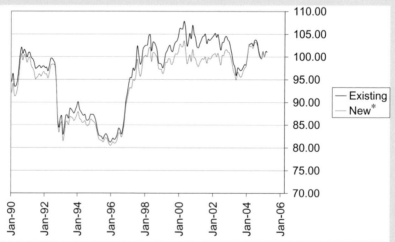

* The shaded line is showing what the adjusted ERI should look like after the proposed corrections.

Source. Bank of England Quarterly bulletin 2004

EUR/GBP	0,6803–0,6804
GBP/USD	1,9162–1,9164
EUR/USD	1,3036–1,3037

The quotation is the banks' buy and sell (respectively) spot exchange rate for one currency unit, expressed in the number of units in the other currency. The difference is the spread, which varies between currency pairs.

The spread in the inter-bank market, expressed as points or 'pips', is the 1/10,000-share of a unit of the currency. For major currency pairs it is usually within a few points. For smaller currency pairs it can be much larger, and the spread will increase in an environment of falling liquidity and large trade size. The spread for customers will be larger that in the inter-bank rate to account for a bank's trading costs. Large corporates, trading in volume will however be given a rate that is close to, if not at, the inter-bank rate.

For currencies that are not directly traded against each other, the exchange rate is calculated via the USD. This can be seen from the following example, where the cross-rate is obtained in the following way:

Spot market exchange rates: GBP/USD = 1,9162–1,9164
USD/SEK = 7, 0540–7,0555

Cross rate: GBP/SEK = (1,9162 * 7,0540) – (1,9164 * 7,0555) =
13,5169 – 13,5212

The exchange rates are normally quoted in one or in one hundred units of the currency, in this example 1 GBP. That is what the customer is quoted, plus the applicable margin in each case, dependent on currency, amount, competition and the relationship with the customer.

❑ 4.2.1.2 Currency information to customers

The banks publish currency rates on a daily basis for the most common currencies (as do most financial newspapers). However, these are by definition historical and, in most cases so-called 'fixing rates', established at 11.00 during the day. For more current information, the seller must turn to their bank. Most banks have special customer desks within their trading teams, which give current currency information and advice, as well as processing customer transactions. The rates they quote give a more accurate picture of the market at that particular time during the day. For larger amounts, it may be beneficial to check with more than one bank but it must be done at almost exactly the same time to get a fair comparison.

Many banks also have their own Internet-based payment and currency information systems, where their customers can make payments and also get account and currency information to their own terminal. This information is constantly updated during the day, although not always in real-time.

More up-to-date currency information can also be obtained through some suppliers, delivering true real-time currency information. These systems, such as Reuters treasury information services, are based on a constant currency updating by banks and brokers, which use these systems as a tool to promote their own quotations and trading teams in this market. These systems give the customer up-to-date currency information, almost as fast as within the banks themselves, as a base for a more profitable currency trading of their own and/or for more effective management of their currency positions. These currency information systems are now widespread, not only among financial institutions, but also among larger corporations.

■ 4.2.2 The forward market

Currencies traded for settlement on a day later than T+2 are traded at the forward rate. The forward contract creates an obligation between a bank and its customer to exchange a fixed amount of one currency for a second currency at an agreed rate and date. The settlement date can be any business day and it is not unknown for forward agreements to stretch a number of years.

The reasons for using a forward transaction could be the same as for a spot transaction, to settle a commercial or a financial transaction, to

INFORMATION BOX

REUTERS
KNOW. NOW.

Reuters' goal is to be the information company our customers value most, by offering indispensable content, innovative trading services and great customer service. Within the area of foreign exchange, Reuters specialises in both key and emerging market currencies and provides you with a comprehensive view of the FX markets.

Reuters 3000 Xtra is a high-speed, high-performance information service for financial professionals. Designed for the most demanding users in business, it delivers a potent combination of real-time information and powerful analysis tools, which gives an unsurpassed view of most financial areas, including the FX and money markets, combined with custom analysis tools.

Reuters Trading for Foreign Exchange brings financial market professionals the ability to quickly and securely execute spot and forward FX with their relationship banks and manage post trade processing through a single sign-on and single STP solution, utilising Reuters unrivalled global desktop footprint in the FX marketplace.

Reuters FX Spot View allows users of 3000Xtra to access, free of charge, comprehensive and real-time FX price data derived from the professional inter-bank market via Reuters Dealing 3000 Spot Matching service.

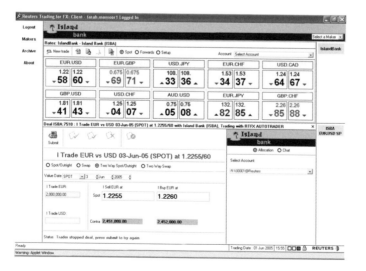

For more information call 0207 2501 122 or see our website www.reuters.com

balance a currency position or as speculation, but with the difference that the settlement is at a future date.

□ 4.2.2.1 Determination of forward rates

Forward rates are usually available for those currencies that can be traded in the inter-bank spot market. However, the rates on the forward inter-bank market are not quoted as currency rates but as differences from the spot rates, so called forward points.

The advantage with this trading system is obvious, forward points are easier to compare over different periods, and they are not changed automatically with the spot rates that are constantly changing. These forward points can then easily be converted to ordinary currency rates, when quoted towards a customer outside the inter-bank market. The forward points are simply added or subtracted to the spot rate, depending if their value are positive (higher offer than bid points) or negative (higher bid than offer points). This will give the forward exchange rates, also often called outright forward rates. For example, if the GBP/USD spot rate is 1,9162–64 and the 3-month forward points are 79-75, the three month outright forward rate would be 1,9083-1.9089, plus the bank's margin.

The forward points are mainly determined by the interest rate differential between the countries whose currencies are involved. This can also be explained in the following way; on a free and unregulated market, a future exchange rate can alternatively be obtained by borrowing the currency to be hedged, which is then sold at spot rate against, for example, GBP, which is then placed on interest bearing deposit for the same period as the loan. In relation to the spot rate, the forward rate is obtained by adding/subtracting the difference between the borrowing and the lending interest rates for the two currencies up until the due date.

However, even if the interest rate differential is the dominant factor behind forward rates, these are also influenced by a number of other factors affecting the currency markets and exchange rates. In particular, when a currency is affected by new or changing economic or political facts or expectations, which suddenly changes its outlook in the short or long-term. In such cases the market participants tend to act accordingly and more in one direction only, with an upward or downward pressure on interest rates and consequently on the forward currency rates. Hence the forward rates will fluctuate as market expectations change.

➢ 4.3 Currency exposure

As can be seen from the currency charts in this chapter, currency movements have been relatively volatile during recent years, making currency exposure an even more important aspect in connection with international trade, as well as foreign investments, particularly if the currency risk is outstanding for longer periods. Even if GBP has developed rather well (seen over a longer time-span) this is not in itself a protection when it comes to new transactions, primarily for two reasons.

Firstly, a historical perspective can never be taken as proof for future currency development, particularly when past development has been strong and a correction might be more likely. Secondly, it is quite usual that these long-term trends are quite opposite to the short-term development, and it is this short-term trend that is more important when evaluating the risk aspects of a new transaction. It is the actual exchange rate at the trading date that is relevant, whether this is done through a spot or forward transaction.

In order to evaluate currency risks, every company must know what types of risk may occur and to decide what risks should be covered in that particular case. The currency exposure for a company, or the 'translation exposure' as it is also called, is often divided into two separate parts, namely:

- Balance exposure
- Payment exposure

Balance exposure is, in principle, primarily an accounting risk, which may appear in the books of a UK company, which is also consolidating foreign subsidiaries. When assets and liabilities for accounting purposes are converted into the consolidated accounts of the group, these figures will be calculated at different exchanges rates, and might then give a distorted picture of the real value of the assets.

For example, assets abroad, which are financed through a foreign currency loan, are normally included in the consolidated statements at the acquisition rate, whereas the corresponding loan is valued at the higher of the acquisition rate and the rate when closing the accounts. Therefore, moving exchange rates will always have an affect on the accounts of the business, either positively or negatively. However, these exchange adjustments may be inaccurate if they do not reflect the true value of the assets and are not accompanied by any cash flow consequences.

Payment exposure on the other hand involves the flow of payments in foreign currencies, both within the parent company and its subsidiaries, in connection with sales and purchases of goods and services, interest payments and dividends, etc. This currency exposure is real and realised when the transactions occur, and the effective exchange rates instantly affect the cash flow of the company and the operating result of the group. In the following text, we will deal with payment exposure only, since this is related to UK trade transactions.

Most companies have different attitudes to currency exposure, dependent on factors such as currency volumes, its composition over time and what currencies are involved. Even the attitude towards risk within the company is important, as laid down in its general financial strategy. Often you will find one of the following three main alternatives when dealing with currency risks:

- To try to keep the currency exposure as low as possible at all times and to cover the risks systematically as they occur, in order to minimise the overall currency risk.
- To aim at a selective coverage to keep the currency exposure within specified limits set by the company. The most common ways of achieving this are covering only certain currencies, only amounts above certain limits, only exposure over certain periods of time or

to use some form of proportionate coverage. A combination of these alternatives is most often chosen.

- Not to cover the exposure at all, an alternative which may be chosen when the volumes and the outstanding exposure is small in comparison with the total business of the company, perhaps in combination with past experience about the strength of GBP.

Most companies use one of the two first alternatives, as is described at the end of this chapter, that is to actively try to limit or minimise the currency risks involved in their trade transactions.

■ *4.3.1 Currency position schedule*

Before any hedging of currency risks can take place, the company must first get a broader and overall picture of the company's present and future currency risks, (ie, proportions, currency, volume, timing and if they are 'firm' or 'anticipated'). This must be done within the framework of a comprehensive set of rules and guidelines on currency risk management specific to each company.

If such management covers several units, for example, foreign subsidiaries, the schedule must be construed in such a way that each unit's position could be monitored while at the same time they are aggregated to a grand total. However, in many larger companies it is common practice to strip the subsidiaries from exchange risks as far as possible or to have them covered internally within the group in order to concentrate all currency risks to the finance department of the parent company.

By using a rolling position schedule for each currency (eg, on a weekly or monthly basis, as shown in *Box 4.4*), the company will get a fair picture of future currency flows and a good background as to how to hedge the net positions. (The shedule is for illustration only, in practice they are mostly computerized with much higher sophistication.) But, in order to make these positions as reliable as possible for management, they should include not only known inflows and outflows but also outstanding offers or tenders together with other less certain transactions (often within brackets) in order to update the

Box 4.4 Practical example of a currency position schedule

		Currency position in USD (000's)					
INCOMING Week No.		**20**	**21**	**22**	**23**	**24**	**25**
Current invoices, due	**1.**	185	20		1.200	70	200
Currency account assets		50			30		
Currency overdrafts							
Other liquid currency assets							
Firm contracts, not delivered	**2.**	150				120	
Firm offers outstanding	**3.**					(100)	
% additional sales (recalc.)	**4.**					(200)	
Others			30		50		
TOTAL INCOMING		**385**	**50**		**1.280**	**190 (490)**	**200**
OUTGOING							
Unpaid invoices	**5.**		170	30			300
Currency loans	**6.**				1.200		
Accepted offers							
Other outgoings							
TOTAL OUTGOING			**170**	**30**	**1.200**		**300**
NET		+385	−120	−30	+80	+190 (+490)	−100
HEDGED			-200	-50	+10	−150	+50
RISK EXPOSURE	**7.**	+185	−170	−20	+80	+40 (340)	−50

1. Incoming payments should be based on earlier experience, and rather too late than too early for slow payers' or uncertain countries. Should the payment arrive earlier than expected, it could always be placed as an interest bearing deposit until used according to the schedule.
2. Same as above to a higher degree, based on the uncertainty of shipment date.
3. Firm offers or tenders must be within brackets until acceptance.
4. Many companies with a stable flow of export earnings over time often use a rolling system where a certain percentage of expected but not yet contracted earnings are firmly included in the schedule. This is described in more detail in *Practical currency management*, at the end of this chapter.
5. Unsettled outgoing payments are easier to calculate and can also be paid earlier with a cash rebate if export earnings are received earlier than expected.
6. Loans in foreign currencies are sometimes used to hedge future export earnings as an alternative to a forward contract.
7. The risk exposure should be reasonably balanced over time, but not necessarily at all times if the balance fluctuates around an acceptable average exposure level.

positions over time. How this can be achieved in practice is shown at the end of this chapter.

➤ 4.4 Hedging currency risks

The most common methods of hedging currency exposure are shown below, in practice, a combination of these alternatives is most often used:

- choice of invoicing currency;
- currency steering;
- payments brought forward;
- forward currency contracts;
- currency options;
- short-term currency loans;
- currency clauses;
- Tender Exchange Rate insurance.

The different alternatives are described below, mostly however from the perspective from the UK exporter, in order to simplify the text, but the conclusions are just as valid for the UK importer.

■ 4.4.1 Choice of invoicing currency

Three different types of currency can be involved in an overseas trade transaction:

- the seller's currency, ie, GBP;
- the buyer's currency, if it is a common convertible currency;
- a third country currency, often USD or EUR.

If not easily agreed at an early stage, the relative market position of the various currencies, along with the competitive situation, will often decide the final choice of currency. If the buyer has a strong and well-known currency, for example EUR, this will facilitate the seller's decision to agree to that currency as a base for the contract – even if

INFORMATION BOX

✳ BANK OF SCOTLAND
PAYMENT & INTERNATIONAL SERVICES

At Bank of Scotland we offer a comprehensive range of international products and services tailored to suit the needs of UK businesses trading overseas.

Our customer-driven service could allow you to deal efficiently and confidently with more companies, in more countries, helping to bring more profit, more consumer appeal and more success to your business.

Our customer-focused team of international services specialists, strategically placed around the UK, are on hand to provide assistance with your international business requirements. Combined with our relationships with trade banks worldwide, we can offer support that helps you to trade almost anywhere in the world.

Our ongoing investment in technology allows us to quickly deal with an optimum package of products such as international payments, currency accounts, documentary services and travel money. Our products are backed by the capability of HBOS Treasury Services plc who provide foreign exchange support to Payment and International Services and directly to our customers.

For more information call us on 0845 604 4499 or visit our website at
www.bankofscotland.co.uk/international

---

the preferred choice was, for example, GBP. However, the seller should, for obvious reasons, be more careful about using other currencies than those commonly used in international trade.

Invoicing in GBP is the easiest way to eliminate the currency risk, provided that the seller has the basic cost structure in that currency. On the other hand, it transfers the currency risk to the buyer, which could make it more difficult for them to evaluate the profitability of the transaction, and may increase the risk for the seller of not getting the business, particularly if the buyer receives other, more competitive offers in their own currency.

In many overseas markets it is also common to use a third party currency, often the USD. This is particularly the case if the local currency is officially or unofficially pegged to that currency, or that it is so widely used in the country that invoicing in USD is normal practice. This is also the case for many business areas, such as energy, raw material, agricultural products, defence materials, shipping and aircraft, as well as within many service areas such as trading, insurance and transport. It may, therefore, often make commercial sense to accept an invoicing currency other than GBP, if the seller can evaluate the currency risk and hedge it. The questions to consider are:

- Is the invoicing currency freely convertible and actively traded?
- Does it have the trading volumes needed to give it market stability?
- Is it stable in the inter-bank markets for loans and deposits?
- Is the forward market working properly for the volumes and time periods that may be applicable to the transaction?

■ 4.4.2 Currency steering

In some cases, the company can influence or manage their own currency position, particularly if having both incoming and outgoing payments in the same currency. It may then be possible to match parts of the payment flows through the choice of currency. If this is a possibility, the company may use one or more currency accounts for that purpose. Such accounts can be opened with most banks and used like any other account, including the use of overdrafts.

How such currency accounts are used in practice is part of the overall currency management within the company, together with the structure of the currency flows and the interest rates that can be obtained for both loans and deposits. These aspects will also decide the use of balances on currency accounts for shorter or longer periods or the transfer back into a GBP account.

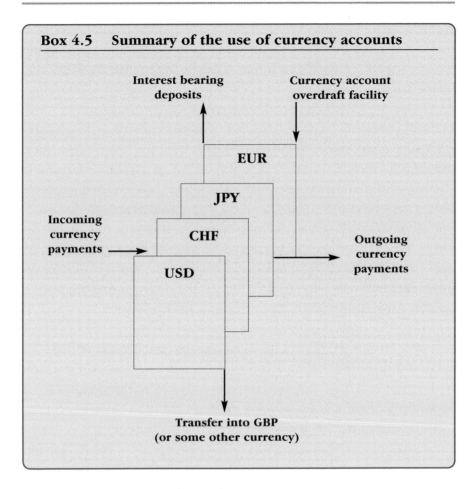

Box 4.5   Summary of the use of currency accounts

4.4.3 Payments brought forward

It is always advantageous for the seller to persuade the buyer to agree to an earlier payment, both from a liquidity and a currency point of view, particularly if invoicing in a foreign currency. However, the buyer will almost certainly see such premature payments as a corresponding disadvantage, unless they can gain some other concession from the seller. For ordinary transactions with a short time span such premature payments, compared to what is considered normal practice, will therefore seldom be agreed.

When it comes to larger transactions and periods longer than ordinary open account terms, and in foreign currency, the question could be more important. The seller could then try to agree with the buyer to divide the payment into part payments (as is shown in *Chapter 8,*

Terms of payment). Such an agreement will normally contain the main part payment at delivery at the latest, even if the seller also has to arrange for a payment guarantee in favour of the buyer, covering any pre-delivery payments.

The seller should also act internally within the company to ensure the early receipt of payments, for example, by more prompt deliveries, sending the invoice and having all the documentation ready for presentation at the bank immediately upon shipment and following that, to have an effective system in place for a tight credit control.

These aspects, together with the right choice of terms of payment at the outset, are some of the most important steps the seller can take on their own, both as a method to make the currency schedule more precise and minimise the currency risks involved, but also as part of effective cash management.

■ 4.4.4 Forward currency contracts

Perhaps the most commonly used method of hedging currency risks is through a forward contract with a bank, whereby the company can fix the value in GBP at an early stage but with delivery of the foreign currency at a later date.

Through the forward contract, the company agrees with the bank to sell or to buy the invoiced currency at a certain rate against GBP with a fixed delivery date. This forward rate may be higher or lower than the spot rate, but it is not what the bank expects it to be at the due date (as described in *Section 4.2.2.1*), it is actually a function of the interest levels and also to some degree of currency, period and market situation, plus the bank's margin.

A forward contract can be issued in one or more parts with separate rates and maturities in order to match the payment flows or to hedge the total risk balance. But it is a fixed agreement with the bank and should normally be done when the underlying contract is signed and/or when payment can be anticipated with some accuracy. If that is not the case – if the payment may be delayed or in the worst case not take place at all – the company may end up with a new currency risk when having to honour the forward contract with the bank.

If in such cases the company cannot use the contract for any other purpose, the bank must be contacted for a cancellation, at a price that depends on currency, volumes and not least the fixed maturity, since both the interest differentials and the banks' margin tend to increase over longer periods.

Forward contracts can be issued over very long periods, for many currencies up to 10 years, even though for commercial transactions, periods from 3–6 months up to a year are most common. These shorter periods are also the most liquid, whereas for longer periods the spreads, and thereby the cost, may increase due to a more illiquid market, but with great variety between different currencies.

If the exact date for the incoming payment cannot be determined in advance, the forward contract can, in most cases, be prolonged or shortened in time after agreement with the bank, even if it involves an additional cost. Another alternative is to arrange the contract at the outset as a period instead of a fixed date during which the currency may be delivered to or from the bank. Such contracts, called 'forward option contracts', will give higher flexibility to the company, but at a somewhat less favourable rate, depending on the length of this open period.

The larger the company or its currency volumes, the more it will tend to arrange contracts not for individual business transactions, but for outstanding balances over time, calculated according to the currency schedule. Such hedging of balances or part balances will always create a higher flexibility and is normally more cost-effective than covering individual transactions. How this is done in practice is shown at the end of this chapter.

■ 4.4.5 Currency options

The currency option (not to be mixed up with the forward option contract described above) is quite different from a forward contract.

The holder of the option has the right but not an obligation to buy or to sell a particular currency at an agreed rate and date. It may therefore be used as an alternative or a supplement to a forward contract.

The currency option would be used in particular when an offer or a tender is outstanding and when the seller does not know if the deal will be won or not. Should that be the case, the company could later make use of the option to cover the currency risk. If the deal is lost, the seller may simply abstain from doing so, or if the value of the currency has changed, the option might have a value of its own and the seller might sell the option contract back to the bank with a profit.

There are two types of currency options:

- Put options and
- Call options.

Purchasing one of these give the holder the right (but not the obligation) to sell (Put) and respectively buy (Call), as in this case GBP, against another currency. The agreed price at which the exchange of currencies takes place under the contract at the agreed expiry date is called the 'exercise price' or the 'strike price'. For example, a UK seller would then purchase a GBP Call option, which gives them the right to buy GBP from the bank at the strike price and sell to the bank the incoming foreign currency in which the transaction is invoiced, and which the seller wants to hedge.

The holder of the option also pays a premium for the contract itself, but normally no additional commission or other charges will be added. This up-front cost can be seen as an insurance premium which is determined by factors such as interest level, the length of the contract, market conditions, expected currency volatility and at what strike price the option shall be exercised, compared to the spot market rate at that time (see *Box 4.6*).

The bank may offer the company a number of different strike prices, both above and below the spot rate at that time, which leaves them with a combination of several strike prices and premiums to choose

Box 4.6   Example of a currency option

The example below is based on the seller expecting to receive an invoice payment in USD in 2 months time. They sign a GBP/USD currency option with the bank with a strike price of 1,7500. In this example, the bank quotes a premium of 2 per cent for an amount of 0.1 million USD.

The seller's alternatives of exercising the currency option or not at the expiry date are shown through the broken black line, which should be compared with a hypothetical forward rate contract (a horizontal line) at a level determined by the forward rate for the same period. The break-even price (the option strike price including the premium) will, in practice, be somewhat higher than the thick black line, depending on the upfront 'insurance premium', but since that premium has already been paid, the seller will consider their alternatives based on the option price alone.

Explanation of the expressions used above can be found in the adjoining text and in the Glossary.

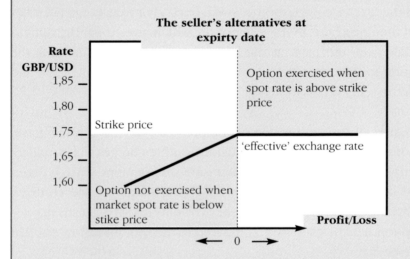

The seller's alternatives at expirty date

Rate GBP/USD

1,85 — Option exercised when spot rate is above strike price

1,80 —

1,75 — Strike price

1,65 — 'effective' exchange rate

1,60 — Option not exercised when market spot rate is below stike price

Profit/Loss

← 0 →

'Loss' is limited to the premium paid, but the seller takes advantage of a better spot market rate.

'Profit' is dependent on the difference between the strike price and the spot market rate – less premium paid.

from. Seen from the seller's point of view, a purchase of a Call option with a low strike price (expressed as units of currency per GBP) will have a higher premium than an option with a high strike price, since it is more likely to be exercised - and will, if exercised, give a correspondingly better rate for the foreign currency.

As a direct comparison between the rate of a forward currency contract and the break-even price for a currency option (when adding its strike price and the premium paid), the option contract will usually be more expensive than the forward contract. But that is to be expected, in an option the company has a choice that is not available in a forward contract. But on the other hand, it the exchange spot rate moves further than the strike price, the owner of the option can earn a substantial profit. (Intrinsic value).

Currency options as a means of hedging a commercial exchange risk have not yet reached the same level as forward contracts for many reasons. This market has not the same depth and liquidity as the forward currency market and it is, therefore, more difficult for the banks to hedge options compared to forward contracts – making the options more expensive. However, if the bank can use a currency option towards a customer as an additional hedge for an imbalance in its own portfolio instead of a new risk to be secured, or as a counter trade for another option transaction, the bank may price the option accordingly.

The option market is understandably also more traded and liquid for the larger currencies used in international trade and for shorter periods, but together with an increased use for commercial purposes, currency options might become more and more competitive. It is estimated that 5–10 per cent (a small but increasing figure) of all commercial currency hedges are done today in the form of options. However, the company should always check the alternatives and see the currency option as one of several methods, which combined should hedge the overall currency position. The option may be more expensive but, in conjunction with other hedges, or for specific purposes, it can be worth the cost.

■ 4.4.6 Short-term currency loans

A loan in a foreign currency is primarily a form of finance, but can also be used by the seller in order to hedge the value of a future incoming foreign currency payment. By immediately exchanging the loan amount into GBP at the spot rate, the seller avoids future currency risks on that amount, and on the due date of the loan it will be repaid by the incoming currency payment. The hedging cost will then be the interest on the loan less the reduced interest cost on the current account. The seller may end up with a total cost for this type of hedging similar to the cost of a forward contract for the same period.

The use of a currency loan as a hedging tool is also part of the total cash management of the company together with other methods used to cap or minimise the total currency balance and overall liquidity.

■ 4.4.7 Bill discounting

Banks may discount Bills of Exchange that the seller receives from the buyer (or sometimes Promissory Notes, which are sometimes used for longer credit periods). Such discounting, as with short-term currency loans, is primarily a method of refinancing, with the currency exchanged at spot rate and the debt being repaid to the bank at maturity out of the proceeds from the bill. The practice of discounting is described more in detail in *Chapter 6, Trade finance*.

■ 4.4.8 Currency clauses

When both commercial parties want to avoid the exchange risk, it can be tempting to use some form of currency clause with the intent of sharing or dividing the risk between them. For example, with a 'cap and floor' agreement, the seller may accept EUR as the invoicing currency, but with a fixed exchange rate floor against GBP. If the EUR weakens below the floor rate during the contract period, the seller would then automatically be compensated through receiving a correspondingly higher EUR amount. The parties could also agree on a similar cap to the buyer's advantage, thereby paying a lower amount if the EUR strengthens above a certain exchange rate against GBP.

When it comes to larger amounts and longer time periods in particular, when the exchange rate developments may be a major issue for the parties, these clauses could be an alternative for sharing the currency risk. But should such currency clauses be made more complicated, what might have been a straightforward agreement at the negotiating table can soon turn into disputes or disagreements later on, when one of the parties wants to make use of the currency clause. A good piece of advice is to stick to the simple 'cap and/or floor-clauses' for shorter periods and for the major currencies only, and to avoid more complicated currency clauses. If such clauses should be discussed, the seller should contact their bank for advice.

■ 4.4.9 Tender exchange rate insurance

The exchange risk during the period when the bid or tender is open is one of the factors that can make the transaction particularly risky. The seller risks losing money when tendering at a fixed price in a foreign currency – while obviously wanting the tender to be successful, the seller could lose out in the contract if the currency weakens during the period between submitting the offer or tender and winning the contract.

Insurance against tender exchange risks are provided by some insurers in the private market, often called 'Tender Exchange Rate Indemnity', and in some cases and for large contracts only, also by the ECGD, the UK's Export Credit Agency. The private market insurance in particular, could be an alternative to currency options if that is not a realistic alternative in the particular case due to costs involved or other practical reasons. Insurance might also be a better alternative than inserting currency or escape clauses in the contract, clauses which often seriously weaken the value of the offer.

These insurance policies are generally construed to mitigate the drawback of having to quote a firm offer in foreign currency with a currency risk that could be outstanding for a long period of time. The insurance conditions are basically quite straightforward, sometimes also with a requirement to pay to the insurer any 'surplus', should the invoiced currency have increased in value during the period. The seller pays an up-front fee, often only a smaller part of the total premium, but only if the bid is successful is the balance of the premium due for payment.

A Tender Exchange Rate Indemnity can be given in the most commonly traded international currencies normally up to a year, but the availability and the cost involved is also dependent on the time period and market conditions at the time of the cover. As in any other currency hedge, many other situations could also arise during the contract period, such as if the contract should fail, be prolonged or abandoned, and the indemnity should also have to cover these eventualities, and will therefore, as any insurance, be based of specified terms and conditions.

➢ 4.5 Practical currency management

The most common methods for hedging currency risks have already been described, but an equally important question is how they are managed and hedged in practical terms within the company, and how the currency aspects are dealt with, during the whole process from negotiation until the sales contract is concluded and payment is received.

Most companies have internal systems for establishing their currency position and rules and limits for dealing with the currency risks. These systems may often be quite simple for the smaller company with a limited currency risk exposure, but often they are much more sophisticated, and highly computerised. It all depends on the volumes and currencies involved, and the more stable the currency flows are over time, the easier they are to forecast, often over long periods ahead.

Many exporting companies with large currency invoicing also have a rolling currency position schedule, comprising both fixed and estimated currency flows, for example, inserted to 100 per cent for contracted deals and with a lower and variable percentage for future non-contracted deals, dependent on probability and the time period covered. Many companies often cover their main positions years in advance on such a rolling basis to achieve the best possible currency rate stability over a longer period.

Such a long term portfolio is constantly updated through new contracts, from a low to a higher percentage if the contract is already in the books, inserted in full for a completely new contract, or reduced with anticipated contracts that were not accepted or did not materialise as planned. When the payment is finally received, it will be booked at the rate of the forward contracts or against other hedges falling due at that time and to the percentage that the hedge covers the individual transaction. Any excess amount not taken against a hedge is booked at the prevailing spot rate.

When determining the internal and calculated rate of exchange to be used within the company in price discussions in offers and tenders, the rates applied are often based on an average currency rate, including the hedges, calculated from the currency schedule over the relevant period. It is then up to the appointed staff to communicate these internal rates within the company as they change. The periods covered in such currency schedules are dependent on the stability of the forecasts, on risk acceptance and how quickly the cost structure to the final customers can be changed. They are also constantly changing with regard to both size and maturity, depending on external currency fluctuations and verified or anticipated changes in company sales.

When it comes to less used foreign currencies, and for smaller or medium-sized export companies generally, the currency transactions are normally smaller and less stable and thereby harder to predict for longer periods. The seller must then often act in another way and establish internal currency rates for individual transactions, instead of on a calculated average currency rate and thereafter, cover the transactions on a case-by-case basis.

As shown earlier, low inflation countries with stable economies often have low interest rates and thereby often a premium in their forward currency rates (ie, higher forward than spot value). The opposite is true for countries that for any reason have higher interest rates (ie, a lower forward than spot value). But irrespective of the method used, the forward currency rates are generally the basis for how smaller companies establish the internal currency rate for individual transactions when preparing an offer or tender and before actual hedging is arranged.

Nowadays the difference between forward and spot rates for shorter periods is relatively small for the more commonly used international currencies, due to a similar economic policy in these countries and consequently less spread in interest rate levels. But, nevertheless, if the seller follows the principle of using the forward currency rate as the basis for offers and tenders, then the following method could be used for covering the individual transaction, with a cautious approach.

For currencies with a forward premium, the seller can use the spot rate as a base for the internal rate, with a percentage increase for longer periods, depending on the angle of the forward premium curve and adjusted to the competitive situation. For currencies with a discount, the actual forward rate can be used as a base, adjusted with a further discount, depending on the volatility of the currency, the period involved and the competitive situation (see *Box 4.7* below).

Other techniques used in setting internal currency rates or covering the currency risk during the quotation stage could be, as an alternative or as a complement, to work with currency options and include the premium in the quotation price. Alternatively the seller could reduce the validity of the outstanding offer or tender, or insert a price clause covering adverse currency fluctuations. But, as pointed out earlier, such clauses have a competitive disadvantage, which needs to be considered.

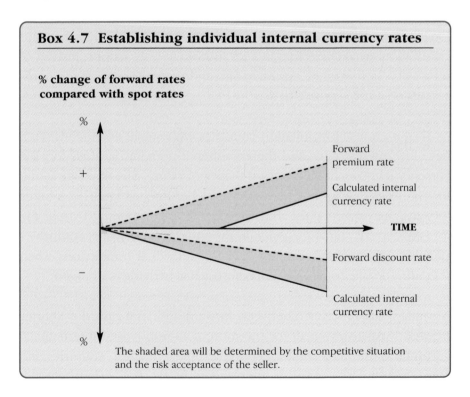

Box 4.7 Establishing individual internal currency rates

% change of forward rates compared with spot rates

The shaded area will be determined by the competitive situation and the risk acceptance of the seller.

5

Export credit insurance

➢ 5.1 A mutual undertaking

Previous chapters have dealt with the different forms of risk that can occur in an export transaction, risks that have to be covered mainly through the terms of payment. But, in many cases, that may be difficult to achieve either because the buyer does not accept the proposed terms, the bank is unwilling to take the risks involved or even the remaining risks may be considered by the seller as being too high. The

---

Box 5.1 Export Credit insurance

Export credit refers to the credit that the seller offers the buyer in the contract for sale of goods and services (i.e. a supplier credit) or credits given to finance such a sale (i.e. a buyer credit).

The risks covered in export credit insurance are normally regarded as divisible into commercial and political or buyer and non-buyer risks. The commercial risk is that which rests with the buyer i.e. their ability to pay for what has been purchased. The political risk is that associated with the buyer's country and includes losses arising from such events as the cancellation of an import licence, war and civil war and the prevention by the authorities in the buyer's country of the transfer of the foreign exchange required to pay the supplier.

terms of payment must be negotiated in the same way as other parts of the contract, in which both commercial parties may have to come to a compromise. In many countries there are established practices relating to the way payments are made and it may be difficult to get agreement from the buyer should the terms differ too greatly from these practices — particularly if they expect other suppliers to offer more competitive terms, sometimes supported by a separate credit risk insurance. The seller may also find it difficult to find financial institutions that are willing to accept the inherent risks in the terms of payment, in particular the political and/or commercial risks in many countries in conjunction with medium or long-term financing.

In these cases it is crucial to try to structure the deal in such a way that enables the seller to maximise the combined cover that can be obtained from banks, financial institutions and separate export credit insurance companies or institutions. The seller should also aim to discover, in advance, what is achievable before commencing negotiations with the buyer. Having the knowledge and capability of structuring such transactions, together with banks and/or insurers, is of vital importance for the seller when dealing with political and commercial risks that might otherwise make the transaction difficult or even impossible to deal with.

> This chapter focuses on how the export credit insurance market works in general terms for UK exporting companies, for short and long periods, together with a description of the two main areas within this sector; the international insurance market and the market for government supported insurance.

Insurance in general is based on a mutual relationship between the parties involved, where both the insurer and the insured (in this case the seller) enter into obligations towards one another. This is a major difference compared with a guarantee or a bond, which is a one-sided obligation based on specified conditions.

There are many forms of export credit insurance created to cover different aspects of an export transaction, for example, coverage from shipment only or also including the production period. Each insurance cover is based on special terms and conditions, which the seller has to check with the preconditions applicable to the individual transaction. The most common of these conditions are related to the seller's risk in the transaction, qualifying or waiting periods or conditions precedent, for example, that a Letter of Credit has been issued, certain permissions in the buyer's country have been obtained or that certain guarantees have been received by the seller.

However, the seller also has obligations towards the insurer. For example, that the uninsured percentage should be retained during the whole insured period or alternatively, that it might be transferred only under certain conditions. Other conditions could be that specified time limits must be adhered to or adverse changes regarding the buyer or the transaction should be reported, and/or that important changes to the transaction have to be approved by the insurer.

Incorrect, misleading or changed and unreported circumstances may, in the worst-case, lead to the insurance being reduced or revoked. The seller must also take reasonable action during the insurance period to prevent or mitigate potential damage or losses under the insurance. It is, therefore, important for the seller to ensure that staff, who might not be aware of the conditions of the insurance, do not make changes or concessions to the buyer that may jeopardize the insurance cover.

If used correctly, export credit insurance can be a crucial part of the whole structure of the deal, whether it is to cover the additional risk of a medium-term credit or ordinary day-to-day short-term export transactions. It is a good idea to compare insurance alternatives from various insurers where available; different risk assessments and alternative risk levels may result in large price differentials.

➤ 5.2 The international insurance market

In the UK, the market for export credit insurance is divided into two basic categories: risk periods under two years, which must be covered through the international insurance market (market sector insurance),

---

Box 5.2 Risks not covered by export credit insurance

Export credit insurance is limited in principle by two factors:

- Percentage of coverage, or inverted, the uninsured percentage that the seller is not allowed to lay-off to any third party.
- Qualifying period — the waiting period before settlement of the claim takes place.

When calculating the size and cost for these uncovered risks, the seller must assume that the maximum risk occurs not only when the delivery obligations have been fulfilled but before receipt of first payment from the buyer. This is also dependent on whether the delivery is in one or more shipments, if the buyer has to pay in one or more part payments, and if separate credit terms are connected to the deal. However, the maximum risk not covered by the insurance can always be determined in advance.

To calculate this, three factors have to be considered:

- Capital risk — that is the capital amount under the insurance, which the seller has to retain as own risk.
- Interest risk — that is the corresponding uninsured parts on any credit given to the buyer, calculated on estimated interest payments during the credit period, multiplied by the average interest rate.
- Settlement risk — that is the interest cost for the waiting period until payment takes place under the insurance.

The seller should also consider other important questions that may vary between insurers (eg, how settlement is made when invoicing in a foreign currency).

---

and longer periods of two years and over, also covered by ECGD (described later in this chapter).

The division into short and longer maturities is primarily related to underlying exports. Goods and services that are not eligible for credit periods of two years or more (ie, consumer goods, raw materials and certain lighter capital goods) must be covered by market sector insurance and cannot be covered by the ECGD due to its statutes. These restrictions are similar, but not identical, as for Export Credit Agencies in other industrialised countries.

For these shorter periods, and in particular periods up to 180 days (which represent the bulk of UK exports to OECD countries and often delivered on open-account payment terms) the commercial risk is the main risk element. In the least developed countries in this category, where both the commercial and political risks tend to increase, the terms of payment are generally shifted from open-account terms to terms based on documentary payments, with stronger control over the goods until payment is received, or supported by a bank guarantee. For non-OECD countries, where the commercial/political risk is even greater, bank guaranteed terms of payment, mostly in the form of Letters of Credit, are often the norm.

This basic payment structure is consistent with the structure of the market sector credit insurance, covering mainly commercial risk on shorter periods, or the combined commercial/political risk on government or semi-official institutions. Political risk cover can sometimes be added to the policy for commercial buyers. The market sector insurance core business is therefore the industrial countries or countries in industrial development in which relevant financial company information can be obtained and where the legal framework and the financial systems are working reasonably well.

A normal condition for obtaining insurance is that it should cover the delivery of goods or services. However, the risks during the production period up to delivery could also be included (normally in ECGD's policies, but more as an exception in the market sector insurance) based on a signed contract between the parties.

Insurance is not only bought by individual exporters but also by banks or financial institutions for a variety of reasons, an example being to mitigate the risk on receivables purchased or discounted from their customers. As with other commercial insurance, those covering export credit risks always contain an element of risk that must be carried by the seller. However, one of the advantages with market sector credit risk insurance, emphasised by the insurers themselves, is that in reality their combined services and not just the insurance, tend to reduce the outstanding risk in the markets in which they operate, for example, through local representation in the buyer's country and more professional supervision.

The advantages of an international network are also used in the marketing of other services provided by insurers in the market sector. For example, issuing of various types of export related guarantees or bonds (mainly contract guarantees/bonds) in competition with the banks, or services related to the credit risk policies, such as credit risk assessment and collection of overdue payments.

The main advantages of private export credit policies, taken from different leading insurance companies, are listed below:

- capped and calculable costs;
- economic security;
- rapid and professional settlement of claims;
- access to experience from various business sectors in many countries;
- professional coverage of clients and outstanding claims;
- access to an international network with local representation;
- large databases with customer information;
- release of administration and resources from its clients;
- increase in borrowing capacity from banks;
- expanding sales to existing customers;
- developing sales into new international markets;
- professional credit management overview of receivables;
- buyer and political risk cover.

The development of more sophisticated models for risk analysis,

INFORMATION BOX

coface Facilitates your global trade

With close to 60 years experience, the Coface Group is the world's largest export insurance group, with subsidiaries/branches in 57 countries and local services in 92 countries. Being a Subsidiary of Natexis Banques Populaires and the Groupe Banque Populaire, Coface is rated AA by Fitch and Aa3 by Moody's.

Coface UK is a leading player in the UK trade credit protection and solutions. We can provide your business with a complete range of solutions for trading on credit in the UK domestic market and in exports.

o **Protection.** Our trade credit insurance policies are designed to meet the diverse requirements of all types of business. Options include national and international cover, selective or complete ledger cover and an option for a guaranteed claim payment within 65 days of the due date. So, whether you are a multinational or a small or medium-sized business, Coface UK has a trade credit solution for your needs.

o **Collection.** Employing our international network of partners and agents across the world, our experience in collections and receivables management is unmatched. We will tailor a programme to meet your needs, whether you require a simple 'off-the-shelf' collection package or a complete outsourcing service.

o **Assessment.** We specialize in providing credit information on all trading entities, from fully incorporated companies right through to sole traders. Using our credit services with information on about 44 million companies world-wide, allows you to make informed decisions about trading on credit terms.

o **Finance.** Receivables finance is available through Coface UK´s subsidiary London Bridge Finance Ltd. Domestic and Export financing services range from off-balance sheet and invoice discounting to full factoring.

Coface UK also issues trade related **guarantee insurance (bonds)**, protecting the buyer if the supplier fails to meet their contractual obligations, or protecting the seller for the fulfilment of payment obligations.

The Coface Group also acts as Credit Risk Agency for the French State, thereby drawing on the knowledge and experience of the state supported credit risk insurance system that is complementing the private insurance markets in international trade.

Coface UK

Egale 1, 80 St Alban's Road, Watford, Herts. WD17 1RP
Telephone: 44 (0)1923 478100
E-mail: enquiries@cofaceuk.com   www.cofaceuk.com

together with new techniques for database handling and the establishment of an international network, has led to a rapid restructuring of this segment of the insurance market, which (apart from a large number of local and specialised insurers) now consists of only a few companies with a global presence.

The cost structure for market export insurance risk cover is based on a number of factors such as risk assessment, customer relations, the volume of business generated and the competition. This means that the premium for individual transactions or for a package of transactions can vary considerably between insurers, even when considering the differences in risk cover and in other terms and conditions that may apply.

Many credit insurance companies or brokers have standardised systems on their websites, so called Credit Insurance Cost/Benefit Analysis, where the seller can do a simple analysis evaluating their total export portfolio. By giving input on the insurable yearly export sales, the average gross margin and an estimated average or worst-case loss ratio, this analysis shows not only the direct cost involved but also what incremental sales are necessary to pay for the corresponding average credit insurance premium.

Not surprisingly, the seller will then probably find that in most of these general and standardised calculations, the premium is a relatively small investment for covering the potential loss and that the additional sales needed to cover this loss are of a magnitude that they justify almost any credit insurance program. This is before taking other indirect advantages into account.

However, even if such standardised calculations do not give the whole picture, the seller should do a study of what would be the cost/benefit in their particular case by using a general credit insurance cover, based on the seller's own pre-conditions and assumptions. A general cover often gives the best outcome in such an analysis due to the business volumes involved and the automatic spread of risk for the insurer, and any new individual deal could be added to the cover at beneficial rates. When this analysis is done, it is easier for the seller to compare other alternatives and to make an informed decision as to whether or not to use such credit risk cover programs.

The insurance policies offered in the market sector are mostly individually structured and can be combined with many other services. The seller should, therefore, check with various insurers to find the optimal combination in each case, either directly or through an insurance broker. By doing so, the seller can also check the various pre-conditions which might be needed for entering into a potential transaction or to cover a risk portfolio, for example, regarding the terms of payment required. This may also give a better picture of the costs involved in relation to different levels of risk coverage, together with a better analysis of how the risk is assessed by an individual insurer. This is why it is so important to establish an early contact with banks and credit insurers when it comes to new transactions, unfamiliar markets or buyers.

■ 5.2.1 Market sector insurance cover

The dominant insurers tend to structure credit insurance policies in the international market in different ways, often also with different product names and including additional, optional services.

One general feature of this market's performance is the tendency to strive to cover not only individual deals or single buyers, but primarily all of the seller's export transactions. This enables the insurer to obtain larger volumes of business with a more diversified risk structure, and take advantage of the international network and additional services included in the offer. The description of the market sector insurance below is, therefore, of a general nature in order to highlight the basic structure of these insurance products. It also highlights the different levels of services, the diversity of services and how these policies can be adapted to the needs of the individual seller based on businesses structure, risk aversion and affordability.

It goes without saying that every request for insurance is evaluated according to the risk involved, which means that certain buyers and/or countries may not be insurable. Or, if they were insurable, it could be at a low percentage indemnity or an almost prohibitive premium.

■ 5.2.2 Standard export credit insurance

Most market sector insurers have designed a range of export credit policies suitable for small and medium-sized businesses, with cover against non-payment of debts due to commercial and/or political risks. These policies are highly standardised in order to be cost-effective, often combining both UK domestic and export sales, based on the individual buyer, with an indemnity level of up to 90 per cent. They are mostly structured and priced in order to induce the company to include most of its receivables, often combined with additional services for a more effective credit control and with collection and litigation support as additional, and mostly optional, services.

In order to facilitate the practical day-to-day handling of the credit limit process, the larger insurers also offer their customers Internet access to their internal underwriting systems, thereby enabling the customers to manage their credit limits on-line in the most efficient way, including:

- applying for credit limits on new or existing customers;
- monitoring current portfolios under existing limits;
- making amendments or cancellations to existing buyer limits.

An additional advantage of standardised insurance – particularly important to small, growing companies – is the access to increased levels of export finance that is obtainable from banks through the added security this cover will give the lender.

■ 5.2.3 Tailor-made credit risk insurance

Many insurers offer more sophisticated integrated insurance packages, tailor-made for larger companies with greater volumes of receivables (both domestic and global). They can also include risk limitations on the turnover covered by the policy, with an enhanced credit assessment and credit control, combined with on-line credit limit management and automatic collection services.

The credit assessment is often based on credit information systems created in-house or in association with other credit information agencies giving information about millions of companies worldwide.

▪ 5.2.4 Managed and guaranteed credit risk insurance

The most comprehensive general credit risk insurance not only covers part or all of the services mentioned, but also provides a payment guarantee, thereby insuring the cash flow of the insured debt. Such insurance may integrate credit assessment, credit insurance and collection — often including even the management and outsourcing of the whole administration of these services.

With such control over the whole debt chain — from invoicing to final payment — some insurers may also be able to guarantee the final claim payment with a waiting period of (normally) 60–90 days, and provide disclosed or undisclosed debt collection services. Policies with a guaranteed claim payment period and a full or partial outsourcing of the administration give the seller other advantages in the form of increased operational and administrative efficiency. These have to be considered in relation to the costs involved.

▪ 5.2.5 Global credit risk cover

Most of the general credit risk policies covered above can be combined with global risk cover, suitable for the company's group requirements. Such cover is tailor-made for companies working through subsidiaries or branches in many countries, enabling each entity to have its policy structured according to local needs and to the law of that country, while at the same time benefiting from the overall global policy between the company head office and the insurer.

▪ 5.2.6 Political risk insurance

Many market credit risk insurers also cover pure political risks associated with trading or investments in countries where such cover may be needed, in particular on the short periods where ECGD is not active. (These political risk policies are also provided by ECGD for medium and long term periods, though in some cases only in combination with their other guarantees or insurance cover.) The most common market insurance policies in this area are:

Contract Repudiation Indemnity or Contract Frustration Policy

There are different names for this kind of cover. It is an insurance that can be combined with the commercial risk on a commercial buyer in many developing countries, covering the political risks caused by a changed or revoked government, or any other public body approval or guarantee. The cover can also include protection for similar events when interference from such institutions makes it impossible for the seller to fulfil their contractual obligations towards the buyer.

Bond/Guarantee Indemnity Insurance

This insurance provides cover against so-called 'unfair calling' of most bonds or guarantees issued on behalf of the seller, related to the export sale. This includes both unfair callings from public buyers, but also (what might be called) 'fair callings' from other buyers, caused by public body or political interference which makes it impossible for the seller to perform their obligations under the commercial contract.

Investment Insurance

This insurance covers events such as confiscation, expropriation, nationalisation or deprivation of the investor's fixed or mobile assets overseas. The cover can also be extended to include war, civil war, strikes, riots, terrorism, regulatory changes, currency inconvertibility, business interruption and the inability to recover leased equipment.

■ 5.2.7 Key commercial credit risk insurance

Apart from the insurance policies mentioned above – which are of a general nature, covering more standardised commercial and political risks – insurance is also available to the seller, which covers specific individual transactions or excess risks. For example:

Key customer risk insurance

Most insurers offer insurance that covers only certain specified parts of the risk in the seller's export ledger. Such insurance may be attractive for sellers with a high proportion of their total sales to just a few buyers. The cover could be structured in different ways, to cover either a percentage of the risk on a particular buyer or a particular transaction.

Excess risk insurance

The seller may want to cap the maximum risk on the total outstanding receivables, while at the same time be able to maintain flexibility for other parts of the portfolio. Such insurance can be made highly flexible, for example, by offering cover only in excess of a certain minimum amount and up to an agreed maximum.

Tender exchange rate indemnity

The exchange rate when tendering in a foreign currency can be a major risk factor, in particular for large amounts and for long periods. Obviously, the seller wants the tender to be successful but may at the same time risk losing money when offering a fixed price if the currency weakens during the period between submitting the tender and securing the contract. This type of insurance was also described as a currency risk cover in *Chapter 3, Bonds and Guarantees*.

➢ 5.3 Export Credit Agencies

Most industrialized but also many emerging market countries have Export Credit Agencies (ECAs) with roughly the same objective - namely to support exports from their own countries. There is however no such thing as a typical export credit agency. Their status vary, some are government departments or agencies and others are private insurance companies (as for example in Gemany and France) which apart from doing insurance business in the market sector, also acts as an ECA on behalf of or on the account of the respective government.

Most ECA´s are part of the The Berne Union, (The International Union of Credit Insurers) the leading international organisation in the field of export credit and investment insurance, with members from both the public and the private sector. The major activities consist of (as taken from their web-site):

(a) Supporting the sale of raw materials, spares and consumer goods on cash or short credit terms. This means underwriting the repayment risks on individual buyers and, often, their banks as well as a whole range of political risks.

(b) Supporting, either by insurance/guarantees or by direct lending, the supply of project and capital goods on medium and long term credit. This often includes underwriting the risks on the viability of the projects themselves, as well as a wide range of other commercial and political risks.

(c) Supporting outward direct investment in various forms, (e.g. equity, loans), made in other countries.

Even if the obligations are guaranteed by the respective state, the ECAs should operate with a reasonable confidence of breaking even in the long term, charging customers premium at levels which are sufficient to cover the perceived market and buyer risks, and cover administration costs. In addition to these costs, some ECAs also include a 'reserve margin' in the premium rate to accommodate potential individual large losses or general country or regional payment moratoriums. The ECAs also make every effort to recover amounts paid in claims – either through the Paris Club of official creditors (*see Glossary*) or directly from individual buyers/borrowers.

Generally speaking, the ECAs also fulfil an important role in supporting the transfer of goods and services and, indirectly provide knowledge and expertise to many countries, particularly developing countries, and in many cases this would not have taken place without this support.

The Organisation for Economic Co-operation and Development (OECD) has regulated the ways in which ECAs are allowed to operate, in order to contain or restrict the competition between the agencies in a race to offer the best terms and conditions in support of their own exports. (The so-called OECD Consensus Arrangement, or just 'Consensus' or the 'Arrangement'). The Consensus rules (described in *Chapter 6, Trade finance*) cover export credit support on periods of two years or more and include the length of credit for different types of goods, repayment structure, minimum advance payments and maximum credit, minimum government supported interest rate levels and premium rates.

It is worth noting that the OECD does not allow ECAs to issue insurance/guarantees for export risks in the most developed OECD countries on periods of less than two years. However, for other countries there is no such restriction, and in these cases many agencies issue insurance/guarantees down to six months.

ECGD, the UK Export Credit Agency, described in the next section, only covers export risks for goods that are eligible for periods of two years or more, irrespective of the buyer's country. Sellers in the UK should be aware of this difference, since their competitors may have such cover from their ECAs where the ECGD cannot participate — meaning that cover has to be arranged through the market sector.

Apart from the OECD, the Berne Union has also implemented guidelines which are to be followed by the ECAs, and include certain restrictions on credits up to five years for different types of goods, which combined with smaller contract values, could result in shorter credit periods than would otherwise be expected. The rules are too detailed to list here, but the seller could always check with ECGD in advance if these restrictions are applicable to their products.

The ECAs also cooperate between themselves in purely commercial matters, mainly in transactions involving suppliers from several countries. In order to facilitate the transaction, one ECA normally takes overall responsibility and covers the whole package (according to its rules) with reinsurance from the other agencies covering their suppliers. The ECGD programme, called the 'One Stop Shop Programme', is a system with many advantages for the project and for the UK lead supplier, who only needs to have contact with one agency which will help coordinate the transaction with other agencies according to the UK rules.

Under an OECD Consultation Process, ECAs also have the role of supervising the OECD rules from a commercial and competitive perspective. Under this process, the agency has to report non-standard cover offered to a seller in its country, which could result in matching from other agencies in support of their suppliers, competing on the same transaction. Therefore, when a buyer is claiming that another supplier offers better credit terms, this can easily be checked with the

ECA. Particularly when an element of foreign aid is involved, which may be the case in exports/projects to the poorest developing countries. Such combined support, which is only given by some countries, (tied-aid finance) could result in extremely low interest levels and longer credit periods.

Individual ECAs have similar, but not identical, rules regarding cover for foreign components of the delivery. Some allow a fixed percentage of maximum foreign contents to be insured and some take it case-by-case, depending on size, structure, buyer country and other supplier countries involved.

The objective for ECGD is to cover UK exports, which, by definition, is when the goods have, or are capable of, obtaining a UK Certificate of Origin from a Chamber of Commerce — although ECGD may consider some limited foreign/local content irrespective of origin. Otherwise, the transaction will be looked at on its own merits, such as total value, percentage and country of origin, and whether these parts could be reinsured with any other agency.

The OECD has recently also issued strict guidelines for a much broader perspective of government supported international trade, for example, its effects on the environment, sustainable development and human rights in the buying country. The larger the transaction and the more it is related to the infrastructure in these countries, the more important these considerations become in order to get the backing of the ECAs.

Illegal practices are also receiving increasingly more attention (ie, facilitation payments, money laundering, bribes and other corrupt practices). These rules are now even included in the law of most industrialised countries, including the UK, and are therefore, enforceable even where such practices have taken place outside the exporter's home country. The area of corrupt practices was discussed in *Chapter 1, Export risks and risk assessment*, but it should be stressed that all agencies, including ECGD, currently demand such statements from applicants for insurance cover. Any material breach of these assurances could have serious consequences on the validity of the cover.

➤ 5.4 The Export Credits Guarantee Department (ECGD)

ECGD is the UK's official Export Credit Agency and is a separate government department. It has been in existence for over 80 years and is one of the leading Export Credit Agencies within the industrialised countries.

ECGD's aim, according to its mission statement, is:

'**To benefit the UK economy by helping exporters of UK goods and services win business, and UK firms to invest overseas, by providing guarantees, insurance and reinsurance against loss, taking into account the Government's international policies.**'

The role of ECGD is to supplement (but not compete with) the insurance cover available from the market sector insurance. This is why ECGD has concentrated its resources on periods of two years and over, and on developing countries and emerging markets where the market sector cover is still very small. The main objectives of ECGD are to provide:

- insurance to exporters against non-payment (described in this Chapter);
- guarantees to banks to assist the financing of exports (see also *Chapter 6 and 7*); and
- insurance to UK companies and banks for overseas investments (see *Chapter 7*).

The majority of ECGD cover in terms of business volume is still for larger transactions, such as defence and infrastructure projects, oil, gas, power generation and transmission, water and the environment, and the transportation and aerospace sectors. ECGD also strives to obtain a larger share of the smaller and medium-sized trade transactions, it can actually support contracts as low as £25,000. It issues guarantees and insurances for a total of £3–4 billion a year, roughly equally split between supplier insurance, supplier and buyer credits, and overseas investment insurance.

ECGD has established standard procedures for dealing with requests or proposals for cover, for both insurance and guarantees, following the normal business cycle of its customers. The first stage is in the form of a **Preliminary Response Letter**, often issued when the seller is in the early internal process of preparing the offer. This letter is without commitment, outlining only basic details for cover (if any) together with indicative terms and conditions.

The second stage is the **Premium Rate Hold Letter**, issued upon request of the seller when preparing an offer or a tender for contract. This is more detailed, specifying the premium (fixed for 180 days) but is subject to certain terms and conditions, and to the business details supplied by the seller.

The third and final stage comes when the contract is secured (subject only to certain conditions and approvals), when ECGD issues a **Letter of Intent/Offer**. This letter/offer specifies the final details and terms and conditions, and will be valid for a period of 180 days to allow time for documentation and fulfilment of all outstanding conditions in the contract, upon which the policy will be issued. With this in mind, it is important for the seller to ensure that any signed contract is conditional upon the final issue of the insurance or guarantee, but also that any material changes thereafter in the commercial contract should have prior approval from ECGD.

As with all insurance policies, a maximum amount of loss is stipulated in each case (denominated in GBP) and within that limit, claims could also be settled in another currency if that is the valid currency of the claim. The insurance premiums are individually set, based on the assessment of the risk and the value and length of the risk period. There is also a premium calculator on ECGD's website which can be used to obtain an estimate of the premium.

> In this chapter we are only dealing with the main insurance policies issued by ECGD. Guarantees given to banks covering export credits are described in *Chapter 6 and* 7, and insurance to UK companies and banks for overseas investments in *Chapter 7*.

INFORMATION BOX

 **How we can help your export business?**

Our Export Credit Insurance policies to exporters and investors can cover three basic risks: buyer default, buyer insolvency and country risk. Our Guarantees to banks enable them to finance your export transaction. We also offer combined packages of risk cover for the exporter and for the financing institution.

We can help you improve your global competitiveness by:
- Offering more competitive credit terms to your overseas buyer.
- Selling more to existing customers.
- Selling to new customers and markets.
- Penetrating higher risk markets.

... and protect your bottom line by:
- Avoiding large unexpected bad debts.
- Improving your cash flow reliability.
- Improving your liquidity.
- Reducing the risk of non-payment.
- Increasing your borrowing potential.

We cover export of Light Capital Goods, Capital Goods, Services and Overseas Investments. To qualify for ECGD support, exporters and investors must be exporting or investing from the UK. This may include foreign owned subsidiaries operating out of the UK. Some foreign goods and/or services as part of an export may be eligible.

However, please note that if you export consumer goods or raw materials, ECGD cannot support this business. For exports of such or other goods that are normally sold on credit terms of less than two years, there are a number of companies in the market that can provide short-term credit insurance.

For existing customers, please contact the personnel in each Business Division, via our website. For customers relatively new to exporting, we have introduced a New Customer Service Team on 020 7512 7887 or email: help@ecgd.gsi.gov.uk

ECGD, London Office:
PO Box 2200, 2 Exchange Tower, Harbour Exchange Square, London E14 9GS
Telephone: 020 7512 7000 E-mail: help@ecgd.gsi.gov.uk
www.ecgd.gov.uk

■ *5.4.1 The Export Insurance Policy*

The Export Insurance Policy (EXIP) covers the risk for the seller for non-receipt of payment under an export contract, due to commercial and/or political risk. The coverage is up to 95 per cent, with a 6-month waiting period, and the seller must always retain the risk on the uninsured part or, as it is formally known, their beneficial interest in the uninsured percentage, which cannot be laid off to any third party.

Commercial risk involves the insolvency of the buyer or failure either to pay or not fulfil obligations in any other way according to the contract within six months from the due date and, as a consequence of this failure, the seller suffers a loss on the insured contract. Political risk involves political, social, economic, legal or administrative events outside the UK, which prevent the buyer fulfilling the contractual obligations, or create difficulties or restrictions of such a nature that the seller cannot fulfil the contractual obligations.

The commercial and political risks can be difficult to separate, and claims under the policy must be dealt with on a case-by-case basis. Nevertheless, it is important for the seller to be able to demonstrate the actual and sequential events to show that every effort was made to fulfil their part of the transaction.

A sub-contractor in an export transaction could also be covered under an EXIP regardless of whether the risk is on the seller or the buyer, as long as the sub-contractor has an insurable risk in the transaction.

An EXIP can be issued in two different forms, either as a **pre-shipment policy** covering the buyer's obligations (including the risk before shipment) or as an **after-shipment only policy**, known as 'Costs Incurred and Amounts Owing Cover'. The pre-shipment policy is by far the most common, since it not only covers payments (if any) before delivery, but also any other contractual obligation, the failure of which makes the seller suffer a loss. Such insurance also strengthen the seller's possibility to arrange additional pre-finance finance through banks or other financial institutions.

A pre-delivery EXIP is frequently used as a supplementary insurance in conjunction with ECGD guarantees given to banks in connection with supplier or buyer credits. This combination of insurance to the seller and guarantee to the bank is explained more in *Chapter 6, Trade Finance*.

■ 5.4.2 The Bond Insurance Policy

It is common practice for the buyer to insist on bonds or guarantees to cover the obligations of the seller, in the same way as the seller tries to cover the payment obligations of the buyer. These contract bonds/guarantees were covered in detail in *Chapter 3, Bonds and Guarantees*.

Since contract bonds/guarantees are an integral part of the terms of payment in the contract, the risks for 'unfair calling' can also be covered by a separate insurance, for example, by a Bond Insurance Policy (BIP) from ECGD. However, this policy is not a stand-alone product — it can only be used if the contract itself is covered or supported by an EXIP or a supplier/buyer credit guarantee from ECGD. The BIP has a high degree of flexibility and is, therefore, suited to almost any contract (except in combination with Tender Bonds when such cover is not applicable).

The most common types of risks in connection with contract bonds/guarantees and those, which the BIP could cover, are:

- Advance Payment Guarantees;
- Performance Bonds or Guarantees;
- On Demand Guarantees;
- Counter-Guarantees and Counter Indemnities.

The 'unfair calling' cover under a BIP protects the seller should the buyer's demand in itself be unfair, because no breach has taken place under the contract. Or the situation could be just as the buyer states, but the reason for the non-fulfilment being due to political events in that country, effectively hindering the seller to perform, for example, through revoked or changed official approvals or permissions, or by many other reasons of a political nature.

In either case, this insurance should cover the above risks, but as with all other insurances, it is up to the seller to show that they have done what they could to fulfil their obligations. The premium for a BIP is based on a risk assessment, the insurance value and on the duration.

This ECGD insurance corresponds to the Bond/Guarantee Indemnity insurance available mainly for short periods on the private insurance markets, as described earlier in this chapter (*Section 5.2.6*).

The commercial risk, sometimes in conjunction with the political risk, is often the main risk for most sellers in their overseas trade. As has been shown in this chapter, there are many different options of how to cover these risks, and with many connected operational services.

It is therefore, generally recommended that each exporter should discuss this matter in detail with an insurer or broker based on their individual trade structure, to establish a strategy and an overall risk policy about how to make use of insurance cover when these risks cannot be fully covered through the agreed terms of payment.

6
Trade finance

➤ 6.1 Finance alternatives

To be able to give or to arrange finance as part of an export transaction is increasingly important, both as a sales argument and to meet competition from other suppliers. This is often the case for heavier capital goods or whole projects, where finance is often an integrated part of the package, but it can also apply to raw materials, consumer goods and lighter capital goods.

The length of credit is often divided into short-term, medium-term and long-term, even though such classifications are arbitrary and dependent on the purpose. Short-term credits are normally for periods up to one year even though the typical manufacturing exporter, as opposed to the larger corporates, would normally trade on short term credits of 60 or 90 days, perhaps up to a maximum of 180 days. Medium-term credits are usually for periods up to five years for large capital goods – and long-term credits for periods over five years.

In general, the buyer often prefers to split the payment for capital goods (machinery and installations with a considerable lifespan) into separate instalments over longer periods, perhaps with the intent of matching the payments against the income generated from the purchased goods. In such cases, the seller may have to offer these longer credit terms in order to be competitive.

The credit period is usually calculated from the time of shipment of the goods, or some average date in case of several deliveries. However, in practice payment is seldom made at that early stage and some form of credit is therefore included in most transactions. The seller may prefer to refinance such credits through ordinary bank credit facilities, especially for shorter periods and smaller amounts. However, in other cases the financing has to be arranged in some other way, which can also affect the structure of the transaction.

Another aspect of trade finance involves ways of obtaining security that will enable the seller to extend such credits, often directly through the terms of payment, or in combination with a separate credit insurance. In most countries such risk policies can be issued either by the private insurance market mainly for shorter periods or by government-supported Export Credit Agencies (ECAs). As explained in *Chapter 5, Export Credit Insurance*, some ECAs offer support for exports of goods and services on credit periods down to six months, whereas in the UK, support given by ECGD only covers goods and services that are normally sold on credit terms of two years or more, leaving the shorter periods to the private insurance sector.

Risk coverage through credit insurance and the terms under which such policies can be issued have a strong influence on how the export credits can be structured, but they also affect the terms of payment and other conditions related to the transaction, particularly for longer periods. *Box 6.1* provides a summary of the most frequently used techniques for financing or refinancing of UK exports and the following text in this chapter will be structured accordingly.

Of the alternatives in *Box 6.1* only one or two may be of interest in each case, depending on the particular area of business or trade cycle of the transaction, that is the period from the time when the first costs are taken for ordering raw material or other goods, until shipment and final payment from the buyer. However, the trade cycle also covers the time from where the first risks have to be incurred, for example, agreements with other suppliers or simply the need to change internal procedures or preparations for the new production.

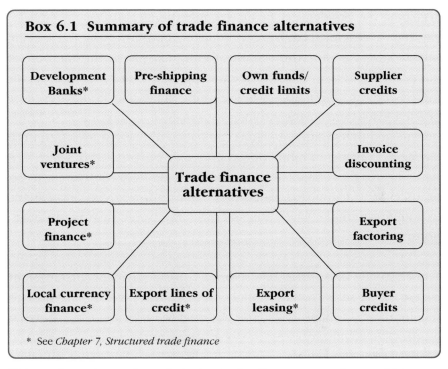

Box 6.1 Summary of trade finance alternatives

- Development Banks*
- Pre-shipping finance
- Own funds/ credit limits
- Supplier credits
- Joint ventures*
- Invoice discounting
- **Trade finance alternatives**
- Project finance*
- Export factoring
- Local currency finance*
- Export lines of credit*
- Export leasing*
- Buyer credits

* See *Chapter 7, Structured trade finance*

This trade cycle can be relatively similar for most products within one and the same company, dependent on the area of business, or it can be unique for every single transaction. The character of the trade cycle will also be different between most suppliers and determines the structure of the terms of payment as well as the method of dealing with different trade finance alternatives.

➢ 6.2 Pre-shipping finance

One of the most important questions relating to the completion of the export transaction (perhaps even one of the most difficult) is how to arrange the pre-shipping finance. In that stage of the transaction the seller only has a sales contract, not a Bill of Exchange or other debt instruments related to the trade, nor any of the documents that comes with the actual delivery, irrespective of the payment terms (eg, copies of the shipping documents or the invoice, showing that delivery has taken place and that a trade debt was created).

For ordinary day-to-day transactions, the most frequent method of arranging the pre-delivery finance requirements is no doubt through existing or additional bank credit limits, without involving the specific sales contract and/or the security, if any, based on the method of payment. However, when business expands or, in case of larger or more complex transactions when existing limits may be fully used or needed elsewhere in the ordinary business, it is important to know how to find the additional means to finance the new transaction until payment is made or until documents can be produced which are necessary for the refinancing. In some cases the sales contract itself can be used for creating that additional finance during the pre-delivery period, for example, when a bank covers the buyer's payment obligations.

The existence of a Letter of Credit (L/C) or a payment guarantee in favour of the seller could strongly facilitate the pre-shipping finance requirements in many ways. The advantages of having the L/C made transferable are also obvious; it will automatically transfer not only the financial cash flow but also the security from the seller to the suppliers who might use the transferred L/C for their own pre-shipping arrangements.

Many banks also extend special export loans on the basis of the L/C to a certain percentage of its value, with the L/C and its future proceeds pledged to the bank as security. This percentage will most certainly vary dependent on many aspects to be considered by the bank, for example, the issuing bank, the size and maturity of the L/C, its terms and conditions, the nature of the goods and perhaps equally important, the knowledge and experience of the seller.

The advantages of a L/C as a pre-shipping finance instrument, also applies to a payment guarantee issued by the buyer's bank in favour of the seller, however, perhaps not to the same degree. The payment guarantee (supposed to be a normal trade-related and conditional guarantee) is more like a credit risk umbrella covering the general payment obligations of the buyer according to the contract. But it does not contain a mechanism, such as a L/C, where the Issuing Bank automatically has to pay, irrespective of the buyer's consent, when certain specified terms and conditions are met. Even though it is less precise than a L/C, most banks will probably nevertheless regard a bank guarantee as an important instrument for increasing the seller's credit limits.

In a mutually advantageous business negotiation and when the commercial parties know each other well, the buyer may even be willing to make further concessions in the payment structure to accommodate the seller and their need for additional pre-delivery finance. In fact, the buyer has already done so indirectly by agreeing to a L/C as a method of payment or by having it made transferable. However, if agreeing to support the seller's pre-delivery cash flow, this could also be done through insertion of a so-called 'red clause' in its terms.

A red clause allows the seller to make use of an agreed part of the value of the L/C before delivering the documents, sometimes earmarked for payment only to be used for some specific purpose. By inserting such clauses in the L/C, this pre-delivery part-payment will, in fact, become an advance payment. Such advance payments are however mostly used as part of an overall part-payment structure with the larger part being payable at shipment and with one part up-front and often one part also as a deferred payment; a split often used in contracts containing more than just delivery obligations, such as installation or maintenance and over a longer period.

Even if an advance payment has to be secured by a trade-related conditional bank guarantee in favour of the buyer, and thus issued under the seller's existing credit limits, it is still to their advantage – both from a cash flow and a collateral perspective. Such a guarantee cannot be drawn upon as long as the seller fulfils the contractual obligations and may, therefore, be issued with other, less stringent security requirements from the Issuing Bank, compared with ordinary lending.

When dealing with pre-shipping finance, one also has to look at the sales contract between the commercial parties and how that could be used as a financial tool. For capital goods in general, the period before shipment could be covered by an ECGD insurance policy, either a stand-alone or a supplementary insurance, called Export Insurance

Policy (EXIP). This insurance would cover incurred costs before shipment, such as raw materials, manufacturing or changes in the production structure, should the buyer not be able to fulfil the payment obligations according to the contract due to default or to the conditions in their country. Even if such insurance is not applicable due to the buying country or nature of the goods, a similar insurance may be obtained on the private insurance market, particularly for short periods. This is described in more detail in *Chapter 5, Export Credit Insurance*.

The existence of separate credit insurance will increase the security of the transaction and will, in most cases, have a strong influence on the bank's decision on additional finance. This interaction between the seller, the insurer and the bank (ongoing during the entire negotiation process with the buyer) may be the key for securing additional pre-finance needed for the transaction.

This procedure also gives the seller feedback on what terms the insurer and/or the bank may be willing to participate and what might be required from the seller and the terms of the contract. Having achieved that, the seller will have secured the support needed from these institutions, covering both the risks involved and the cash needed as pre-shipment finance.

➢ 6.3 Supplier credits

Supplier credits are a commonly used method of trade finance, both for shorter and to a certain degree also for medium-term periods. Its structure is determined by both the length of the credit, its size, the buyer's country and the method of payment agreed in the sales contract – details that determine not only the seller's credit risk exposure but also the structure required by the financial institution, should the credit have to be refinanced at a later stage.

The seller's own possibility of issuing supplier credits are determined by how they can be refinanced, either through existing bank limits for smaller amounts and shorter periods, or by separate discounting or refinancing of the finance instrument that becomes available at shipment or shortly thereafter. The credit terms that can be offered by the seller are also important as a sales argument and as a competitive advantage – or at least a means of being on equal footing with competitors.

Sometimes the terms of such short credits can be made particularly advantageous for the buyer as part of the offer, even if the seller compensates for that in another part of the contract. The problem for the buyer is that it is not easy to see if the price was increased through the favourable credit terms, and if so, by how much. There is also a risk that the seller may overcompensate for the risks in their credit offer if the buyer is unfamiliar or if the seller cannot evaluate the commercial risk correctly. The buyer, on the other hand, may ask for a quotation to include both cash against delivery and a supplier credit alternative in order to be able to make a fair comparison.

The buyer may even start the negotiations based on cash against delivery or short-term open account terms to allow for new and longer credit negotiations, when the price discussions are more or less concluded. It will then be more difficult for the seller to add the credit costs to the price and these will have to be part of a separate negotiation in which the buyer again tries to get the best solution – or arranges the finance elsewhere or in the worst case, choses another supplier altogether.

Irrespective of how the negotiations proceed, there are some general questions that the seller must evaluate before offering a supplier credit, such as:

- To what degree is the requested credit changing the commercial and/or the political risk involved in the transaction?
- Can the buyer be expected to take any open credit costs?
- Should the financial costs be included in the original price offer or should the seller be proactive by keeping the credit terms open as a separate question to be discussed with the buyer?
- How can such a credit be refinanced?
- In the case of foreign currency invoicing, how should the currency risk be evaluated and covered?

In many cases, for shorter periods and smaller amounts, these questions are easily dealt with whereas, in other cases, they might be one of the major aspects of the transaction.

■ *6.3.1 Short-term supplier credits*

The most common form of short-term supplier credits are by short-term open account payment terms, that is, the contract is based on a future payment transfer, and the invoice specifies the date when payment must be received at the seller's account. However, the seller has no other security for the buyer's payment obligations. Sometimes, particularly for periods over 3–6 months, even short-term credits are arranged through a Bill of Exchange to be accepted by the buyer at delivery, thereby replacing the open credit by a documented debt instrument, payable at a specified later date.

Even on open account and shorter payment terms (30–90 days), and even if that is not agreed with the buyer, the seller may nevertheless enclose a Bill of Exchange payable at sight with the invoice, showing the delivery date together with a fixed payment maturity date. This Bill of Exchange could have its value even if it is not to be accepted by the buyer because it combines more directly the sales contract with the invoice and the buyer's payment obligations. This is the same procedure as used in connection with documentary collections, payable at presentation.

The seller should also evaluate whether it would be beneficial to offer both cash against delivery terms and short-term credit on favourable terms as two alternatives, however, if choosing the latter alternative, it should be conditional upon the buyer's acceptance of a Bill of Exchange at shipment date. A short, well-documented supplier credit could have advantages for both parties, compared to open account payment terms, for the following reasons:

- it could be an extra advantage from a sales perspective;
- the buyer can use the credit for improved cash-flow management, perhaps at more favourable terms, however, with the strict obligation to pay at maturity – with the risk for noting and protest of the accepted bill if not paid;

- the seller has the advantage of an accepted finance document that is easier to refinance at an earlier stage, if needed;
- the seller can plan liquidity more exactly at the outset, knowing that payment on maturity is highly likely; and
- the seller may wholly or partly include interest in the Bill of Exchange, compared with a later overdue interest (which in practice is very difficult to receive).

The difference between open account payment terms and the accepted Bill of Exchange is also greater than one might first expect (even with the same payment date). With open account terms, the buyer has a stronger case for negotiating with the seller prior to payment, should it be considered that the delivery was not in accordance with the agreement. It could be anything from time of delivery to shortcomings in the quality or quantity of the goods – the main point is that the buyer may refuse to pay until the matter is resolved.

However, by accepting the Bill of Exchange at the time of shipment, the buyer has an unconditional obligation to pay, irrespective of any real or alleged shortcomings discovered later in the delivery. If the claim is correct, the buyer will probably get compensation, however, the bill must be paid at maturity, irrespective of the ongoing discussions with the seller. The buyer does not then have the same strong bargaining power as in the situation above.

When documentary collection is used as the method of payment together with supplier credits, the documents will be released against acceptance of a Bill of Exchange with a fixed maturity. The documents are exchanged against the bill, normally without any further security for the seller unless it is also agreed that it should be guaranteed by the buyer's bank. But, if the supplier credit is given as part of a L/C (with documents against acceptance), the banks involved will determine the procedure and will also check the correctness of the documents. When they are approved, the Bill of Exchange will be accepted, (by one of the banks as a Banker's Acceptance and not by the buyer) and can then easily be discounted by the seller.

□ 6.3.1.1 Refinancing of short-term supplier credits

The most common method of refinancing short-term supplier credits is simply by using the seller's existing bank credit limits, often the current account. This refinancing is normally done at a floating interest rate as any other domestic borrowing and in this way, the banks are the main refinancing source of the shorter end of trade finance.

The banks may also refinance or give advance payment to documents under collection to a certain percentage of the collection value (up to 70–80 per cent) often under a separate and more favourable trade-finance limit, to be used for trade documents until payment is received. The documents/bills are also mostly pledged to the refinancing bank as additional security.

The accepted short-term trade Bill of Exchange, normally three to six months, may also be discounted by the seller's bank under the same trade-finance limit. These discounted bills are generally with recourse to the seller, unless guaranteed by an acceptable third party or a bank. (A special form of bill discounting is 'forfaiting', which is commented on separately in *Section 6.3.3*).

When invoicing in foreign currency, the seller may also use a short-term currency loan as a way of covering the exchange risk – apart from the liquidity aspect and a potentially lower interest level in that currency. The loan is exchanged into GBP at spot rate and is repaid by the incoming foreign currency at maturity date.

> When delivery/shipment is completed, the seller has a contractual claim on the buyer (which is not necessarily verified by a Bill of Exchange but usually through the invoice only). Such an invoice can also be used as the refinancing instrument in two main ways, by '**Invoice discounting**' and '**Export factoring**'.
>
> Due to the frequency of refinancing ordinary day-to-day export transactions using the invoice as security (or part security) these two methods of refinancing the supplier credits are described separately in *Sections 6.4* and *6.5*.

■ *6.3.2 Medium or long-term supplier credits*

Supplier credits of two years or more are usually arranged in connection with the sale of machinery, vehicles, equipment or other capital goods or services, and with credit documentation that tends to become more complex than for shorter periods. In these cases a separate financial documentation is often used, with or without supplementary Bills of Exchange – or promissory notes with the same but more summarised wording compared to a complete loan agreement, as in the example in *Box 6.2*.

When Bills of Exchange or promissory notes are to be refinanced externally, the seller often has a prearranged facility from a bank or financial institution, specifying the details, including the security required, for such refinancing to take place. In any case, the seller is likely to have such refinancing agreed as part of the transaction, with all preconditions in place before delivery.

With longer supplier credits, two questions are important for both commercial parties to agree upon, namely:

- the choice of currency; and
- the choice of fixed or floating interest rate.

The choice of currency need not be the same as the invoicing currency, even if that is normally the case. However, if the parties agree to a separate financing currency, they also have to agree at what future date the exchange from invoicing to financing currency shall take place. If the invoicing is in GBP and nothing else is agreed to the contrary, the buyer will stand the currency risk until the date when the conversion into the financing currency takes place, determined by the spot exchange rate that day.

The buyer's possible currency deliberations are described in *Chapter 4, Currency risk management*. The outcome may be a 'neutral' third party currency, often USD, which also has good liquidity over longer periods and, therefore, is possible to hedge at reasonable terms. However, if the currency of the credit is not the buyer's home currency, then the buyer takes the currency risk, or the hedging cost, until final maturity (often with a substantial risk or cost if it is either not hedged at all or hedged against a weaker currency).

Box 6.2 shows an example of a promissory note, being the last note in a medium-term supplier credit over five years with ten equal, semi-annual instalments, with interest based on a fixed rate. And, as can be seen from the last paragraph in the example, a bank guarantee as well as a Currency Transfer Guarantee from the Central Bank may sometimes be required in order to make the promissory notes acceptable for refinancing.

It should also be pointed out that generally it is more difficult to structure Bills of Exchange or P/N based on a floating interest rate, principally due to the terms of the Bills of Exchange Act, which state that such an instrument should represent a 'sum certain in money', ie, for a specific value. (See also *Chapter 2, Figure 2.2*) This can be achieved with a fixed rate, but floating is more difficult, and in such cases, separate series of instruments for principal and interest are often used.

The choice of fixed or floating interest in a medium or long term supplier credit is primarily a choice of the buyer, if a fixed rate alternative can be obtained through the refinancing bank. That is most likely in the larger trade currencies, either as direct refinancing or through interest swaps which are separate contracts with the bank, exchanging floating for fixed interest rate under a fixed period of time. Such contracts in the larger trade currencies can be obtained at reasonable rates for very long periods. However, a separate swap agreement must also be approved by the bank, which may result in a request for additional security from the borrower since the bank would be entering into a new interest risk.

The different refinance options on shorter periods are often easy to arrange, as shown above. However, on longer periods the market for commercial (purchaser) risks, especially in conjunction with political risks, is more restricted. This is the main reason why, in these cases, guarantees from a credit insurance company or from ECGD are some-

Box 6.2 Example of a promissory note*
(Issued under a medium-term supplier credit agreement)

Promissory note No. 10

For value received, Bayala Machinery Group Bhd, 2 Jalan Tong Shin, 50201 Kuala Lumpur, Malaysia, (the Buyer), hereby irrevocably and unconditionally promises to pay, on June 21st, 2009, to Pierson & Henders Ltd, 4 West Regent Street, London EC2 4LP, (the Seller), or order, the principal sum of onehundredandthirtyfivethousand USdollars (USD 135.000) and to pay interest on said amount from and including the date hereof at the rate of five per cent (5 per cent) per annum. Interest shall be payable annually in arrears on the 21st of June each year, commencing on June 21st 2005, calculated on the exact number of days and a year of 360 days, and any overdue payment should be calculated on a day to day basis at an interest rate of 8 per cent, until payment is made. Both principal and interest is payable in USD at First Commercial Bank, 3 Tower Hill Street, London EC2 3JK, in favour of the lawful holder of this Note, without set-off or counterclaims and without any deduction for present or future withholdings or taxes.

This Note is one of a series of ten (10) Promissory notes in the aggregate amount of USD 1.350.000, of the like form and tenor except their number and date of maturity, issued pursuant to the Contract Number DN/8318/26, entered into between the Buyer and the Seller on Febr.3rd, 2004. The contract is covering sixteen (16) 280 KW Diesel Generating Machines, the delivery of which is fulfilled according to contract and unconditionally approved by the Buyer by signing this Note.

This series of Notes is to be covered by a separate Bank Guarantee issued by Bank of Berhad, 304 Sultan Road, 50230 Kuala Lumpur, Malaysia, a Currency Transfer Guarantee by the Central Bank of Malaysia and by a legal opinion issued by the law firm Derr & Whitney, Kuala Lumpur.

The laws of the United Kingdom shall govern this note, and the courts of England should settle any legal dispute.

Date and Signatures

*** This example is an illustration only, any debt instrument should always be subject to legal scrutiny in each particular case.**

times so important for making supplier credits work in practice over longer periods, particularly when the political risk is a main issue. This is described in below.

☐ 6.3.2.1 Supplier Credit Financing facility from ECGD

The Supplier Credit Financing (SCF) scheme passes the payment risk on to the bank, which in turn is guaranteed by ECGD. The seller receives the full credit value at presentation of the documents, including proof of shipment – often without recourse. The buyer can secure two years credit or more for capital goods and services (depending on the goods and contract value) sometimes at preferential rates under the Consensus fixed interest rates (*see* Box 6.5), or at market terms (Pure Cover), based on floating rate or fixed interest rate. Minimum contract value is £25,000 with 85 per cent credit and semi-annual instalments.

SCF cover is given to eligible banks participating in the scheme under a Master Guarantee Agreement, outlining the general terms and conditions under which separate supplier credits with individual terms are to be linked. The seller's chosen bank asks for a preliminary and conditional approval from ECGD as a base for the seller´s final negotiations with the buyer. At a later stage, usually when the contractual terms have been finally agreed, a full application is made to ECGD, which forms the base for the underwriting process. After mutual acceptances, the bank will issue its facility letter, confirming finance of the supplier credit, for example, against the following documents:

- Bills of Exchange, promissory notes or other financial document;
- proof of shipment according to contract;
- standard warranty clauses to be agreed by the seller; and
- any other documentation as specified in the facility letter.

ECGD normally require the bills or notes from a private buyer to be guaranteed by an acceptable third party (often through aval/guarantee from commercial banks or a standby L/C). For public buyers, guarantees may also be needed from the relevant authority, depending on circumstance. The bills/notes must be unconditionally guaranteed and thereby not affected by any commercial dispute between the seller and the buyer, if the finance is to be without recourse to the seller. They must also be freely negotiable in order to allow the transfer of its rights from the seller to the refinancing bank.

The SCF is often combined with a supplementary cover under an Export Insurance Policy (EXIP) in favour of the seller, covering the pre-delivery risk period and thereafter, up to the refinancing of the bills/notes (the pre-credit period). Such policies can also cover payments that are not to be included in the supplier credit itself, such as foreign components or local payments. Goods produced in the UK may contain foreign components up to the limit where they can obtain a UK Certificate of Origin, in order to qualify for cover. Support for other foreign components or sub-deliveries will vary dependent of percentage, country of origin, market and interest rate scheme.

The SCF rules are not described in detail in this handbook, more information can be obtained through contacting one of ECGD's underwriters, the helpdesk or the website (www.ecgd.org.uk). This website also provides a premium calculator, which gives an estimate of the premiums for any individual insurance or guarantee – based on some given assumptions. The insurance or guarantee premiums are, in practice, based on an individual risk assessment and on the length of the commitment and may, therefore, vary considerably.

■ 6.3.3 Forfaiting

In many countries the refinancing of medium or long-term supplier credits is done by the commercial banks and by separate export banks, specialising in trade finance and often owned or supported by the governments. However, in the UK, this is left to the private finance market but longer periods are also often backed by guarantees from ECGD, as described above.

This market refinancing also includes the special forfaiting institutions, which have a long history in the UK in financing international trade – even if they do not have the same importance today due to increased competition from commercial and international banks. Forfaiting basically means the surrender of an unconditional future right for a trade-related claim through accepted and freely negotiable bills or notes, for the receipt of prompt payment.

Forfaiting, whether through specialised departments within the banks or through a few traditional independent forfaiting houses, is a special type of discounting of trade-related and mostly fixed interest bills and notes without recourse to the seller, both individual short-term bills or a set of bills covering longer periods. When it comes to risk evaluation of both individual buyers and countries, the forfaiters have gained vast experience in trading these negotiable financial instruments, also spreading the risks through risk participation and distribution through domestic and international credit risk insurers, using reinsurance and syndication techniques.

The diversity of the operations, often with specialisation in different areas, countries, commodities and time periods, together with various experiences and risk attitudes, may create different credit decisions in different situations. However, forfaiting risks are generally based on security in the form of first class corporate risks, acceptable land risks, bank guarantees, Standby Letters of Credit, undertakings from ministries of finance in the case of sovereign buyers, with or without currency transfer guarantees from a Central Bank. What might be acceptable to one bank/forfaiter may not be acceptable to another. If a deal is acceptable, they will issue a firm or a conditional facility letter to the seller, specifying the terms and conditions for discounting and the interest level to be applied.

Forfaiting may not necessarily require larger transactions to be a cost-effective solution, however, the procedure is quite simple; at receipt of the bills or notes according to the terms in the facility letter, the net amount is paid to the seller without recourse.

➢ 6.4 Invoice discounting

Invoice discounting is the simplest form of invoice finance, aside from ordinary lending, and can briefly be described as the provision of finance against the security of a bulk of receivables and, in this respect, it is relatively similar to factoring (described below). The major differences are that invoice discounting is a lending facility where the title to the invoice remains with the seller and that factoring is mostly combined with associated services offered alongside the funding. Invoice discounting gives payment of a certain percentage of the total receivables to be discounted, whereas factoring is mainly based on individual invoices. Invoice discounting is, therefore, often used as a cheaper alternative to factoring when the seller already has an internal system in place for effective sales ledger and credit control functions.

Invoice discounting can accommodate most of the seller's invoices based on open account payment terms on a rolling basis, however, it is mostly confidential, and the buyer is unaware of the facility and the seller is normally responsible for collecting the payment and for the sales ledger administration.

The use of invoice discounting is an increasingly important form of invoice finance for shorter periods, particularly for sellers using open account payment terms. This finance covers the stage after the pre-shipment period when delivery is effected and invoices can be produced, demonstrating the completion of the seller's obligations according to the contract, and that the buyer has incurred an open account debt. Many institutions – banks, credit insurers and specialised finance institutions – provide different forms of invoice discounting, therefore, the term 'provider' is used below.

Some providers integrate invoice discounting with other services, such as credit information, credit insurance and debt collection, in order to make this combination more competitive and easy to use at a reasonable price. And even if these 'packages' are constructed somewhat differently, this combined service has even more similarities with factoring, seen from the seller's practical point of view. These additional services are not dealt with here but can be found under their respective headings in other parts of this book.

The major features of an ordinary invoice discounting facility used for trade finance purposes are:

- The buyer is usually unaware of the invoice discounting facility arrangements between the seller and the provider.
- The provider will arrange the opening of a separate bank account in the name of the seller, where all trade payments must be paid. This account, along with the invoices, will be pledged to the provider as security.
- The seller is normally responsible for the sales ledger and for the collection of sums due for payment, however, some providers also offer these services. The sales ledger works like an invoice pool where new and approved invoices are included, and paid invoices together with unpaid and long overdue invoices, are excluded.
- The seller is required to send regular notifications or copies of invoices to the provider, together with any other agreed documentation in order for that institution to keep a 'mirror image' of the pool of eligible invoices.
- The provider will make available to the seller an initial payment against invoices at an agreed percentage and the remaining percentage, when the buyer has paid the invoice in full.
- The provider will send the seller regular statements in order for the seller to check against the export invoice ledger.
- As security for the provider, besides the pledged account, the seller will be required to provide a detailed sales ledger analysis on a regular basis, which will be compared with its own records. The seller will also approve independent audits of its ledger as required by the provider.

Invoice discounting is suitable for most companies and is particularly useful for the smaller and medium-sized companies. It may cover both domestic and export transactions within mostly European and neighbouring countries where open account payment terms are normally practiced. And, while additional services such as collection and risk coverage often are optional, these services taken together as a package may have an obvious advantage for the seller, both from an efficiency, risk and cost point of view.

Invoice discounting is mostly a 'with recourse' form of lending and is a form of lending up to a certain level of the face value of the invoices,

INFORMATION BOX

Lloyds TSB Corporate trading globally

Whether you are a business with substantial international presence or simply with the desire to develop and grow into overseas markets, Lloyds TSB Corporate are able to provide access to a variety of international services. Our comprehensive cash management and trade finance services will help your business through many of the situations you will face.

Lloyds TSB Corporate has a formidable international reputation and is a Moody's AAA-rated institution with a considerable network of alliance partners across the globe. This ensures that they are able to deliver an expert funding, liquidity and payment service to a wide variety of corporate businesses and financial institutions.

Lloyds TSB Corporate are able to do this because they have:

- an experienced and focused Financial Institutions team, based in London, who work with around 1200 banking groups worldwide;

- cross border payment capabilities and a strong UK based payment network;

- UK based cash and trade teams who work with corporate businesses to deliver excellent cash management and financing solutions;

- a Structured Export Finance team who, working with Export Credit agencies, other banks and exporters, are able to deliver specialist trade finance services;

- an International Advisory Service that provides consultancy in financial services to other banks/agencies/government ministries and institutions across the world.

This all ensures that their customers are able to rely upon a secure and reputable conduit for all global banking and funding needs, with access to international expertise in a variety of forms - practical, advisory, experience – all supporting UK exporting and importing businesses.

For more information about Lloyds TSB Corporate's international trade capabilities contact simon.harris@lloydstsb.co.uk in the Financial Institutions team or colin.hemsley@lloydstsb.co.uk in the Corporate Transaction Services team.

often 70–90 per cent, based on the risk assessment of the provider and even up to 100 per cent if covered by credit insurance. In case of non-payment, and after an agreed waiting period, the seller will have to repay the advance including accrued interest, normally in the form of deductions on later incoming invoice payments.

The risk assessment and the discounting percentage offered to the seller is based not only of the invoices themselves and any credit risk insurance, but also on their average distribution regarding amounts, buyers and countries. As with any other form of lending, the provider will obviously also consider the general credit standing of the seller and their experience and track record of similar transactions, and the aggregate of these criteria will determine the established percentage lending value and the cost structure.

In most cases, invoice discounting can be used as an ordinary overdraft facility at the seller's discretion, set by the volume and specified lending value of the underlying eligible invoices, forming a pool of available borrowing under the facility at any time. As the value of the pool of invoices fluctuate, more or less money will be available, and in the case of maximum utilisation in conjunction with reduced total invoice value, the seller may even have to repay money in order to keep the agreed percentage. Many banks also offer this service to be used via the Internet, which also facilitates the practical day-to-day handling of the facility.

The cost for invoice discounting is dependent on the services involved, the finance often charged as an overdraft facility, with additional handling charges, based on turnover and work involved, together with costs for any other additional service.

➤ 6.5 Export factoring

Factoring is a special form of short-term financing where a company (the factor) purchases the seller's receivables and assumes the credit risk, either with or without recourse to the seller.

In its original form, the seller entering into a factoring agreement, agrees to sell the receivables to the factor, often also relieving the credit control and debt collection functions, which are assumed by the factor against a fee. In such a case, the factor also gains the title of the invoice and takes the future decisions, if any, regarding collection and other measures, including the legal work in case of non-payment. The seller will display a notification on the factored invoices, informing the buyer that the invoice has been sold to the named factor, together with instructions on how payment is going to be made directly to them. The seller also sends copies of the invoices and the shipping documents to the factor.

The factor starts with a credit assessment of the seller and the general structure of their trade and previous export experience followed by an assessment of the different buyers, including any insurance cover, in order to establish individual lending limits on the buyers and a total credit limit for the seller. Factoring could have the following advantages for the seller (banks and other providers often include some similar services based on the invoice discounting structure):

- a higher risk coverage than other finance alternatives;
- more punctual payments from the buyers, being pre-notified of the sale of the invoices to the factor;
- the borrowing value of the invoices could be higher than through bank lending, thereby increasing the seller's total liquidity;
- the seller can use additional administrative systems to reduce workload.

Export factoring is mostly in the form of 'with recourse factoring' with up to 90 per cent of invoice value, with the provision that if the buyer fails to pay the invoice after a set period of time, the factor will be repaid by the seller – normally through deduction from later invoice payments. But sometimes export factoring can also be provided also as 'non-recourse factoring', where the factor will stand the risk in the event of bankruptcy or liquidation of the buyer, but normally not in case of slow payment only. Most such non-recourse factoring is secured by a separate credit insurance or similar security, and the seller will in these cases never be requested to repay the advance to the factor, however they will may have to pay interest for the agreed waiting period after due date, normally 60–90 days as specified in the factoring agreement.

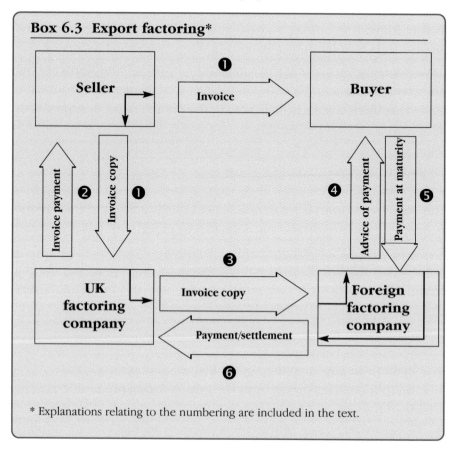

Box 6.3 Export factoring*

* Explanations relating to the numbering are included in the text.

It is often said that export factoring is more expensive than the corresponding or similar bank services (mainly invoice discounting), however, such a comparison could be misleading and not quite relevant. Apart from the interest charged, a flat service fee is also charged on every invoice factored, the size of which is dependent on workload, services included, involved factors (see below) and the total factoring turnover. This charge can range from substantially below 1 per cent up to four to five per cent, and the seller should therefore do a cost/revenue valuation in relation to the services offered – and needed – compared with other alternatives.

In most cases, factoring should lead to more punctual payments, better control of outstanding receivables and less administrative workload for the company, however, the question for the seller is often to what degree they can make effective use of these additional services, compared to the cost involved. The factoring services are generally more efficient on slow payers and in these cases the use of a special factoring company can have an effect – and the seller avoids straining the business relationship.

Whether or not the use of factoring will increase the total liquidity of the company is also dependent on whether the invoices are included as part of the security pledged to the bank at the outset and if so, at what value. However, for a rapidly expanding company, a purchase of the receivables by a finance company, often at a higher rate than offered by the bank, should increase the seller's total available credit limits, even if at a higher cost.

In practice, there are two basic forms of export factoring, either the so-called 'two-factor export factoring', where the seller's factoring company uses local correspondents within a chain of cooperating factors, or 'direct export factoring', without such a local factor involved. In Europe, where most of the potential export factoring clients are located, there are two main cooperating groups of factoring companies, Factor Chain International (FCI) and International Factoring Group (IFG), through which many UK commercial banks, or their subsidiaries, are handling their factoring businesses.

However, some major international companies within the area of credit risk management services, also offer similar services within their own organisation through a network of branches around the world, offering in-house combinations of not only purchase of invoices but also credit information, credit insurance and debt collection. (See also the information box from Coface in *Chapter 5.2.*)

Box 6.3 shows the two-factor alternative, in which a UK factoring company cooperates with a domestic factor (either an independent company or the branch of that UK company) in the buyer's country. The use of domestic factors or branches of an international organisation will often increase the overall cost structure, but has the advantage of a local presence, knowledge of the buyers and the local procedures to collect the money according to local law and common practice, including debt recovery.

There are also other and more institutional reasons why factoring may be more commonly used in the future; not least developments within the EU (with the largest volumes of UK export factoring) with its gradually increased structure of harmonised laws, rules and procedures. This development has given advantages of scale also for larger suppliers of credit risk services, enabling them to be more competitive also in the area of international trade finance.

➤ 6.6 Buyer credits

Buyer credits are given directly to the buyer or the buyer's bank in connection with the export transaction, but not directly by the seller. This enables the seller to receive cash payment at delivery and/or at different stages of construction or installation as specified in the contract. Buyer credits are normally used for larger individual transactions, particularly when the transaction involves more than just delivery of goods, or covers a longer contract period and often when the delivery is tailor-made to the specifications of the buyer.

Buyer credits are given to the buyer's bank (bank-to-bank credits) for further on-lending to the buyer, or directly to the buyer (bank-to-buyer credits) mostly covered by a guarantee from the buyer's bank or from any other third party. However, since this difference is relatively small from the perspective of the seller, we shall deal with both these forms as bank-to-buyer credits below.

In industrialised countries, buyer credits are usually arranged on pure market terms, however, outside these countries transactions of this nature are seldom possible to finance on longer terms on the open market, but often need to be backed by a credit guarantee, usually issued by ECGD. The seller should then co-ordinate the commercial negotiations with the buyer and with both the chosen bank and the insurer so that the contract and the corresponding loan agreement can be developed in parallel during the negotiating process.

Box 6.4 Supplier and buyer credits – a comparison

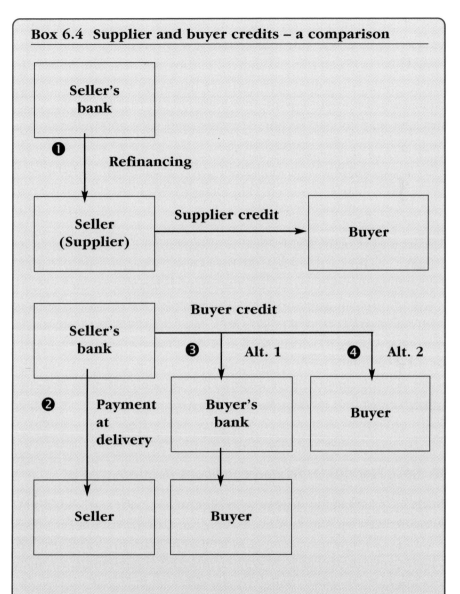

1. Refinancing is done through a bank or some other financial institution, ie, a specialised forfaiting company, with or without recourse to the seller.
2. Credit amount is normally 80–85 per cent of contract value; the buyer pays the remaining part payment at or before delivery directly to the seller.
3. The seller's bank has the buyer's bank as counterpart in this case, which forwards the credit to the buyer, often with the same/similar documentation.
4. With bank-to-buyer credits, the seller's bank has the buyer as a direct counterpart in the same way as the seller in the commercial transaction, and will in these cases request a third party guarantee, normally from the buyer's bank, covering the obligations under the credit agreement.

One of the important aspects of buyer credits is how they relate to the underlying contract. Financial credits are normally unrelated to the obligations between the commercial parties, and that also applies to buyer credits when the buyer normally has to approve the delivery in connection with entering into the loan. Should that not be the case, the loan may contain recourse clauses until such approval, but it is more likely that this contractual risk on the seller is covered outside the loan agreement by a separate performance guarantee issued by a bank in favour of the buyer in order to separate the commercial contract and the financial credit.

The loan agreement and its final wording have to be approved by all parties – the buyer, the seller, the banks and the credit insurer if applicable. It is normally based on the same principles as an ordinary international loan agreement, but also includes the relevant parties of the commercial contract, in order for the two agreements to harmonise during the disbursement period. Thereafter, they should be seen as two totally separate agreements. However, in some cases that is not possible due to the structure of the commercial transaction, and in such cases, the lending bank has to have recourse to some other party, often the credit insurer, guaranteeing the loan. (See 6.6.1).

■ 6.6.1 Normal terms and conditions in buyer credits

Buyer credits can be arranged in almost any way and with terms decided between the parties, as long as it done on market terms without government support. However, when such support is needed, which is mostly the case in connection with buyer credits to many countries, either as insurance to the seller and/or guarantee to the lending bank, then the credit terms must comply with the Consensus-rules. These are described in *Box 6.5* and below are additional comments on ECGD rules relating to such supported buyer credits.

The exported goods should qualify for credit periods of at least 2 years, with 15 per cent of the contract value as advance payment and a maximum of 85 per cent credit, with disbursement, repayment and interest structure according to Consensus. However, for buyer credits covered by ECGD, the minimum contract value is normally £5 million, since this type of financing is mainly reserved for larger, complex and tailor-made transactions, which are difficult and costly to arrange.

The ECGD offers, at its own discretion, two types of guarantee cover to the bank offering the buyer credit, 'Simple Cover' when loan funds may be used only for scheduled and due payments after delivery or any other performance according to contract, and 'Complex Cover' which also covers termination and arbitration payments related to contractual disputes, should any unexpected event occur during the lifetime of the loan. A supplementary Export Insurance Policy (EXIP), basically insurance on the non-payment by the buyer can give added protection for the seller during the pre-credit period and also cover payments not included in the buyer credits.

Buyer credits may be given in GBP or most other trade currencies, at both floating and fixed-term rates. Officially supported rates may also be given (see *Box 6.5*) based on an ECGD mechanism called Interest Make Up (IMU), to cover the difference between the banks floating rate funding cost plus margin and a fixed rate, which may then be offered to the borrower. However, other finance techniques are also available to offer competitive market fixed rates for long-term credits and larger amounts through the international money or capital markets. If possible, offers can also be made to provide the loan, or part of it, in the buyer's local currency, (see *Chapter 7, Section 7.3*).

ECGD also arranges 'One Stop Shop' agreements with other ECAs, with the agent of the largest supplier acting as coordinator for all the suppliers, and then using its own terms and conditions and documentation for the transaction. Such solutions have big administrative advantages for the completion of the transaction, with only one insurance counterpart for the lead supplier – not least in larger transactions, based on buyer credits arrangements.

The loan agreement in a buyer credit contains the same standard clauses as in every other international loan, such as conditions precedent, default clauses and applicable law, along with legal opinions regarding both the loan and the contract, showing that they are compatible, legally enforceable and duly executed. It must also contain confirmation of receipt of the stipulated advance payments as well as documents or guarantees and all the relevant details of the commercial contract, such as disbursement and repayment clauses, interest rates and other costs involved. The disbursement clauses have to be properly documented. Most buyer credits are based on disbursement in one payment directly to the seller or related to the seller's successive performance. The loan amounts are payable against certificates of completion countersigned by the buyer, according to a preliminary draw-down plan and timetable as an appendix to the agreement.

Apart from the loan agreement, some other agreements must also be signed as an integrated part of longer buyer credits, if backed by an insurance cover. Firstly, a 'Premium Agreement', between the insurer (often ECGD) and the seller, specifying not only the premium and other costs for the issued insurances towards the seller, but also the recourse clauses applicable (described below). Secondly, a 'Support Agreement' must be signed between the bank and the insurer, specifying the terms and conditions for the guarantee of the loan, to include the coverage of 100 per cent and the obligation to pay to the bank both principal and interest due. The support agreement also covers the obligations of the bank towards the insurer in operating the loan.

■ 6.6.2 Recourse to the seller

Under a Support Agreement, the ECGD (or any other insurer) is obliged to pay the bank in case of a default in payment under the buyer credit, regardless of the reason. This could be an alleged non-performance of the seller or a dispute under the contract and the insurer normally requires recourse to the seller, at least during the period up to final acceptance from the buyer. However, such recourse is never total and is limited in a number of ways. Firstly, there are many occurrences outside the UK of an economic, legislative, administrative or political nature, for which the seller cannot be held responsible. Such events can equally affect the buyer – most events that are normally referred to as political or in some cases commercial (purchaser) risks.

Box 6.5 The Consensus — a summary

The OECD has stipulated a number or guidelines for restricting state-supported export credit competition between the countries, often referred to as the 'Arrangement' or the 'Consensus'; it contains guidelines for minimum and maximum credit periods, amortization structure, minimum advance payment and above all, minimum interest rates.

The minimum credit period is 2 years, with repayment in equal quarterly/half-yearly instalments (plus interest); the first 3–6 months after the starting point of the credit, which normally is acceptance or the 'mean acceptance date' in the case of several deliveries. It could also be commissioning or physical possession relating to whole projects. A minimum payment of 15 per cent has to be paid before the starting point of the credit.

Buyer countries are divided in two groups, Group I consisting of the industrialised countries and some other some OPEC countries, and Group II including most developing countries. This classification is made automatically based on World Bank statistics of per capita GNP.

The maximum credit period is for countries in Group I up to 5 years, however, in exceptional circumstances this may be extended to 8.5 years after international pre-notification, which means that other competitors should get the same advantage, so called 'matching'. For countries in Group II the maximum credit period is 10 years, but for certain commodities and lower contract values, shorter periods may apply.

The minimum level for state-supported fixed interest rates is based on CIRR (Commercial Interest Reference rates), which are revised monthly, based on the assumption of what they might have been if finance was available. The two types of CIRR are Contract CIRR and Pre-contract CIRR, which is 20 basis points higher. The advantage for the seller with the Pre-contract CIRR is that they can submit a cost-free offer to the buyer based on a fixed interest rate at the date of the application to ECGD, which can then be held during the negotiations for up to 120 days. The Contract-CIRR must be applied for before signing the contract and will be the rate applicable at contract date, so in this case the parties will not know the exact rate in advance. After contract, the rates so determined will be held for another 180 days to allow time for credit documentation.

Further information can be obtained directly from ECGD: **www.ecgd.gov.uk**

The recourse requirements are also limited in size, related to the perceived risk in the transaction. It is usually fixed at a percentage of the maximum liability under the guarantee, with a minimum recourse limit of normally 10 per cent. This might be much higher in the individual case, based on a number of factors such as the complexity of the transaction, the seller's financial standing and earlier experience of similar transactions.

The seller will eventually be released from the recourse, either through confirmation from the buyer that the terms of the contract have been fulfilled, or should that not be forthcoming, when the seller has successfully shown that that is the case.

7

Structured trade finance

The expression 'structured trade finance' is often used in many different situations and is not generally defined, however, in this book it has the meaning of prearranged or tailor-made trade financial techniques or structures, mostly designed for larger transactions or projects, arranged by, or in cooperation with, specialised financial institutions.

Due to its flexibility and importance as a source of refinancing most international trade transactions, this chapter also describes the international money market.

➤ 7.1 The international money market

Apart from purely domestic finance, based on local bank GBP base rate lending, the market commonly used for refinancing of trade finance is the international money market or markets, since they operate within financial centres in different time zones. The international money market is a market for short-term currency loans and deposits, whereas the expression 'capital market' refers to long-term periods, usually only for larger amounts and with fixed interest, for example, through bonds and other long-term instruments.

The money market is not a physical marketplace but more a general description of the trade itself, carried out in different currencies between numerous lenders and borrowers. The major banks, both in the UK as well as internationally, play a central role in the inter-bank money market, through maintaining an internal money trade, which is crucial for both liquidity and stable market conditions – in the same way as banks operate in the currency market. For short-term loans and deposits in different currencies, this inter-bank money market is often referred to as the name of the financial centres where the main banks are operating. For example, the London Interbank Market, where the corresponding interest rates are referred to as London Interbank Offered Rates (LIBOR).

Similarly, inter-bank money markets are also established in other financial centres, particularly in the respective local currency. The interest rates in these markets are then referred to in a similar way, for example, SIBOR in Singapore, HIBOR in Hong-Kong, PIBOR in Paris and STIBOR in Stockholm. London is by far the largest money market place in the European time zone and is also the financial centre to which most commercial contracts or agreements are referred to regarding interest rates in general for most currencies. However, other market places are often used for reference interest rates for a single and local currency in commercial contracts, for example, STIBOR for lending or borrowing in Swedish Krona.

Market forces in a liquid money market will create almost identical interest rates at one and the same time. In particular, the LIBOR-rates at 11.00am are often referred to as the reference interest rates for that day for most trade-related currencies and for periods normally between 1 and 6 months or up to a year. They are also quoted in the newspapers as the established short-term international interest rates for the most common currencies. As the market interest rates changes continously during the day, more accurate information is also available, either through the bank's own internet-based information system, or through direct contact with the bank's trading departments. For participants actively trading directly in the market, there are also specialized on-line systems available on the market, described in *Chapter 4*, with almost identical and instantly updated currency and money market information as is available within the banks themselves.

So, when referring to floating interest rates in trade finance, these are often based on these interest fixings, even if the details have to be specified in each individual case (eg, USD LIBOR 3 months interest rate, at 11.00am on a given date). To be even more precise, many loan agreements also often refer to interest quotations from one or two major banks in that market as specific reference banks in order to get the interest rate absolutely identified and fixed without referring to a general marketplace. The total interest rate, towards the customer, also includes the margin as applied by the lending bank(s) in each individual case, or as specified in the loan agreement.

Trade finance transactions are generally based on bills or notes related to supplier credits, but more frequently on separate loan agreements when it comes to buyer credits and structured trade finance transactions, as described in this chapter. Shorter-term Bills of Exchange are often combined with a fixed interest for the entire period until due date, with the combined capital amount and interest rate added to a fixed amount to be paid at maturity. The promissory notes are often made in the same way, but for longer periods they have to be more detailed and are usually designed as small loan agreements, based on either floating or fixed interest rate.

When it comes to buyer credits (bank-to-bank or bank-to-buyer credits) and other forms or structured finance, a separate and detailed loan agreement is, however, generally used for these often longer periods. If based on a floating interest rate they also contain a clear definition on how the interest should be calculated and fixed for each short interest period, with a successive number of roll-over-periods of, for example, three or six months until final maturity. The borrower can often choose the length of these roll-over-periods and at the end of each such period interest is due together with amortisation, if any.

Many loan agreements also give the borrower the option to change currency at the end of each interest period, however, combined with a maximum amount expressed in one base currency in order to cap the total outstanding loan in case of adverse currency exchange movements. This structure with different optional currencies, floating or fixed interest rates and variable loan periods, can be adapted to suit the

Box 7.1 Short and long-term interest rates for some larger trade currencies

Similar to currency rates, also interest rates often show a different development in the short term as compared to their long term trend. It is the perspective during which the transaction should be financed that is important, the period during which one of the contracting parties may stand the interest risk, dependent of the structure of the financing. In order to illustrate this difference, the diagrams below show the interest development for some larger trade currencies. The graphs also illustrate the interest difference between GBP and the other currencies, one of the aspects to consider when choosing the financing currency.

A. The short term perspective (LIBOR 3 month for GBP, USD, EUR and JPY)

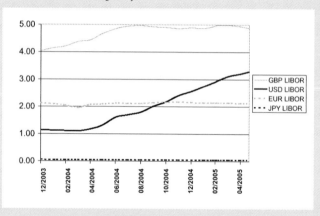

B. The long term perspective (LIBOR 3 month for GBP, USD, EUR and JPY)

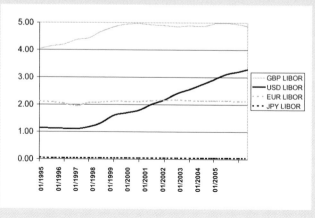

changing circumstances of the borrower during the lifetime of the loan and makes the international money market a very flexible source for short, medium or long-term trade finance, based on a variety of financing techniques.

One of the advantages with longer-term loans based on short-term roll-over- periods is that they are simple to use and so flexible that, in principle, they can be adapted to any trade or financial transaction for almost any period. The disadvantage for the borrower on longer periods can be the floating rate, which makes the credit costs difficult to evaluate in advance, but this problem is also easily solved in most cases.

In *Chapter 4, Currency Risk Management*, the forward points system was described as the basis for establishing currency forward rates. The technique is similar for exchanging floating interest rates into fixed rates through interest swaps. A five-year loan agreement based on, for example, three-month LIBOR may, at any time during the loan period, be changed into a fixed interest rate loan. This is done through a separate interest rate swap agreement with a bank, whereby the borrower agrees to receive the floating rate needed to service the loan and deliver fixed interest rates to the bank under the swap agreement.

However, such a swap agreement also contains an additional risk for the bank should the borrower default during the period of the loan, thereby not being able to deliver the fixed interest. It is, therefore, subject to a separate credit decision within the bank but the technique and the market liquidity makes it possible to hedge the interest rate for long periods, in the most traded currencies, up to five or ten-years, thereby eliminating the potential disadvantage of using the money market's short-term interest rates.

It should finally be mentioned that most of the medium/long term bank financing guaranteed by ECGD or some other ECA, are also based on the short term funds available on the international money markets, irrespective of whether these longer term export credits are offered as floating interest rates or as the officially supported Commercial interest Reference rates(CIRR), as described in Box 6.5.

➢ 7.2 Export leasing

Leasing is a medium-term form of finance of machinery, vehicles and equipment, with the legal right to use the goods for a defined period of time but without owning or having title to them.

The export lease is normally divided into two separate categories:

- The operating lease – where the lessee is using the equipment but where the risk of ownership rests with the lessor, and where, in most cases, the equipment consequently remains on the books of the lessor.
- The financial lease – where the practical risk of ownership rests with the lessee, and the lessor, from the outset of the lease, expects to recover from the lessee both capital cost of the investment as well as interest and profit during the period of the lease, and where in most cases under the tax laws of most countries, the equipment has to stay on the books of the lessee.

The distinction between these types of leases are, however, not always that clear in reality and many leases are frequently structured in one way while at the same time being defined in another, usually due to potential tax advantages.

When the sales contract between the supplier and the lessor, and the leasing contract between the lessor and the lessee are signed, the equipment is usually delivered directly from the supplier to the lessee, who is the end-user of the equipment. Following approval of the delivery by the lessee, the lessor remits the payment to the supplier. The equipment, together with the leasing contract, constitutes the security for the lessor, sometimes together with a limited or a full supplementary repurchase agreement with the supplier, but most of the risks, rights and obligations in connection with the use of the equipment rest with the lessee.

The lessee leases the equipment on a period that corresponds to its economic lifetime, normally three to seven years, or any other period agreed, with monthly or quarterly lease payments, based on annuities,

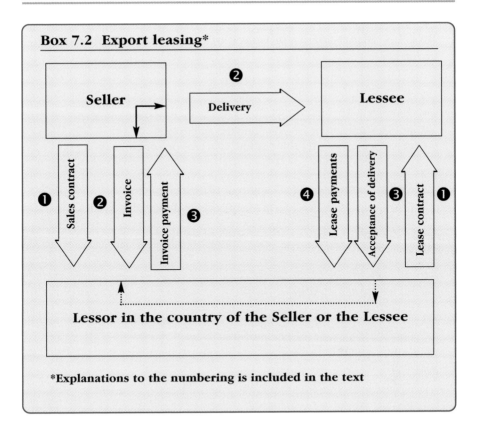

Box 7.2 Export leasing*

Seller

② Delivery

Lessee

❶ Sales contract

❷ Invoice

❸ Invoice payment

❹ Lease payments

❸ Acceptance of delivery

❶ Lease contract

Lessor in the country of the Seller or the Lessee

*Explanations to the numbering is included in the text

which could be adapted to the lessee's own fluctuating liquidity situation during the year. At the end of the lease period, the equipment is to be returned to the lessor or prolonged for a newly agreed period, however, the lease contract could also include an option for the lessee to buy the equipment at the prevailing market value at that time or at a fixed percentage of the original lease value.

This is, in short, a general description of a lease; the principles are basically the same irrespective of whether it is a domestic transaction or an export lease, the main difference being that in the latter case the parties are located in different countries. On the other hand, that difference could have a major impact on the transaction and how it is executed, as explained below.

The most common form of export lease is when a leasing company in the buyer's country is buying the equipment and leases it to a lessee in the same country. Such a lease is often arranged in local

Box 7.3 Short-form summary of an international lease contract

§ 1
– Definitions, parties involved and the description of the equipment.
– Conditions precedent for executing the agreement.
– Terms of lease and for prolongation, cancellation or termination.

§ 2
– The lessee's receipt and final approval of the equipment.
– The terms for the lessee's right of use of the equipment.
– Requirements for a separate service agreement between the supplier or any local agent of choice in the country of the lessee.

§ 3
– Choice of currency, the lease calculation and terms of payment.
– Rules for default interest.

§ 4
– Geographical area for the equipment to be used and rules for movement.

§ 5
– Rules for VAT-payments for leases and residual values.
– Rules for payments of import duties or any other taxes.

§ 6
– Conditions, if any, for transfer of the lease agreement.

§ 7
– Discharge for the lessor against claims from the lessee for fault or deficiencies in the equipment and the lessee's responsibility for any third party claims or damages in the country of operation.

§ 8
– Rules for insurance and arrangements in case of damage or total loss.
– Rules for current inspection of equipment by selected third party.

§ 9
– Lessor's right to repossess the equipment.
– Rules in case of use of lease option or return of equipment.

§ 10
– Rules for legal actions, applicable law and definition of force majeure.

§ 11
– Guarantees, or other security, if any, to cover the obligations of the lessee.

currency and with other parts of the contract also adapted to local conditions. It may be arranged or initiated by the seller as part of the offer and normally leads to cash payment for the seller upon acceptance of the delivery by the buyer (the lessee), but with continued responsibility for any contractual repurchase, partial guarantee or other undertaking the seller may have to enter into with the foreign lease company.

In some countries and particularly for larger individual transactions it is a common occurrence to use the benefits of state subsidised export credits in the country of the seller to reduce the cost of the lease, and that is particularly the case when the delivery is part of a larger project and coordinated or supported by some international or regional agency or development bank.

When the lessor and the lessee are located in separate countries, the expression 'cross-border leasing' or 'international leasing' is often used. This type of lease is sometimes structured in order to take maximum advantage of differences in tax and depreciation rules between countries in order to produce the most competitive solution, often generating an effective total cost for the lessee, lower than the best commercial interest rates. In order to produce such results, the lease agreements are sometimes structured to involve more parties than the original ones, for example, an investor in a third country who might legally, and from a tax perspective, also be the formal owner of the equipment, thereby creating depreciations in several countries on the same equipment.

Such leases are frequently used in connection with 'big ticket' deals such as aircrafts, large computers, ships, railway carriages and other rolling transportation vehicles. But, at the same time, the local authorities have understandably tried to prevent the excessive use of such tax-driven solutions and there is a constant battle between financial engineers on one side, trying to find new solutions and the tax authorities on the other side, trying to cap their use for tax purposes. Most cross-border leases are, however, considerably less complicated and are used for more ordinary-sized equipment as an alternative to other medium-term trade finance solutions, in which ownership, depreciation and other tax aspects may be important but not crucial to the execution of the transaction.

Even for more ordinary cross-border leases, detailed knowledge of the legal consequences are crucial, as are the tax implications, for example, regarding VAT, should it be paid or not and in what country and by whom? The aspect of legal ownership also has to be addressed, which may be dependent on other factors, such as length and size of the lease in relation to its value and estimated lifespan, including residual value and repurchase agreements, if any. These aspects are also included in the basis for considering if the transaction is to be deemed as a commercial or a financial lease, which may have economic consequences for both the lessor and the lessee.

Legal ownership is thus an important factor to consider in each case, not only in relation to pure economic advantages and commercial and political risks, but also with regard to legal and economic consequences in case of damages and claims from any third party (which may be governed in accordance with the laws of the country where the equipment is used).

Within European countries, where most of the lease transactions in relation to UK trade are made, the applicable law for governing the lease contract is becoming increasingly similar but, in other markets, where that might not be the case, the lease is usually arranged through a local lease company in order to avoid these and any other third party risks. If the lease is part of, or connected with, larger projects it will probably become a part under the general framework governing the project as a whole.

A cross-border lease can be arranged in most international trade currencies, based on floating or fixed interest rates in accordance with the structure of the annuities in the contract. Other advantages for the buyer could be a 100 per cent finance, flexible annuities and the use of a source of finance that will not affect the existing credit limits with their banks. The buyer may have an option to replace the equipment for newer versions and may also benefit financially from other tax benefits in their country. It is then up to the buyer to compare these advantages with the cost for leasing compared with other financial options and, for the seller to explore these options with a leasing company in the UK, in order to be able to offer the most competitive financial solution.

➢ 7.3 Lines of credit and local currency finance

■ 7.3.1 Lines of credit

As mentioned earlier, buyer credits are usually arranged in connection with larger, often tailor-made transactions with ECGD support and often require the size of at least £1 million or more contract value to be cost-effective. This is one reason why many UK banks have established separate lines of credit for smaller transactions directly with some foreign banks, mainly in the larger emerging market countries with an established UK trade pattern.

Lines of credit can cover a range of contracts based on finance through a buyer credit and backed by an ECGD guarantee given directly to the UK bank that has arranged the credit. The advantages for the seller is that these lines of credit are already in existence at the time of the negotiation with the buyer and that the finance is almost ready to use and can cover low value contracts, down to about £25,000.

Each established line of credit specifies the framework for the financing, such as goods, currency, minimum and maximum value of contracts, conditions precedent, applicable law and most other standard clauses in an ordinary international loan agreement. However, the credit terms must be consistent with the OECD Consensus rules, since they are generally backed by an ECGD guarantee. This established framework also makes it easier to incorporate the details of each commercial contract in a new loan agreement in a fairly standardised form. Such lines of credit are intended as general purpose lines to be used to finance a number of contracts from different UK exporters, but could also equally be used as a framework for financing a single specific project with deliveries from a number of UK suppliers.

Provided the credit meets ECGD's risk standards, the lines of credit will be established under a Master Agreement between ECGD and an approved bank, specifying both the premium to be paid and the mutual rights and obligations under which these lines of credit should be used. The Master Agreement also specifies the administration of the loan and the guarantee.

More details on banks and countries where such lines of credit are in existence can be found on www.ecgd.org.uk under *Country Cover Indicators*, and the seller can then find out in advance if such limits are available in the particular case.

■ 7.3.2 Local currency finance

Most of the export credit alternatives available directly to the buyer have so far been described as based on finance in the most traded international currencies, which implies a currency risk for the buyer unless that risk could be hedged or balanced by a matching inflow in the same currency. For buyers in industrialised countries this is usually not a problem. However, to hedge a strong currency against a domestic (and often weak) emerging market currency, with a potential and often constant devaluation risk – or convertibility risk due to change of law or regulations – can be very expensive. The buyer is seldom in the fortunate position to have a constant inflow of foreign currency or being able to generate such earnings out of the purchased goods. Consequently, many buyers in these countries have taken huge currency losses from overseas export credits during recent years.

For that reason, many buyers outside the industrialised countries may prefer finance in their own local currency, either for the whole credit amount or part of it, despite the higher interest rate usually incurred. The financial consequences of a local currency credit could at least be more calculable, even with a floating interest rate. Such local finance for UK exports would however probably not be available to the buyer without a guarantee and ECGD has therefore introduced a scheme, based on the buyer credit structure with up to 100 per cent unconditional guarantee to the financing bank. This scheme has already been used in some Asian and African countries. Such loans are raised in the buyer's country and financed by a local bank, based on the Consensus credit terms. The ECGD guarantee with its AAA-rating will also have favourable balance sheet implications for the lending bank and the loan (which will need to be managed by a UK-based agent bank) should always attract the finest rates in that market.

However, such loans will normally have to be at floating rates and market terms without official interest rate support, due to the uncertainty of swapping these rates into fixed rates, at a reasonable cost, for the periods required. Other criteria have also to be fulfilled due to the implications for the country concerned. The local currency has to be convertible and the local market needs the capacity to support the finance without major impacts. It also has to be approved or at least acceptable to the local financial authorities.

If the commercial contract is in GBP or some other commonly traded currency, which is usually the case, at some point in time there has to be a conversion into the local currency of the loan agreement. The parties have to agree when the exchange should take place and, consequently, who should stand the currency risk during the period between signing the contract and the time of conversion into local currency.

➤ 7.4 Project finance and joint venture

■ 7.4.1 Project finance

Project finance is normally related to larger individual private or public sector projects, for example, factories, power plants, larger construction or infrastructure projects, sometimes even of national interest in the buyer's country. True project finance schemes are generally based on the revenues of the project to a high degree, mostly secured on its assets and less on the creditworthiness of the buyer, as this party is frequently a single purpose company or a partnership with limited equity.

From experience, such projects can take years until a signed contract and effective loan agreement stage is reached, sometimes also due to internal political or local controversy as to its real or alleged social, economic or environmental consequences. Such projects also incur more pre-contract costs than ordinary export contracts, not only due to their length in time but also through feasibility studies and appraisals, legal and technical costs and necessary approvals by a number of local authorities.

In many large projects, the financing or rather, the assets together with other forms of security for such finance, is the key question. The World Bank, its subsidiary IFC or some of the regional developments banks are often involved in larger projects of national interest, together with international banks and the national ECAs from the supplier nations. But the final solution for the project finance will inevitably be as complex and tailor-made as the project itself.

Due to the cost and work involved, UK projects backed by ECGD, or some other government body, should usually have a minimum support value of £20 million, but the credit periods may be up to 14-years with highly flexible loan structure and amortisation periods. Some other requirements are that the support should be given as senior debt and a risk sharing on an equal basis with other lenders.

It is not within the scope of this handbook to elaborate more on this often highly complex area, but more information about project finance and the criteria and preconditions for participation from the ECAs in project finance transactions can be obtained directly from ECGD.

■ 7.4.2 Joint ventures

In many developing countries and/or emerging market countries, the seller could also be asked to participate as co-owner of the project, or even be required to do so in order to get the contract. The buyer may have many reasons for such a request and government authorities may even have it as a requirement of the successful bidder for giving import licences or currency approvals. But, in other cases, it could even be advantageous for the seller and their future business prospects with a particular buyer or with the long-term goal of establishing a permanent base and a competitive advantage in the country or region.

Box 7.4   Business opportunities

One of the practical services offered by UK Trade and Investment, the government organisation that supports companies in the UK conducting business internationally and overseas enterprises seeking to locate in the UK, is **Business Opportunities Services**. This is a free internet-based system matching UK businesses with international business opportunities gathered by the Government's network of British Embassies, High Commissions and Consulates worldwide.

To benefit from this service, UK businesses need to register on the website (www.uktradeinvest.gov.uk) and profile themselves to receive opportunities relevant to their products/services from specific markets around the world. UK customers have the added option of being alerted by e-mail, if they wish, when new opportunities come in to match their profile.

The information is divided into the following categories:

- Specific Private Sector Opportunities
  Specific export sales opportunities; it also includes enquiries from overseas agents and distributors looking for UK principals.

- Tenders/Public Sector Opportunities
  Public and private tender opportunities, including invitations to pre-qualify.

- Joint Venture, Invest, Co-operative Partnering
  Opportunities
  Details of overseas opportunities for manufacture under licence, joint ventures, or to co-operate in production, management, finance, investment and distribution.

- Multilateral Aid Agency Opportunities
  Details of overseas agreements proposed or approved by the Multilateral Funding Agencies.

- Market Pointers
  Early notification of potential opportunities overseas.

See **www.uktradeinvest.gov.uk** for more information.

The buyer may hope that a joint venture will give not only capital or equity advantages, but could also see the benefits of technical know-how and management along with the international marketing expertise which an international partner can contribute. The authorities can also look for potential advantages in the form of a widened infrastructure, additional exports and the creation of new jobs.

The establishment of a joint venture often requires significant management resources from the seller and it may take years before the advantages can be seen and, before that, many legal, cultural and management differences may have to be solved. On the other hand, many host nations clearly see the advantages of joint ventures and can back them in many ways through local support or market benefits. Today, most countries accept foreign majority ownership as well as foreign management, which may increase the potential value for the international company of such ventures but also mitigate any potential internal frictions.

In order to facilitate the creation of joint ventures in the developing countries, the World Bank and in particular its IFC (*see section 7.5*), participate actively in assisting such joint ventures or partnerships. Many industrialised countries have also established similar corporations on a smaller scale in order to promote and/or support companies from their own country in forming such joint ventures in primarily the developing countries.

In order to support UK overseas long-term investments, amongst other in joint ventures, ECGD can provide insurance cover to UK companies and investors against the political risks on loans and equity, or on a guarantee given for these purposes, or directly to banks that have given or arranged such loans. This program, Overseas Investment Insurance scheme (OII), is described later in this chapter.

➤ 7.5 Multilateral development banks

Over many years, a number of multilateral and regional development banks have been established, with the main purpose of supporting projects vital for the economic development within the region. The best known of these institutions is no doubt the World Bank with headquarters in Washington and its International Development Association (IDA), which participates in lending to the poorer developing countries on 'soft terms'.

The IFC, which is also part of the World Bank Group, is active in promoting projects for the development of private industry by participating as shareholder or lender in joint ventures or projects vital to the country, and with reasonably good prospects. The World Bank Group also includes the Multinational Investment Guarantee Agency (MIGA), guaranteeing the political risks for investments and projects in many developing countries.

A number of regional development banks were also set up, based on the same principles as the World Bank, but with a more regional purpose. That is the African, Asian, Inter-American and Islamic Development Banks and their development funds for lending on 'soft terms' to projects of special importance for regional development. These institutions also have finance agencies similar to the IFC-model to promote the private industry within their regions.

The development banks not only participate in projects as a lender or a guarantor but frequently also, and more directly, in feasibility studies and promotion of the project itself, even as co-arranger. Their involvement often takes place together with international banks and ECAs from the exporting countries, but also in cooperation with local governments, which often are the borrowers or the guarantors of the loan. This will give these projects a high political and financial priority within the country and an added reassurance to co-partners, suppliers and creditors that they will be financially secured, not only during the construction phase but also during the entire repayment period.

The development banks can only cater for a small part of the finance requirements from the developing countries, therefore, they have also contributed to the development of different forms of leveraged finance, such as co-joint or parallel financing techniques with other

---

Box 7.5   Some larger regional development banks

Regional development banks are important for promoting and supporting larger international trade transactions and projects in their respective regions, and more information about their activities can be found on the web-sites listed below.

It is recommended that the seller trading in the areas covered by these institutions do study these web-sites, since they often give indirect valuable information and links to other local institutions that could be of interest.

African Development Bank (AfDB)
www.afdb.org

African Development Fund (AfDF)
www.afdb.org

Asian Development Bank (ADB)
www.asiandevbank.org

Asian Development Fund (ADF)
www.asiandevbank.org

European Bank for Reconstruction and Development (EBRD)
www.ebrd.com

European Investment Fund (EIF)
www.eif.org

European Investment Bank (EIB)
www.eib.org

Inter-American Development Bank (IDB/BID)
www.iadb.org

International Bank for Reconstruction and Development (IBRD) World Bank
www.worldbank.org

International Development Association (IDA) World Bank
www.worldbank.org/ida

International Finance Corporation (IFC), World Bank
www.ifc.org

Islamic Development Bank
www.isdb.org

Multinational Investment Guarantee Agency (MIGA), World Bank
www.miga.org

Nordic Investment Bank
www.nib.int

sources of finance, for example, international major commercial banks, special export banks and aid agencies from industrialised countries.

The development banks have a high international rating due to their ownership, capitalisation and proven financial record and are therefore often able to offer their borrowers even better than market terms, for example, through lower interest rates and longer repayment periods.

The projects supported by the development banks are often very attractive and therefore, competitive for potential suppliers, not least since they receive cash payment through the financing arranged by the banks. The rules for tender for projects financed by or through the development banks may vary but, in principle, they all require open and international tenders. The UK exporter can monitor these tenders and projects through the services provided by UK Trade & Investment, see *Box 7.4*.

It is not within the framework of this book to describe these development banks in detail, additional information can be found on their websites, as shown in Box 7.5. It should however be mentioned that many industrialised countries have special schemes for combining foreign aid with subsidised credits for projects in the poorest countries, often also supported by the regional development banks.

These combined aid and subsidised credits will result in particularly good terms for the borrower, far beyond the best market terms available, but are generally given only in conjunction with deliveries of goods from their own country. Even if practised by some other industrialised countries, the UK Government has long since taken a strong stance against this form of 'tied aid finance', involving aid elements in a finance offer which only supports the industry of a particular country, due to its negative effects on competition on equal terms and its distortion of the pattern for free international trade.

■ 7.5.1 *European Bank for Reconstruction and Development (EBRD)*

The EBRD (established in London 1990) is a development bank with a somewhat different profile than the other development banks and will be described in greater detail since it is probably more relevant for many UK suppliers and overseas investors. The bank is owned by the member countries of the OECD but also by many emerging market countries and has a capital base of not less than EUR 20 billion.

The bank primarily covers countries from central Europe to central Asia, including many former Soviet republics. From its sources, the goal is described as follows:

'To provide financing for banks, industries and businesses, both in new ventures and investments in existing companies. It also works with publicly owned companies, to support privatisation, restructuring state-owned firms and improvement of municipal services... and promote policies in these countries that will bolster the business environment'.

The EBRD is the largest single investor in the markets in which it operates, and even if its core business is the finance of larger projects – the bank has committed more than 20 billion to more than 800 single projects – it is involved in many other areas as well. It participates in co-financing and in this way facilitates domestic funding for other financial institutions or banks, and by supporting local commercial banks, equity funds and leasing consortiums, the bank is involved in more than 200,000 smaller projects since it started some 25 years ago.

Apart from the role of supporting projects and individual local banks, the EBRD also has an important role in supporting international trade in general, both imports and exports, through its Trade Facilitation, 'TF-Programme'. Through this programme, described below, it provides credit facilities in the form of guarantees in favour of international banks, covering the political and commercial risk of the local bank or buyer in the region.

When negotiating for contracts in these countries, the commercial parties may together contact the EBRD or the buyer's bank, to request support for the potential transaction. Through its TF-programme, the bank is an important risk provider in these countries, which has already benefited a number of UK export transactions. Potential UK

INFORMATION BOX

European Bank
for Reconstruction and Development

The trade facilitation programme

The EBRD's Trade Facilitation Programme promotes foreign trade with central and eastern Europe and the CIS-countries. Through the programme, the EBRD provides guarantees to international confirming banks. In so doing, it takes the political and commercial payment risk of transactions undertaken by issuing banks in the countries where the EBRD operates. The programme can guarantee any genuine trade transaction associated with exports from, imports to, and between the EBRD's countries of operations. Over 80 issuing banks in the Bank's region of operations participate in the programme together with about 500 confirming banks throughout the world.

The programme is an excellent business development tool. It provides:

- cover for a broad range of trade finance instruments
- unconditional guarantees payable on first written demand
- guarantees of up to 100 per cent of the face value of the underlying trade finance instruments
- uncommitted trade finance lines and transaction approval on a case-by-case basis
- attractive fee levels that are agreed separately for each transaction
- a fast and simple approval procedure to issue guarantees
- short-term loans to selected local banks for on-lending to local exporters and importers

Guarantees may be used to secure payment of a number of finance instruments issued or guaranteed by issuing or confirming banks for trade transactions. These guarantees cover a wide range of goods and services, including consumer goods, commodities, equipment, machinery, and construction as well as technical and other services.

For more information contact

EBRD

One Exchange Square, London EC2A 2JN   Telephone 020 7338 6000,
Trade Facilitation Programme Email: tonnay@ebrd.com

www.ebrd.com

sellers or suppliers should be aware of the possibilities the EBRD can offer when exporting to these countries, not only in the form of projects, but also for more ordinary trade transactions.

■ 7.5.2 The European Investment Bank (EIB)

The EIB is the European Union's long-term financial institution and is, as such, both an EU institution and a bank. Its primary purpose is to finance capital investments in the member states and candidate countries, but also to support the EU's external partnerships and development policies. Even though 85 per cent of its lending is to member or candidate states, the remainder is spread to many countries in Africa, Latin America and Asia, who have a special relationship with the EU or are important to its trade and investment structure.

The EIB's basic financial facilities are venture capital and individual loans or structured finance facilities for larger or medium-sized new projects and for upgrading existing infrastructure with parts, new technology or increased capacity, with credit periods of 4 to 20 years. For member states, these facilities can also be supplemented by venture capital or guarantees, funded through its own fund, the European Investment Fund (EIF).

The EIB also finances loans for small and medium-sized enterprises (SMEs) through Global Loans to countries outside the EU. This scheme has a structure where a domestic bank or financial institution, mainly located in developing countries, can receive a line of credit under which they are mandated to extend credits for eligible purposes as defined by the EIB. The required purposes for such loans are defined within a broad spectrum of the infrastructure and industrial sectors in the country, targeted on the part-finance of investments, works, goods or services, undertaken by private companies with EU interest, such as subsidiaries or joint venture. These lines cover single deals from EUR 40,000 and upwards, and have resulted in thousands of individual transactions each year.

The support given by the EIB as project loans or under the Global Loans is not directly focused on facilitating EU trade, even though many such trade transactions related to investment goods from EU suppliers are financed by the EIB, directly and indirectly, through its 'EU-interest' clause. But, in all its financing, the EIB also verifies a fair process of international tendering and non-discrimination to its member states and their companies, an important element in many cases where otherwise such discrimination to the disadvantage of EU suppliers might have taken place.

The EIF is the risk capital arm of the EIB Group. Its main objective is to support the creation, growth and development of SMEs, and also to support the emergence of a performing and homogenous European venture capital market.

➤ 7.6 Investment Insurance

This form of insurance covers events such as confiscation, expropriation, nationalisation or deprivation of the investor's fixed or mobile assets. The cover can also be extended to include war, civil war, strikes, riots, terrorism, regulatory changes, currency inconvertibility, business interruption, and the inability to recover leased equipment. This cover can be obtained from both the private insurance market sector and from ECGD. Due to its considerable proportions and its importance for UK investors and suppliers, this book will describe the ECGD scheme below – but the structure of the market sector alternatives are, however, relatively similar.

The ECGD scheme is called Overseas Investment Insurance (OII), and is in short a risk cover against certain political risks in connection with UK overseas investments (whereas the commercial risk is up to the UK investor/supplier to assess and to cover separately, if needed). However, the cover can extend to breach of contract, where the host government or a local authority causes the underlying reasons.

The scheme provides cover for:

- UK overseas direct investments as shareholder equity, loans or guarantees;

- bank loans to an overseas company with UK interest, when used for investment or purchase of UK goods;
- bank portfolio loans in some cases, even without UK interest.

The OII has, over time, become very important for UK investors and stands now for almost 25 per cent of ECGD's total business volume (approximately £700–800 million per year). The investors are often UK export companies creating production, storage or sales facilities abroad to strengthen the business opportunities in the region.

The scheme covers long-term investments, individually as low as £20,000, with a cover for up to 15 years, under which period of time the investor can apply for annual renewals at unchanged terms and conditions, including premiums, even if the situation in the country deteriorates. At the same time, the investor must take the long view on the investment in order to benefit from the cover, with an *intended* investment period for at least three years, or in the case of loans, with the same duration.

The cover not only includes the normal political risks such as transfer of currency, war, civil war, expropriation, etc. mentioned above, but could also include the indirect consequences in case such events damages or prevents normal business operations related to the investment.

8

Terms of payment

➤ 8.1 Terms of payment and cash management

Through the terms of payment, the objective of both parties is to optimise the outcome and profitability of the transaction within the
framework of an established and acceptable risk level. However, from the
seller's perspective, the terms of payment can also be used as an additional sales argument to strengthen their competitive edge, in the same
way as in other parts of the contract. This makes it important to understand the structure of terms of payment and how they could be used in
conjunction with guarantees, different forms of finance solutions and
separate export credit risk insurance. Such a framework also raises the
question of how to use the capital resources in the most efficient way?
Anyone who controls these matters, will be a better negotiator and will be
more able to conduct a more profitable business.

In most cases, effective cash management means minimising the use of
capital, whilst using the resources available to support the core business of the company. However, good cash management could
therefore, for example, also involve the seller offering the buyer a
medium-term supplier credit to be more competitive, providing the
risk structure is controlled and that such credit is needed to obtain the
contract.

Effective cash management could also include the seller taking the decision to delay, restructure or cancel a transaction if the risk structure is above an acceptable level, for example, if the buyer is not fulfilling part of the contract through a late or incorrect issuing of a L/C. This is why the structure and wording of the terms of payment are so important – particularly when things are not developing according to plan and when both parties are scrutinizing the wording of the terms of payment. There must never be any doubt as to how the seller, for example, can or may act in different situations without risk of damages, callings under guarantees or other actions taken by the buyer.

It is through the correct structuring of the terms of payment, in conjunction with any additional security arrangement that both parties should be able to determine, in advance and with a high degree of accuracy when, where and how payment will be made. That will also determine what capital resources are needed during the different phases of the transaction, which is the basis for all cash management, particularly in international trade (compared with domestic business) where some risk elements are more difficult to evaluate.

The different structures of practical terms of payment shown below must of course be adjusted to the individual preconditions in each case. When the dates of payment can be established within a narrow timescale, they can also be incorporated into the payment flow of the company in advance, with optimal effect on its liquidity planning for both parties – making the necessary capital need easier to calculate and finance, and any currency risk easier to cover.

The following text has been presented with a deliberate bias towards the seller's perspective, mainly due to the special risk structure that the seller usually has to cover through the terms of payment. However, this simplification also ensures that the text is generally more accessible so that both UK exporters and importers can formulate individual terms of payment based on their own perspective and preconditions.

➤ 8.2 Contents of the terms of payment

When negotiating with the buyer, the seller needs to determine the detailed terms of payment to be included in the contract. This can be a complicated process in which, initially, both parties could have different views. The terms of payment are often among the remaining areas to agree.

In order to enter the negotiations it is essential to have enough prior knowledge about the details of the terms of payment and what minimum requirements the seller must adhere to in order to maintain the expected level of security. The minimal requirements for the terms of payment are as follows:

- when payment should take place (time of payment);
- where payment should take place (place of payment); and
- how payment should take place (method of payment).

In the case of several payments, each part has to be treated as a single terms of payment – this also applies to guarantees issued under the contract.

■ 8.2.1 Time of payment

The seller and buyer may have different views on when payment should take place:

- The buyer may want to make the best use of a competitive situation by having the seller also finance the purchase through a shorter or longer-term supplier credit at attractive terms.
- The seller would probably prefer payment on delivery or with a shorter deferred payment covering the shipping period.

The negotiations will determine at what time the payment will take place, or in case of larger contracts or longer contract periods, when the different part payments should take place – both before and after delivery – mostly along with the larger part payment on delivery.

However, the possibility of offering supplier credits has become increasingly important as a sales argument. Even with smaller transactions it is quite normal to offer short-term credit for 60–90 days (which also covers the period of transportation). When dealing with larger transactions, both the seller and the buyer have a common interest to have the deal financed through a third party, often separate bank-to-bank or bank-to-buyer credits. This will give the seller cash payment on delivery while the buyer gets bank financing (often on better terms than what they could have achieved on their own) which could at best also wholly or partially balance the cash flow generated from the purchased goods.

The size of the transaction, the delivered goods and the length of the discussed credit and the security for it, will finally decide what credit terms can be offered and may bridge the gap between the different views of time of payment.

■ 8.2.2 Place of payment

The question of where payment should take place has to be defined, since it determines the fulfilment of the obligations of the buyer. This also relates to what form of payment is used. L/Cs are normally payable either at the Issuing or the Advising Bank, which means that the respective bank takes responsibility for transferring the payment to the seller – but only after the documents have been approved.

The situation is similar when a documentary collection is used as a method of payment – the difference being that the buyer in this case has fulfilled their obligations when paying or accepting a Bill of Exchange against the documents at the collecting bank. It is then up to this bank to transfer the payment according to the instructions from the seller.

In the relatively few cases when payment by cheque is agreed upon, it has to be made clear whether the seller accepts a commercial cheque or only a bank cheque (often also referred to as a Banker's draft). It is up to the parties to decide if the buyer's obligations are fulfilled when the cheque has been sent, when it has been received by the seller or when it has been cleared in the banking system and the payment is available to the seller in cleared funds. This includes the question of who has to cover the postal risk, should the cheque be delayed or even lost.

In the case of a bank transfer, the place of payment has to be decided by the parties involved. The seller wants the payment to be received by their bank before accepting that the buyer has fulfilled the payment obligations, whereas the buyer can find equally that that is the case when having paid the amount at their local bank. For payments within most OECD countries, this may only be a matter of 2–3 days difference, with the reliable and fast international transfer systems most banks operate in these countries through the SWIFT-system. However, there are also other reasons why the place of payment should be clearly defined.

Irrespective of the transfer system used, the payment out of a country might also be dependent on currency regulations or be delayed by other reasons, such as incorrect handling or slow practices in general, bank strikes or other forms of *Force Majeure*, or simply insufficient or incorrect payment instructions from the buyer.

The question of where the buyer fulfils the payment obligations in connection with open-account payment terms is always a matter the parties have to agree on. If no such agreement is made, disputes may arise later on, and may then have to be decided by the applicable law. In most countries, it is the law that the debt should be paid at the domicile of the creditor, which is the seller. It is, therefore, also in the buyer's interest that the place of payment is stated in the terms of contract, particularly with larger amounts, when every interest day may be of importance. The place of payment should, in most cases, be defined as being at the premises of the seller's chosen bank, and proper IBAN and BIC codes (see *Chapter 2, Section 2.2.2*) should be included in the terms of payment to secure an accurate and rapid transfer.

Box 8.1 Some useful time definitions in the terms of payment

To avoid future disputes it is important that all timely events in the terms of payment are related to certain clearly defined points on the time axis of a contract.

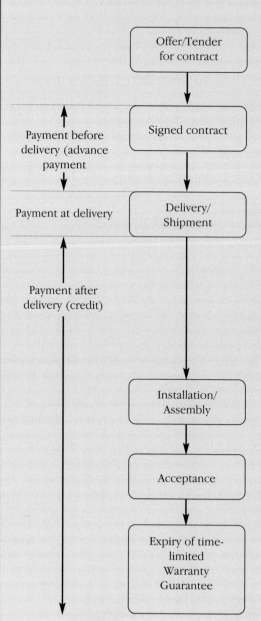

The contract date is often the starting point for calculating the timing of the advance payment, issuing the L/C and for delivery.

The shipment date is often defined through the date of the Bill of Lading or other shipping documents. The shipment date (or average shipment date in case of several deliveries), is normally the starting point for credit periods or deadlines for installation or final completion or acceptance.

The acceptance of delivery, installation, test period, completion or any other contractual obligation is often the starting point for any Warranty Guarantee.

■ 8.2.3 Methods of payment

How payment is made is dependent on the role of the banks involved and affects the security offered to both the buyer and the seller. As described in *Chapter 2, Section 2.1*, payments can, in principle, be divided into two main categories, 'clean payments' and 'documentary payments'.

Clean payments (bank transfers and bank or corporate cheques) are primarily used when the parties have agreed on open-account payment terms (see definition in *Chapter 2, Section 2.2*), meaning that the buyer has to pay according to the contract after receiving the seller's invoice specifying the payment date. With the absence of any other security for payment offered by the buyer, it is obvious that the clean payments (or rather the bank transfers) are regularly used within industrialised countries and/or in conjunction with other security, for example, credit insurance.

Documentary payments are, on the other hand, used in situations other than those mentioned above, when the need for additional security is greater, whether the underlying reason is the buyer, their country or the nature or size of the individual transaction. The documentary payments are divided into documentary collections (bank collections), when the buyer has to pay or accept a Bill of Exchange in order to obtain access to the shipping documents or L/Cs, where the seller also is guaranteed payment if the documents presented are in accordance with the terms of the L/C.

➢ 8.3 Structure of the terms of payment

Based on what has been written about when, where and how a payment is to be made the parties can, in principle, design many different combinations. Examples of some frequently used terms are given in this section, showing what they should contain, as a platform for adapting them further, according to the specific situation.

However, no examples are given for the use of cheques, the reason

Box 8.2   Detailed country information

Before deciding the detailed terms of payment that should be proposed in each particular case, the seller should try to get the best background information possible about the buyer and the economic and political structure in the importing country. Particularly in emerging economies or developing countries, the main risk is often both political and commercial and the terms of payment have to be structured accordingly.

Country information can be bought from specialised credit report companies, but another source of detailed information can be obtained free of charge from UK Trade & Investment from their website **www.uktradeinvest.gov.uk** (*see* also Introduction).

This website contains information, country by country, on most aspects that are important to the potential seller:

- country profile and key facts;
- market profile — visiting and social;
- customs and regulations;
- selling and communications;
- main export opportunities;
- the public procurement market;
- export related events;
- connections to other trade-related websites;
- new regulations/requirements on imports;
- local contact information.

For each country there is a specific contact to which the seller may turn for additional information or advice. This information, together with the additional banking, financial and insurance experience obtained from larger commercial banks and global credit risk insurers, form a solid background when deciding on the terms of payment in an individual transaction.

Informative country information can also be obtained from the larger export insurance companies, for example, Coface, through their country rating, which can be found on **www. trading-safely.com** (for more information on Coface see the Information Box in *Chapter 5*).

being that this form of payment is not that frequently used in international trade (apart from smaller advance payments, where they are often used) and has no main advantage over a bank transfer. Should, however, payment through corporate cheques be allowed by the seller (as is sometimes practised by some large buyers due to its cash management advantages) this has to be agreed on a case-by-case basis between the parties, and then follow the basic structure of the bank transfer, as shown in *Box 8.3*.

■ 8.3.1 Bank transfer (bank remittance)

To ensure that the payment shall have been received by the seller's bank at maturity, it is up to the buyer to arrange the payment through their local bank some days prior to this date. The possibility of receiving overdue interest for shorter periods is often limited in practice, but the mere mentioning of it could have a positive affect on a timely payment. (See also *Section 8.3.2* below, where the open account transaction is secured by a separate bank guarantee)

Box 8.3 Structure of terms of payment in open account trading

'Payment through bank transfer, which shall have reached (*name and address of the seller's chosen bank — with full details of the BIC and IBAN codes*), not later than 90 days from date of invoice, which shall be the same as the date of shipment. Interest on arrears at $x\%$ p.a. is charged from maturity date until payment is received.'

■ 8.3.2 Bank guarantee

As an additional security to the open-account sale (without using the documentary forms of payment), the terms of payment could stipulate that the buyer should arrange a bank guarantee covering the payment obligations according to the contract – particularly if the transaction includes a longer supplier credit.

A bank guarantee has to be issued under the existing credit limits with the buyer's bank, but it should, in reality, come without any additional risks for the buyer (in case of a conditional guarantee), providing they fulfil the payment obligations already agreed.

Such a clause could have the following wording in the terms of payment:

Box 8.4   Structure of terms of payment combined with a bank guarantee

---

'The buyer has to arrange a payment guarantee issued by . . . (*the name of the buyer's bank*) for £15,500 in favour of the seller, covering the buyer's payment obligations according to contract . The guarantee shall be advised through . . . (*the name of the seller's bank*) and shall have reached that bank not later than 30 days from date of contract and be valid for 30 days from last delivery as stipulated in the contract.'

The above wording, referring to the underlying sales contract, makes it a conditional guarantee, payable only after the applicant's approval (the buyer in this case) or after the Issuing Bank has been satisfied that the buyer has defaulted in the contractual payment obligations.

■ 8.3.3 Documentary collection (bank collection)

By specifying the chosen collection bank at the buyer's location in detail, as the example below indicates, the documents could often be sent directly to this bank by the seller's bank without delay.

Unless the buyer's bank is not a particularly small local bank, it is normally advantageous for the seller to agree on using the buyer's main bank, where the buyer might also have to give good reasons for unduly delaying the payment or acceptance. However, it should also be advantageous for the buyer to have the documents sent directly to their own bank.

> **Box 8.5 Structure of terms of payments based on docu-
> mentary collection**
>
> ---
>
> 'Payment through documentary collection at first presentation of documents through *(complete name and address of the chosen bank at the domicile of the buyer, where the documents should be presented)*.
>
> Payment should be effected against presentation of the following documents:
>
> - at sight Bill of Exchange drawn on ... *(the buyer)*;
> - invoice in three copies;
> - certificate of UK origin;
> - insurance policy, covering ... *(value and risks)*;
> - full set clean on board Bill of Lading, blank endorsed.
>
> All collection charges (alternatively, bank charges outside the UK) are to be paid by the buyer. Interest on arrears $x\%$ p.a. will be charged on overdue payments and is to be paid together with the documents.'

The expression 'clean on board' in a Bill of Lading is a standard expression indicating that no damage or defective condition of the goods or their packing could be noticed at the time of loading. As a document of title, it should also be endorsed in blank or to any other party as per instructions of the buyer.

It is important to agree in advance which documents the buyer needs and it is up to the buyer to decide if additional details should be included in the terms of payment. For example, latest shipping date, port of loading and destination in the Bill of Lading, or endorsement instructions for the shipping and insurance documents. However, overly detailed specifications are not necessarily beneficial for the seller who might want some flexibility in shipment and documentation details (whilst still adhering to the stipulations in the contract).

Box 8.6   Summary of the structure of the terms of payment

Listed below is the basic structure of some of the most commonly used terms of payment, grouped in order of their advantage to the seller.

TERMS OF PAYMENT	COMMENTS
A: Payment before delivery	
1. Without advance payment guarantee.	1. Gives the highest security for the seller.
2. Against contractual advance payment guarantee.	2. As above, based on due fulfilment of the contract.
3. Against an 'on demand' advance payment guarantee.	3. Gives less security for the seller.
B: Payment at delivery	
1. Letter of Credit, documents against payment.	1. High security — dependent on the strength of the Issuing Bank – and if confirmed or not.
2. Documentary collection, document against payment.	2. Dependent on the buyer honouring the documents — and which documents are included.
C: Payment after delivery	
1. Letter of Credit, documents against acceptance.	1. Same security as **B** but with later payment.
2. Payment secured by payment guarantee.	2. The security is dependent on the Issuing Bank and the wording of the guarantee.
3. Documentary collection, documents against acceptance.	3. As **B** above, but after release of documents, the risk is on the buyer until payment.
4. Bank transfer.	4. Risk on the buyer until payment.

■ *8.3.4 Letters of Credit*

In most cases it is satisfactory to specify the terms of payment as shown in *Box 8.7* below, as long as there is a clear reference to the underlying contract. The same comments to the documents apply as for a documentary collection, detailed in *Box 8.5*.

The L/C is often issued is such a way that it may at first glance appear to be in accordance with the contract, but nevertheless contains minor details that could make it difficult for the seller to totally comply with its terms – or create uncertainty if that will later be the case. The seller should, therefore, have the right to have amendments made in order to be able to comply with the terms of the L/C, as long as they do not violate the contract.

Box 8.7 Structure of terms of payment based on a Letter of Credit

'Payment through an irrevocable Letter of Credit, payable at sight with and confirmed by ... *(the agreed Advising Bank)*. The Letter of Credit shall be issued by ... *(the agreed Issuing Bank)* and shall have reached the Advising Bank in form and substance acceptable to the seller in accordance with the contract, not later than 60 days from the date of the contract.

The Letter of Credit, which must give reference to the contract number and date, shall be valid for three months and be payable against the following documents:

* at sight Bill of Exchange, drawn on the Advising Bank
* invoice in three copies;
* packing list;
* certificate of UK origin, issued by ...;
* full set of clean on-board marine Bill of Lading, blank endorsed and showing ... *(shipping date, ports, etc.)*.

Partial shipments and transhipments are not allowed. Bank charges outside the UK are to be paid by the buyer.'

Detailed examples of Letters of Credit are found in Chapter 2, Box 2.15 and 2.16.

■ 8.3.5 The importance of timing in connection with Letters of Credit

Both the detailed agreement about the L/C as well as the subsequent handling of documents require a high degree of consideration and knowledge in order for the seller to obtain the advantages and security upon which the transaction is based.

Unfortunately, it is very common for buyers, particularly in developing countries, to vastly underestimate the time it takes to get all the necessary approvals and permissions in order for the Issuing Bank to issue the L/C. This delay will immediately affect the seller and the planning of production and delivery. At some point in time a decision may also need to be taken between having to take additional costs without having the security on which the transaction is based, or to postpone the production, delivery or some other obligations in the contract, which could jeopardize the whole deal.

With this in mind, it is crucial that all time limits and other delivery variables agreed by the seller are based not on the date of the contract but on the time when the seller has received and approved the L/C and other conditions to be met by the buyer, and that their own obligations will only come into effect when this is achieved.

➤ 8.4 Composite terms of payment

With larger and often more complex transactions over longer periods, it is normal for the payment to be divided into part-payments in order to satisfy both parties. The combination of the size of the transaction and the time period between first delivery by the seller to final acceptance by the buyer could otherwise lead to unacceptable risk and liquidity consequences for both parties.

The risk for the seller increases through the nature of the product and the size of the transaction, particularly if the goods are tailor-made with a long timescale between production and final delivery. However, the buyer will in these cases also take an increased commercial risk in case of payment before the final acceptance of the delivery. The terms of payment that are built around these transactions will, therefore, follow the sequences of the contract itself, from contract date, production and delivery periods, installation, test runs, acceptance by the buyer and final warranty periods. Such terms are also often combined with different forms of guarantees, covering both the seller's and the buyer's mutual obligations during this period.

With regard to machinery and equipment, it is relatively common that both the payment before delivery and on/after completion varies between 10–15 per cent in order to achieve a reasonable balance between the parties, with a main payment at delivery of about 75 per cent.

As can be seen from the example in *Box 8.8 below*, the seller has agreed to a non-confirmed L/C, which would indicate satisfaction with the credit standing of the Issuing Bank and the political risk in that country. In this example, the parties have also agreed to let a separate inspection company have the final say when the last payment is to be released, which will also be the time when the seller has fulfilled their contractual obligations. Separate instructions have to be given to the inspection company to carry out such an inspection.

In the example in Box 8.9 below, the bills will, when released, not be covered by the Letter of Credit, but by a separate guarantee by the Issuing Bank, issued directly on the bills. It can also be presumed that the seller has an additional firm offer from a bank or a forfaiting house to discount the bills without recourse to them at their release. However, the wording of the terms of payment must always be checked against such offer so that the seller can be absolutely sure that all conditions can be met when presenting the bills for discounting.

Box 8.8 Structure of a simple composite terms of payment

'10% of the contract value through bank transfer to be received by... *(the Advising Bank below)* not later thank 30 days from contract. The amount is to be paid to the seller against an advance payment guarantee issued by the Advising Bank in favour of the buyer, according to the text *on page xx in the contract.*

75% of the contract value on delivery through irrevocable Letter of Credit, payable at sight with ... *(the agreed Advising Bank).* The Letter of Credit shall be issued by ... *(the agreed Issuing Bank)* and shall have reached the Advising Bank in form and substance acceptable to the seller in accordance with the contract, not later than 45 days from the date of the contract. The Letter of Credit, which must give reference to the contract number and date, shall be valid for 3 months and be payable against the following documents:

- at sight Bill of Exchange, drawn on the Advising Bank
- invoice in 3 copies;
- packing list;
- certificate of UK origin, issued by ...
- full set of clean on-board marine Bill of Lading, blank endorsed and showing ... *(shipping date, ports, etc.).*

The Letter of Credit shall permit partial shipments and tranship-ments.

15% of the contract value upon signed installation certificate, issued by ... *(the name of a control and inspection company agreed by the parties)* to have reached ... *(the Advising Bank)* not later than 30 days from such signing.'

All bank charges outside the UK are to be paid by the buyer.

Box 8.9 Structure of composite terms of payment combined with a long-term supplier credit

'5% of the contract value before delivery, through a bank transfer which shall have reached ... *(the Advising Bank below)* not later than 30 days from contract date. The amount shall be paid to the seller against a conditional advance payment guarantee in favour of the buyer, issued by that bank.

10% of the contract value at delivery through an irrevocable Letter of Credit, payable at sight with ... *(the agreed Advising Bank)*. The Letter of Credit shall be issued by ... *(the agreed Issuing Bank)* and shall have reached the Advising Bank in form and substance acceptable to the seller in accordance with the contract, not later than 45 days from the date of the contract. The Letter of Credit shall be valid for 3 months and be payable against the following documents:

- at sight Bill of Exchange, drawn on the Advising Bank
- invoice in 3 copies;
- packing list;
- certificate of UK origin, issued by ...;
- full set of clean on-board marine Bill of Lading, blank endorsed and showing ... *(shipping date, ports, etc.)*.

The Letter of Credit shall permit partial shipments but not tranship-ments.

85% of the contract value after delivery through 10 Bills of Exchange, of the same amount and half yearly due, drawn on and accepted by the buyer, avalized by ... *(the Issuing Bank)* and provided with a transfer guarantee by the *Central Bank of* ... The bills shall be placed in deposit with *(the Advising Bank)* at the same time as the Letter of Credit is issued. In each bill is to be included interest at x% p.a. calculated up to its final maturity.

The bills shall be fully negotiable and payable in the UK, and the Letter of Credit should contain irrevocable instructions that the bills are to be released to the seller when 90% of the value of the Letter of Credit has been disbursed. Before releasing the bills, the Advising Bank shall provide the bills with the seller's verified signature and blank endorse-ment but also with the respective date of maturity, the first bill maturing 6 months after the date when 90% was disbursed under the Letter of Credit and the rest maturing successively semi-annually thereafter.'

All bank charges outside the UK are to be paid by the buyer.

➢ 8.5 The final design of the terms of payment

The main purpose of the terms of payment is to establish the payment obligations of the buyer including when and how these obligations occur in relation to the seller. This risk analysis has been thoroughly dealt with in earlier chapters, along with the function of the terms of payment and also the liquidity aspects and the capital requirements needed for the conclusion of the transaction.

In reality there are, of course, other main factors that must be considered, including the payment practices in the importing country; the knowledge and earlier experience of the buyer and his business; and the competition the seller can expect to face in winning the contract.

These aspects together with the details of the actual transaction, will finally help the seller decide which terms of payment they should include in the offer or propose in the negotiations. Yet the terms of payments are only one aspect of the contract that has to be negotiated. Both parties will value all these parts differently and have to be prepared to compromise on certain questions.

The final structure and design will, therefore, also be dependent on the seller's evaluation of the importance of the deal and its potential profitability compared to the risks involved. When doing so, it will also test their ability to cover these risks through the terms of payment combined with available guarantees and insurance. The seller who has this knowledge will be able to make both better, more profitable and more secure international business transactions.

■ 8.5.1 Make use of the experience of the banks and other export institutions

In practice, previous experience is important when preparing risk assessments and when deciding on both the method of payment and the detailed terms of payment but it is equally important to know the normal payment practice in different countries. The banks have a comprehensive network of branches, subsidiaries, affiliates or

---

Box 8.10 Terms of payment in the quotation

SUNDALE ALARMS LTD

123 Sundale Road, Birmingham BS1 123
Registered: 012345670

Date	**Reference**
2005-06-18	Q 3203/HA

Your date	**Your reference**
2005-06-10	AC 201/TH

Attending to this matter
S Sayers

LAMJASSA MOHAMMED ED FILS
Attn: Mr. Kihal Sherif
17, Rue Mekki Ali
ALGER
Algeria

Quotation for Alarm Systems

Dear Mr. Sherif,
We refer to your letter of June 10, 2005 and want to make you the following offer for our Alarm Systems, type Soundstrong 1300, subject to a detailed contract documentation.

You will find a complete technical description in enclosure No. 1, which is the same as the one given to Mr. Ali El-Bakr when he was visiting us this spring.

Quantity: 300 units Soundstrong 1300 with standard equipment according to enclosure No. 1.

Price: USD 175 per unit, including standard equipment.

General terms: See enclosure No. 2.

Delivery terms: C & F Alger, Incoterms 2000

Terms of payment: Payment through irrevocable at sight Letter of Credit in USD, issued by Banque Extérieure d'Algerie, Alger within 30 days from order and payable at and confirmed by the UK Commercial Bank Ltd, London. The Letter of Credit shall be valid for 2 months after our acceptance of the L/C terms. All bank charges outside the UK are to be paid by the buyer.

Delivery terms: Shipment from the UK within 1 month from receipt of approved Letter of Credit.

Packing: The goods are packed for export with 10 units per carton and 10 cartons per wooden case.

This quotation is valid until July 18, 2005. We hope it will be of interest to you and look forward to receiving your order.

Yours faithfully,

SUNDALE ALARMS LTD

Roger B Staines   Stephen Sayers

correspondents in most countries, along with a constant flow of international payments and documentary transactions that pass through their businesses every day. That gives them a good picture of how different payment methods work in different countries, but also what experiences other sellers have had – surprisingly few sellers take the opportunity to make full use of this experience.

The final general advice is, therefore:

- Do not hesitate to ask for help from your bank or one of the companies or institutions participating in this handbook – they will be pleased to advise you.
- If you are uncertain, ask for assistance in the detailed design of the terms of payment.
- For those companies that do not have enough knowledge or expertise in international trade, make use of the Education, Training and Business Information services that are available through The Institute of Export.

Trade financial glossary of terms and abbreviations

This glossary contains most of the trade finance related words and expressions used in this handbook or directly related to its contents. In order to make the content less complicated and more precise, the comments are made from the point of view of the seller unless stated otherwise.

Where entered, the numbers within brackets refer to the corresponding chapters and sections in the text.

A

Acceptance	Time draft accepted by the drawee, thereby creating an unconditional obligation to pay at maturity.
Acceptance Letter of Credit	A Letter of Credit, which requires the seller to draw a term draft to be accepted by the Nominated Bank upon presentation of documents, whereby the seller receives a Banker's Acceptance instead of payment. **(2.5.2)**
Advance payment	Trading method where the seller receives payment before delivery, either as part of an agreed composite payment structure or due to low or unknown creditworthiness of the buyer.**(6.2)**
Advance Payment Guarantee	Undertaking on behalf of the seller to repay the buyer in case of non-fulfilment of their contractual obligations. **(3.2.1)**

Advances	Payments made available by a third party to the seller earlier than at maturity date, often secured by the underlying trade documents. See also Discounting and Invoice discounting. **(6.2)**
Adverse business risks	Negative, corrupt and unlawful business practices related to international trade, ie, bribes and money laundering. **(1.4)**
Advising Bank	A bank, usually in the seller's country, which authenticates the Letter of Credit and advises it to the seller. **(2.5)**. The expression is also used when a bank authenticates a bank guarantee in favour of the beneficiary. **(3.1.2)**
Air Waybill (AWB)	Transport document in airfreight as a receipt of goods and evidence of the freight agreement. AWB is not a document of title and is not needed to claim the goods. **(2.4.1)**
All risk insurance	A common insurance clause in policies to be presented under collections and Letters of Credit.
Amendments	Alterations to the original instructions in a collection, or of the original terms and conditions in a Letter of Credit. The seller has the right (in an irrevocable Letter of Credit) to refuse such amendments. **(2.5.11)**
Annuities	Lease payments, based on a combination of interest and amortisations of the underlying financial costs. **(7.2)**
Applicant	The party at whose request a bank issues a Letter of Credit. Sometimes also called account party. **(2.5)** See also Principal.
Assignment	A method where the seller transfers the rights of proceeds, often under a Letter of Credit, to a third party.
At sight	A notation on a draft (Bill of Exchange), indicating that it should not be accepted but paid upon presentation. Often used in collections and Letters of Credit. **(2.5.2)**
Avalise (Aval)	Where a guarantor, often a bank, issues its guarantee directly on an accepted Bill of Exchange or other financial instrument, thereby undertaking the payment obligations with the drawee on a joint and several basis. Other terms are Bill Guarantee and Guaranteed Acceptance. **(3.2.2)**
Availability	A Letter of Credit may be available for presentation of documents against payment at sight, deferred

payment, acceptance or negotiation. See these terms. **(2.5)**

B

B/L	See Bill of Lading.
Back-to-back Letter of Credit	An arrangement where the seller offers an existing Letter of Credit as security to their bank for the issuance of a secondary Letter of Credit in favour of their supplier(s). **(2.5.5)**
Balance exposure	An often unrealised currency risk exposure within the company, reflecting different methods of calculating assets and debts for accounting purposes. **(4.3)**
Bank Cheque	Cheque issued by a bank and sent directly by the buyer to the seller as a method of payment. **(2.3)** Also often referred to as a Banker's Draft.
Banker's Acceptance	A time draft drawn on and accepted by a bank, often in connection with a Letter of Credit. See also Acceptance Letter of Credit.
Banker's Draft	See Bank Cheque
Bank Guarantee	An unconditional undertaking by a bank, on behalf of the principal to pay a certain amount in money to the beneficiary under certain conditions. **(3.1)**
Bank-to-bank Credit	A buyer credit given by a third party (often the seller's bank) to the buyer's bank for on-lending to the buyer to pay cash to the seller for goods delivered. **(6.6 & Box 6.6)**
Bank-to-buyer Credit	A buyer credit given by a third party (often the seller's bank) directly to the buyer to pay cash to the seller for goods delivered. Such credits normally demand a corresponding guarantee from the buyer's bank, covering the obligations of the buyer. **(6.6 & Box 6.6)**
Bank identifier Code (BIC)	The same as the SWIFT-address and used as identification of accounts, often in connection with bank transfers. **(2.2.2)**
Bank remittance	See Bank transfer.
Bank transfer	The most common method of payment where the only role of the banks is to transfer funds according to payment instructions by the buyer. Also called Bank Remittance. **(2.2 & Box 2.4)**
Barter trade	Trade of goods and services without the use of money. **(2.6)**
Bid Bond	See Tender guarantee.

Bill of Exchange	Commonly used trade financial instrument, drawn up by the seller and, after acceptance by the buyer, being an unconditional payment obligation to pay at a specified future date. Also called Draft. **(2.4.3 & Figure 2.2)** A bill is often referred to as a 'draft' until it has been accepted.
Bill Guarantee	See Aval/Avalise.
Bill of Lading	Transport document issued by the carrier for shipment by sea. The Bill of Lading is a document of title, which means that the goods will not be released to the buyer (the consignee) other than against this original document. **(2.4.1)**
Blank endorsement	A transfer of rights without specifying the new party, making the document, usually a Bill of Lading or an insurance policy a freely negotiable document. **(2.5.10)**
Bond	A synonym to guarantee — which is the term generally used in this book. **(3.1.1)**
Bond (Guarantee) Indemnity Insurance	The general term for an insurance cover against the risk for 'unfair calling' under a Demand Guarantee. **(5.2.6)**
Bond Insurance Policy (BIP)	The standard ECGD insurance covering 'unfair callings' under contract guarantees issued on behalf of the seller. **(5.4.2)**
Break-even Price	The currency price needed at maturity in order to make the currency option profitable — calculated on strike price, premium and commission, if any. **(4.4.5)**
Business Opportunities Service	A free internet-based information service, offered by UK Trade & Investment, matching UK businesses with international business opportunities. **(Box 7.4)**
Buyer Credit	Any arrangement where a third party, usually a bank, in agreement with the seller, refinances the transaction, giving the credit directly to the buyer or their bank for direct cash payment to the seller. **(6.6)**

C

Call option	A term used in connection with currency options, where the UK exporter purchases a GBP Call option to hedge the incoming currency. **(4.4.5)**. The opposite is a Put option —see that term. See also Currency options.

Cap and floor	A currency hedge technique, whereby the currency risk is restricted to an upper and lower limit. **(4.4.8)**
Capital goods	Industrial durable goods used for production of other goods for consumption, a distinction important in connection with credit risk insurance. **(5.2 & 5.4)**
Cash cover	A term used when the Applicant of a Letter of Credit is required to deposit money in favour of the Issuing Bank as security.
Certificate of origin	Verifies the origin of the goods delivered. Often issued by a Chamber of Commerce in the seller's country. **(2.4.3)**
Charter party Bill of Lading	A special form of a Bill of Lading issued by the vessel owner, which may restrict its nature as a document of title (not normally allowed under a Letter of Credit).
CIS-countries (Commonwealth of Independent States)	A political grouping of 11 former smaller Soviet states, included in the programmes of support from the European Development bank. **(7.5.1)** See also EBRD.
Claim Document	The document giving evidence for a claim to be presented under a Bank Guarantee. **(3.3)**
Clean Bill of Lading	A Bill of Lading without indication that goods are damaged and/or in unsatisfactory order at the time of loading. **(2.4.1 and 8.3.2)**
Clean collection	Collection in which only a financial instrument is included, often the Bill of Exchange. **(2.4.3)**
Co-joint financing	A form of leveraged finance between development banks, commercial banks and Export Credit Agencies in order to increase the scope for additional projects and investments in developing countries. **(7.5)**
Collection accounts	Accounts held by the seller in banks in other countries to be used for incoming payments from buyers in that country. **(2.2.4)**
Collection Bank	Bank in the drawee's country, which is instructed to release documents to the buyer (the drawee) against payment or acceptance. Also called Presenting Bank. **(2.4)**
Combined Transport document	See Multimodal Transport Document. Such a document may or may not be a document of title. **(2.4.1)**

Commercial documents	A general term for documents produced in connection with the delivery of goods or services, as compared to Financial documents — see that term. **(2.4.3)**
Commercial Interest Reference Rates (CIRR)	The minimum level for state-supported fixed interest rates according to the Consensus rules. See Consensus. **(Box 6.6)**
Compliant Documents	Documents presented which fully comply with the terms and conditions of the Letter of Credit. **(2.5.11)**
Composite terms of payment	An expression used in this book when payment is to be effected in separate tranches related to the underlying structure of the commercial transaction. **(8.4)**
Commercial risks	Also called purchaser risks, covering not only the possibility of non-payment by the buyer, but also the risk for non-fulfillment of all other contractual obligations, including those necessary for the seller's own performance. **(1.3)**
Commitment	In connection with Letters of Credit, banks undertaking in advance to the seller to confirm Letters of Credit, which may be issued by certain banks during a specified period of time, usually against a fee. **(2.5.4)**
Compensation trade	The sale of goods and services with payment often in a combination of money and other goods. **(2.6)**
Conditional guarantee	See Demand guarantee.
Confirmation	A procedure whereby a Confirming Bank, normally upon the request of the Issuing Bank, assumes towards the seller the liability for payment, acceptance or negotiation of correctly presented documents under a Letter of Credit. **(2.5.4)**
Confirming Bank	The bank confirming the Letter of Credit to the seller. See Confirmation.
Complex cover	The extent of cover (more comprehensive) in a guarantee issued by ECGD, extended to banks in a buyer's credit. **(6.6.1)**
Consensus	Guidelines issued by OECD establishing a common practice for the use of state-supported export credits. **(Box 6.6)**
Consignee	The party to whom goods are to be delivered, usually the buyer, the Collecting Bank or the Forwarding agent. **(2.4.1)**

Consignor	The party who delivers the goods to the consignee according to a freight agreement. **(2.4.1)**
Contract CIRR	A form of state-supported interest rates. See Consensus. **(Box 6.6)**
Contract Frustration Policy	See Contract Repudiation Indemnity.
Contract Guarantees	Guarantees directly linked to the course of events in an underlying commercial contract. **(3.2.1)**
Contract Repudiation Indemnity	Credit insurance covering the political risks of changed or revoked approvals by an authority in the buyer's country, preventing the transaction from being correctly performed. Also called Contract Frustration Policy. **(5.2.6)**
Convertible currencies	Currencies that can easily be exchanged against the main international currencies on a free and unrestricted market. **(4.1)**
Corporate cheque	A cheque issued by the buyer and, in the context of this book, sent to the seller as a method of payment. **(2.3)** See also Bank cheque.
Correspondent Bank	Banks in other countries with whom UK banks have account relationships or arrangements to verify signatures or authentication. **(1.3.1)**
Counter Trade	The sale of goods where the transaction is dependent on a corresponding purchase of other goods within a common framework. **(2.6)**
Credit Guarantee	Undertaking by a bank to guarantee any credit, loan or other obligation assumed by a subsidiary or affiliate of the principal or any third party, not capable of entering into the obligations on their own merits. **(3.2.2)**
Credit Insurance (Credit risk Insurance)	Insurance against loss due to the inability or unwillingness of the buyer to pay for goods delivered. Credit risk insurance may cover a variety of risks, both commercial and political. See also these terms. **(5.1)**
Cross border leasing	An expression used in lease transactions, when the lessor and the lessee are located in separate countries. Also a general expression for larger, more complicated leasing transactions using tax rules advantages in different countries. **(7.2)**
Cross rate	The price of one currency in terms of another as calculated from their value against another major traded currency. **(4.2.1.1)**
Currency accounts	Accounts held by the seller in foreign currency with

	their bank in order to balance currency flows/transactions without unnecessary currency exchanges. **(4.4.3 & Box 4.8)**
Currency clauses	The use of special agreements between buyer and seller in order to cap or split the currency risk between the parties during the period from firm offer to contract date or invoice payment. **(4.4.8)**
Currency exposure	The real currency risk affecting the liquidity position, to which the company is exposed at any period of time. **(4.3)** See also Balance exposure and Payment exposure.
Currency hedges	Methods of minimising currency risks and/or currency exposure. **(4.4)**
Currency options	A currency hedge different from a forward contract since the currency option is a right, not an obligation, to buy/sell one currency against another at a fixed rate within a specified period of time. **(4.4.5)**
Currency pegging	Officially or unofficially determined fixed or capped rates for the currency of one country against another currency, often the USD. **(4.1)**
Currency position schedule	The comprehensive schedule over the company's total currency risk exposure, containing both fixed and anticipated risks. **(4.3.1)**
Currency risk	The risk connected to invoicing in a foreign currency, which, when payment is received, may result in a lower amount in GBP than anticipated. **(4.3)**
Currency spread	The difference between the bid and offered rate quoted by banks in a freely-traded foreign exchange market. **(4.2.1.1)**

D

D/A	Abbreviation for 'documents against acceptance'.
D/C	Abbreviation for Documentary Credit, synonymn for Letter of Credit (which is the expression used in this book).
D/P	Abbreviation for 'documents against payment'.
Default	Failure to pay an accepted financial instrument on maturity date or to perform any agreed contractual business obligation.
Deferred payment	Payment made to the seller at a specified date after shipment or presentation of documents under a

	Letter of Credit, but without the use of a draft accepted by a bank. See also Acceptance Credit. **(2.5.2)**
Demand guarantee	Undertaking by a bank to pay to the beneficiary the amount on first demand without their proving the right to the claim and without the consent of the principal. **(3.3)**
Development banks	Regional and mostly well-capitalised banks, owned by the participating countries, which support projects vital for the economic development of that region. **(7.5)**
Development funds	Regional and mostly well-capitalized funds, subsidiaries of the development banks, that lend on 'soft terms' to projects of special importance for regional development. **(7.5)**
Direct export factoring	An arrangement where the seller's factoring company (the factor) has direct contact with the buyer without the use of a local correspondent. **(6.5)**
Direct guarantee	A guarantee issued directly to the beneficiary by the seller's Bank without using a local Issuing Bank. **(3.1.2 & Box 3.2)**
Discount rate	An expression often used when the forward exchange rate of a currency is lower than its spot value (the opposite is a Premium rate). **(4.5)**
Discounting	The purchase (with or without recourse) of an accepted termed (usance) Bill of Exchange against an amount less than its face value. **(2.5.2)**
Discrepancies (in documents)	Non-presentation, non-consistency or other reasons why documents may not be approved under a Letter of Credit. **(2.5.10)**
Documents against acceptance (D/A)	When the buyer is requested by the Collection Bank to accept a termed Bill of Exchange that accompanies the documents instead of payment at sight. **(2.4)**
Document against payment (D/P)	When the Collection Bank notifies the buyer about the documents for collection and requests them to pay the amount at sight as instructed by the seller's bank. **(2.4)**
Documentary collection	Where banks, acting on behalf of the seller, present documents for collection to the buyer against cash payment or acceptance. **(2.4)**
Documentary Credit	See Letter of Credit.

Documentary payments	A general reference to the two main documentary methods of payment, documentary (bank) collections and Letters of Credit. **(2.1)**
Document of title	Transport document where the carrier undertakes not to release the goods other than against this original document. See also Bill of Lading. **(2.4.1)**
Double insurance	Where the seller takes a subsidiary transport insurance, should the buyer not fulfil their contractual obligation to insure the goods. **(1.2.2)**
Draft	Synonym for Bill of Exchange. **(Figure 2.2)** Draft is the term often used in connection with Letters of Credit. See also Bill of Exchange.
Drawee	Party on whom the Bill of Exchange is drawn and who is required to pay at sight or accept the bill. **(2.4.2)**
Due date	Maturity date for payment.
Duty-exempt Guarantee	Undertaking by a bank, on behalf of the principal, to pay any Customs duty for goods intended to be only temporarily brought into the country, but not brought out within the specified period. **(3.2.2)**

E

EES-countries (European Economic Space)	A definition of European countries comprising more than the EU-states. **(2.2.2)**
European Bank for Reconstruction and Development (EBRD)	The EBRD is a development bank, supporting countries from central Europe to central Asia, including many former Soviet republics. **(7.5.1)**
The European Investment Bank (EIB)	The EIB is the European Union's long-term financial institution for finance of capital investments in member states and promoting international trade and investment. **(7.5.2)**
Export Credits Guarantee Department (ECGD)	The ECGD is the UK's official Export Credit Agency. **(5.4)**
EU-payments	Bank transfers between most European countries, made in a specific format and according to rules stipulated by the EU. **(2.2.2)**
Endorsement	Transfer of rights on a trade or a financial instrument, mostly made on the back of the document. See also Blank endorsement
Exchange rate index (ERI)	An index published by the Bank of England, showing the value of GBP expressed in terms of a

	currency basket, determined by the commercial trade of goods and services. **(4.2.1.1)**
Exercise price	See Strike price.
Expiry clause	A clause in a bank guarantee, limiting its duration. **(3.5.2)**
Expiry date	The expiry date under a Letter of Credit is the last date at which the seller can present documents to the Nominated Bank. **(2.5)**
Export Credits	Credits that the exporter offers the buyer for sale of goods or services or credit given by third party to finance such transactions **(5.1 and Box 5.1)**
Export Credit Agencies (ECAs)	Government owned or supported insurance institutions focusing on export risk cover for sellers/suppliers from that country. **(5.3)**
Export loans	Advance payments by banks, based on the security of a Letter of Credit, up to a certain percentage of the L/C amount. **(2.5.13)**
Export Insurance Policy (EXIP)	The standard ECGD insurance to the seller, covering commercial and political risks. **(5.4.1)**
Export Factoring	A method of short-form refinancing where the factoring company (the factor) purchases the seller's receivables and assumes the credit risk, either with or without recourse to the seller. **(6.5)**
Export leasing	Medium-term export finance facility for machinery, vehicles and equipment in particular, with the legal right for the lessee to use the goods for a defined period of time but without owning or having title to them. **(7.2 & Box 7.2)**
Export risks	Risks that may affect the individual export transaction and which the seller must evaluate and cover prior to the execution of the contract. **(1.1.2 & Box 1.1)**
Express payments	Urgent payments through the SWIFT-system, making the transfer available to the seller quicker than normal payments, but at a higher fee. **(2.2.3)**
Extend or pay	Where the beneficiary threatens to claim under a demand guarantee unless it is prolonged. **(3.5.3)**

F

Facilitation payments	A form of corrupt practice in international trade where payments are made to officials or employees in the buyer's country or elsewhere in order to smoothen, hasten or facilitate the contract. **(1.4)**

Factor	Synonym for factoring company, see Export Factoring.
Financial documents	Documents related to the financial aspect of the transaction and the payment, (ie, a Bill of Exchange) as compared to the commercial documents.
Financial lease	An arrangement where the practical risk of ownership rests with the lessee and where the lessor, from the outset of the lease, expects to recover from the lessee both capital cost of the investment as well as interest and profit during the period of the lease. **(7.2)** The opposite is Operating lease – see that term.
Financial risks	An expression for increased financial, liquidity and cash management impacts as a consequence of entering into a new commercial transaction. **(1.7)**
First demand guarantee	See Demand Guarantee.
Force majeure	Various specified conditions, including 'Acts of God' which cannot be avoided through due care by the commercial parties and therefore may excuse them from performance. **(1.5.1)**
Forfaiting	Purchase of negotiable trade financial instruments, mostly avalised Bills of Exchange, without recourse to the seller. See also Avalise. **(6.3.3)**
Forward (exchange) contract	A contract between the seller and the bank, in one currency expressed in terms of another currency at a rate fixed at contract date with execution at a future date. **(4.2)**
Forward exchange market	The market for currency exchange transactions with delivery at a future date, but with the rate determined at transaction date. **(4.2)**
Forward option contracts	Forward (exchange) contracts that can be settled within a period of time instead of at a fixed date. (Not to be mistaken for a Currency Option, see that term). **(4.4.4)**
Forward points	The trading technique in the inter-bank forward exchange market, where rates are expressed and quoted as differences in points from the spot rates. **(4.2.2.1)**
Forwarding Agent's Certificate of Receipt (FCR)	Transport document indicating receipt of goods from the seller and the arrangement of transportation according to instructions. It is not a document of title. **(2.4.1)**

Freely negotiable	A statement, often in a Letter of Credit, giving the seller the right to present the documents for negotiation at any bank.**(2.5.3)**
Full set	Documents (often the Bill of Lading) with more than one original, where all originals shall be presented (often under a Letter of Credit or collection).

G–H

Global Loans	EIB line of credit facilities to local domestic banks, mainly in developing countries, under which they are mandated to extend credits for international trade transactions. **(7.5.2)**.
Guarantee	See Bank Guarantee.
Guaranteed Acceptance (Aval)	The undertaking of a bank, on behalf of the buyer (the drawee), to guarantee an accepted Bill of Exchange or Promissory Note, either directly on the bill or note (Aval) or through a separate guarantee. **(3.2.2)**
Hard currency	The currency of a nation with economic strength and a long-term reputation for currency stability, which results in a high acceptability in international trade and currency markets. **(4.1)**
Hedge	An expression used for reducing outstanding currency or interest risks or fluctuations through compensating transactions.

I

IDA	The International Development Association (IDA), part of the World Bank, provides long-term interest-free loans and grants to the poorest developing countries. **(7.5)**
IFC	IFC, International Finance Corporation, a member of the World Bank Group, is the largest multilateral source of loan and equity financing for private sector projects in the developing world. **(7.5)**
International Bank Account Numbers (IBAN)	A fixed bank account numbering standard, according to EU rules, often used in connection with bank transfers. **(2.2.2)**
International Chamber of Commerce (ICC)	The world's only truly global business organisation, based in Paris. They are also the issuing institution of generally accepted rules governing guarantees, documentary collections and Letters of Credit. **(1.1)**

Import licence	Document issued by authorities in the buyer's country in order to control or restrict the importation of goods. **(2.4.3)**
Incoterms	International accepted trade delivery clauses (*Incoterms 2000*) issued by International Chamber of Commerce (ICC). **(1.1.3)**
Indirect guarantee	A guarantee issued to the beneficiary (often the buyer) by a local Issuing Bank based on a Counter Guarantee from an Instructing Bank. **(3.1.2 and Box 3.2)**
Inspection certificate	Frequently used document where an independent third party verifies the quality, quantity or other aspects of the goods prior to shipment, in most cases upon instruction from the buyer. **(2.4.2)**
Instructing Bank	The bank forwarding instructions on behalf of the Principal to a local bank (the Issuing Bank) to issue a guarantee in favour of the Beneficiary. **(3.1.2)**
Inter-bank currency market	The market(s) established between major commercial and international banks for dealing in currencies (spot and forward), thereby also establishing inter-bank currency market rates. **(4.2)**
Inter-bank money market	The market(s) established between major commercial and international banks for dealing in short term loans and deposits in most trade currencies, thereby also establishing inter-bank money market rates. **(7.1)**
Interest Make-up	An ECGD arrangement, whereby officially supported fixed interest rates can be given to the borrower, where such support may be available according to Consensus rules. **(6.6.)**
Interest swap	An arrangement with a third party, usually a bank, where a commercial party wanting to hedge the interest rate, agrees to exchange (swap) floating into fixed interest rate, or vice versa, during a fixed period of time. **(7.1)**
International leasing	See Cross Border Leasing.
Intrinsic Value	Term used in connection with currency options and describes the amount, if any, which could be realised if the option was to be sold at spot market rate. **(4.4.5)**
Investment insurance	A form of insurance covering a number of long-term political risks, potentially affecting the value or performance of an overseas investment. **(5.2.6)**

Invoice discounting	Arrangements for provision of finance against the security of trade receivables, usually with recourse to the seller. See also Advances. **(6.4)**
Irrevocable Letter of Credit	A Letter of Credit, which cannot be cancelled or amended during its validity without the approval of all parties concerned. **(2.5.1)**
ISP 98	International Standby Practices, rules covering Standby Letters of Credit, issued by the International Chamber of Commerce. **(3.4 and Box 3.8)**
Issuing Bank	The bank issuing a Letter of Credit on behalf of the Applicant (the buyer). Also called the Opening Bank. **(2.5.4)**. The expression is also used when issuing a Bank Guarantee on behalf of the Principal. **(3.1.2 and Box 2.12)**

J–K–L

Joint and several guarantees	The normal form of bank guarantee, where the Beneficiary, at their discretion, can claim either the Guarantor or the Principal.
Joint ventures	Arrangements in primarily many developing and/or emerging countries, where the seller participates as co-owner in a project or in a larger export scheme to and within the local country. **(7.4.2)**
Jurisdiction	The place agreed on in contracts and financial instruments where disputes, if any, should be settled legally. **(3.5.1)**
Key Customer Risk Insurance	Insurance policies covering and capping the outstanding risk on certain key risks in the seller's export ledger. **(5.2.7)**
L/C	Abbreviation for Letter of Credit.
Legalisation	Certification of documents, normally done by an official or appointed representitive of the buyer's country. **(2.5.8)**
Lessee	The contractual end user of the machinery/equipment in a lease contract. **(7.2)**
Lessor	The owner and contractual counterpart to the lessee in a lease transaction. **(7.2)**
Letter of Credit (L/C)	A method of payment whereby an Issuing Bank upon instruction from the buyer, authorises the seller to draw a specified amount of money against the presentation of compliant documents within a specified time period. Often also called Documentary Credit. **(2.5)**

Letter of indemnity	A bank guarantee issued on behalf of the buyer in favour of the shipping company against their delivering of the goods without presentation of the original Bill of Lading. **(3.2.2)**
Letter of Support, Letter of Comfort or Letter of Awareness	Different forms of undertakings, but not in the form of a guarantee, normally issued by a parent or group company, indirectly supporting credit or other obligations assumed by subsidiaries or affiliate companies. **(3.2.2)**
London Interbank Offered Rates (LIBOR)	The inter-bank money market in London for trading in short-term loans and deposits in the most traded currencies, thereby establishing this market's lending interest rates. **(7.1)**
Lines of Credit	Arrangements by eligible UK banks establishing ECGD guaranteed credit lines with local banks in mostly developing countries, to be used for financing of small and medium-sized UK export transactions. **(7.3.1)**
Local currency finance schemes	Arrangements, whereby local banks can arrange local finance supported by ECGD guarantees, to be used for the financing of UK exports. **(7.3.2)**

M–N–O

Master Letter of Credit	The term for the original Letter of Credit, based on the security of which a second Letter of Credit is issued. See also Back-to-back L/C and transferable L/C. **(2.5.5)**
Matching	The offering of government supported credit risk insurance cover to suppliers in one country on the same terms as offered by other government agencies to their exporters. **(5.3)**
Maturity	Due date for a term Bill of Exchange or other financial instrument. **(Figure 2.2)**
Method of payment	The agreed form of payment to be used by the buyer, either open account payments through bank cheque or bank transfer, or by documentary collection or a Letter of Credit. **(2.1)**
Money laundering	A process, also carried out in connection with international trade, through which the proceeds of criminal activity are disguised to conceal their actual origins. **(1.4)**
Multimodal Transport Document	Transport document evidencing shipment of goods by more than one means of transportation. **(2.4.1)**

Negotiable document or instrument	A document or financial instrument where rights and obligations are freely transferable to another party. **(6.3.3)**
Negotiation	Purchase of drafts under a Letter of Credit by the Negotiating Bank, which the Issuing Bank has undertaken to reimburse, however, often with recourse to the seller until documents are finally approved by the Issuing Bank. **(2.5.3)**
Negotiating Bank	The bank authorised by the Issuing Bank to negotiate compliant documents under a Letter of Credit. See also Negotiation. **(2.5.3)**
Nominated Bank	An expression used in the ICC rules for a bank authorised by the Issuing Bank not only to negotiate but also to pay or to accept drafts as the case may be. **(2.5.3)**
Non-compliant documents	Where the documents presented, or their details, are not in accordance with the terms and conditions of the Letter of Credit. **(2.5.10)**
Non-convertible currencies	Currencies not traded freely on an international currency market, often restricted by internal regulations and currency controls. **(4.1)**
Non-negotiable documents/ instruments	Documents or financial instruments where rights and obligations are not freely transferable to another party.
Non-tariff barriers	A general phrase describing non-regulated and often disguised barriers to international trade, mostly practised by individual countries to protect own trade or industry. **(1.5.1)**
Non-recourse financing	See Project Finance.
Notify party	The party who is to be informed by the carrier about the arrival of goods at the destination.
Noting	The first stage in protest of a dishonoured Bill of Exchange.
Ocean/Marine Bill of Lading	See Bill of Lading.
Organisation for Economic Co-operation and Development (OECD)	An international state organisation helping governments to implement common economic and social solutions globally and establishing common rules for government support of trade and industry. **(5.3)**
On board Bill of Lading	Notation on the Bill of Lading that the goods have been loaded on board the ship. Often a requirement in the Letter of Credit. **(8.3.2)**

'On their face'	An important expression when dealing with documents and Letters of Credit, indicating that banks examine the presented documents with reasonable care, but without responsibility for their accuracy or genuineness. **(Box 2.17)**
Open account (payment terms)	Payment terms often including a short-term suppler credit, extended to the buyer at shipment without any written evidence of indebtness. **(2.2)**
Opening bank	Expression sometimes used instead of (Letter of Credit) Issuing Bank. **(Box 2.12)**
Operating lease	An arrangement where the lessee is using the equipment but the risk of ownership rests with the lessor who also retains a financial risk in the arrangement. **(7.2)**
On demand guarantee	See Demand Guarantee.
Outright forward rates	Another expression for forward exchange rates normally quoted to customers as compared to the forward points quotations between banks. **(4.2.2.1)**

P

Parallel financing	See Co-joint financing.
(The) Paris Club	An informal group of official creditors whose role it is to find co-ordinated and sustainable solutions to the payment difficulties experienced by debtor countries. **(5.3)**
Payment exposure	The currency exposure resulting from in and outgoing flows in foreign currency within the company, often reflecting the potential and real currency risk. **(4.3)**. The opposite is Balance exposure – see that term.
Payment Guarantee	Undertaking, normally in the form of a bank guarantee, on behalf of the buyer, to pay for the seller's contractual delivery of goods or services. **(3.2.2)**
Performance Guarantee	A common guarantee, covering the seller's delivery and performance obligations according to the contract. **(3.2.1)**
Points	The spread in the inter-bank currency market between the buying and selling rate **(4.2.1.1 and 4.2.2.1)**. See also forward points.
Political risks	The risk for a commercial transaction not being performed due to measures emanating from the

government or authority of the buyer's own or any other foreign country. **(1.5)**

Postal risks	The risk of cheques or documents not being received by the counterpart, with risk for non-performance and/or payment disputes and delays. **(2.3)**
Pour aval	See Avalise.
Pre-contract CIRR	See Consensus. **(Box 6.6)**
Premium	The up-front fee the buyer of a currency option pay to their counterpart, usually a bank, similar to an insurance premium. **(4.4.5)**
Premium rate	An expression often used when the forward exchange rate of a currency is higher than its spot value (the opposite is a discount rate). **(4.5)**
Presenting Bank	The bank presenting the documentary collection to the buyer and collect payment. See Collection Bank.
Pre-shipping finance	Finance earmarked for manufacturing or other costs for an export transaction until shipment, often based on the structure of the sales contract and/or supported by the chosen method of payment. **(2.5.13 & 6.2)**
Principal	Party instructing a bank in a collection or when issuing a guarantee. **(3.1.1)** See also Applicant.
Product risks	Risks, including manufacturing and shipping risks, which are related to the product itself, and which the seller has to evaluate and cover in order to be able to fulfil the contractual obligations. **(1.2)**
Progress Payment Guarantee	Undertaking on behalf of the seller to repay payments made by the buyer according to contract but where the buyer, because of the seller's non-fulfilment, cannot make use of the delivery until completion. **(3.2.1)**
Project finance	Finance arrangements for larger projects, generally based on the revenues of the project to a high degree, mostly secured on its assets and less on the creditworthiness of the buyer. Often called non-recourse financing. **(7.4.1)**
Promissory note	A form of financial instrument in international trade and mostly more detailed than a Bill of Exchange, where the buyer irrevocably promises to pay to the seller according to a fixed schedule. **(6.3 & Box 6.3)**

Protest	The formal procedure after noting of an dishonoured bill, where the notary public issues a formal protest, which can be used in legal proceedings.
Purchaser risks	See Commercial risks.
Put option	A term used in connection with currency options, where a company purchases a GBP Put option for a scheduled payment in foreign currency. **(4.4.5)**. The opposite is a Call option — see that term.

R

Rail Waybill (RWB)	Rail transport document as receipt for goods and evidence of freight agreement. RWB is not a document of title and is not needed to claim the goods. **(2.4.1)**
Recourse	The provision whereby a refinancing party reserves the right against the seller to reclaim any amount not paid by the buyer (drawee) on maturity date of the refinanced instrument. **(6.1-6.6)**
Red clause Letter of Credit	A Letter of Credit containing a clause that authorises the Advising or Nominated Bank to make an advance payment to the seller prior to delivery of conforming documents. **(2.5.5)**
Reduction Clause	A clause that automatically reduces the undertaking under a bank guarantee in line with the successive fulfilment of the obligations by the Principal or in any other way, stated in the guarantee. **(3.5.2)**
Reference Banks	Banks selected in a loan agreement to be used as quoting banks to establish the reference interest rates. **(7.1)**
Reference interest rates	The recognised money market rates for most trade currencies, established on an inter-bank market at a specific time during the day, or established in any other way as specified in a loan agreement. **(7.1)**
Repurchase agreements (A)	Trade in which payment is made through products, generated by the equipment or goods being delivered by the seller. **(2.6)**
Repurchase agreements (B)	Arrangements used in leasing transactions as additional security for the lessor, where the original supplier agrees to repurchase or arrange in some other way for the equipment in case of default of the lessee. **(7.2)**

Retention Money Guarantee	Undertaking on behalf of the seller to comply with any obligation after delivery such as installation, start up, etc, but where the buyer has already made payment. **(3.2.1)**
Revocable Letter of Credit	A Letter of Credit, which can be cancelled or amended during its validity period before presentation of documents, without the approval of the seller. **(2.5.1)** See also Irrevocable Letter of Credit.
Revolving Letter of Credit	A Letter of Credit that is automatically reinstated after each drawing, however, with some restrictions on total amount or number of reinstatements. **(2.5.5)**

S

Sight bill	See At sight.
Silent Confirmation	A confirmation of a Letter of Credit to the seller made by the Advising Bank or some other party, but without the instructions to do so from the Issuing Bank. **(2.5.4)**
Simple cover	The extent of cover given by ECGD in a guarantee to refinancing banks in a buyer credit. **(6.6.1)**
Soft currencies.	The opposite to hard currencies, see that term.
Spot exchange rate	The fluctuating market price of one currency expressed in terms of another currency, for immediate delivery. **(4.2.1.1)**
Spot market	The market for currency exchange transactions with delivery immediately or typically within two banking days. **(4.2.1)**
Standby Letter of Credit	As opposed to an ordinary commercial Letter of Credit, the Standby Letter of Credit is usually drawn on only in cases where the applicant fails to perform a specified obligation. The Standby Letter of Credit is often used as an alternative to a bank guarantee. **(3.4)**
Strike price	Also known as the exercise price, which is the stated price at which the holder of a currency option has the right to exercise the option at maturity **(4.4.5)**
Structured trade finance	In this book a reference to ad hoc trade finance techniques, often arranged by or through specialised financial institutions. **(7.2-7.6)**
Subsidiary insurance	See Double insurance.

Supplier credit	Arrangements where the seller is extending a fixed credit period after delivery to the buyer to pay for the goods, often but not necessarily evidenced by an accepted financial instrument. **(6.3)** See also Open account.
Supplier Credit Facility (SCF)	A guarantee issued by ECGD given to eligible UK banks, covering the refinancing of medium or long-term supplier credits. **(6.3.2.1)**
Surety bond	An undertaking from a third party, often an insurance or a surety company to pay a certain sum of money or under certain conditions with the alternative obligation to fulfil or arrange for the completion of the underlying commercial contract, should the Principal default in their obligations. **(3.1)**
Society for Worldwide Interbank Financial Telecommunication (SWIFT)	An international co-operative bank network for payments and messages. **(2.2.3)**

T

Tender exchange rate insurance	The use of insurance in order for the seller to cover the outstanding currency risk between the period of a firm offer until acceptance, if any, from the buyer. **(4.4.9 and 5.2.7)**
Tender Guarantee	Undertaking on behalf of the seller to stand by the offer/tender, should it be accepted. **(3.2.1)** Often also called Bid Bond.
Term Bill	Bill of Exchange to be paid at a later due date. **(2.4.2)**
Terms of delivery	The detailed terms and conditions agreed between the parties to govern the delivery of goods. The rules set by ICC, *Incoterms 2000*, are by far the most commonly used in international trade. **(1.1.3)**
Terms of payment	The complete terms and condition agreed between the commercial parties, related to the buyer's payment obligations, including the chosen method of payment. **(8.2)**
The trade facilitation programme	The EBRD's programme for promotion and support of foreign trade with central and eastern European and the CIS-countries. **(7.5.1)** See also these abbreviations.

Third party documents	Documents under Letters of Credit (and collections) issued by other parties where the seller must be certain these can be correctly issued for presentation under the Letter of Credit (or be included in the agreed collection documents) **(2.5.8)**
Trade practices	Established trade rules in a country or as agreed by the commercial parties. The rules set by ICC are by far the most commonly used in international trade. **(1.1)**
Trade refinancing	Any arrangement where the seller is using receivables or separate finance instruments to offload a trade credit given to the buyer. **(6.3.1.1)**
Transfer risk	Restrictions caused by government authorities, preventing the buyer from purchasing the foreign exchange for local currency and/or transferring the currency out of the country. **(1.5)**
Transferable Letter of Credit	Permits the seller to transfer under certain conditions the rights and obligations under the Letter of Credit to one or more of their suppliers. **(2.5.5)**
Transfer Guarantee	A separate undertaking issued by a Central Bank or authorised commercial bank, guaranteeing both the allocation and the transfer of foreign exchange out of the country. **(3.2.2)**
Two-factor export factoring	An arrangement where the seller's factoring company (the factor) makes use of a local factoring company for the direct contacts with the buyer. **(6.5)** See also Direct factoring.

U–V–W

Unconditional guarantee	See Demand guarantee.
Unconfirmed Letter of credit	The Issuing Bank always guarantees a Letter of Credit, but if unconfirmed, no other bank has the obligation to pay, accept or negotiate compliant documents when presented by the seller. **(2.5.4)**
Undertaking to provide guarantee	Undertaking to have the relevant guarantee issued if the offer is successful. Often issued by a parent or group company in support of a subsidiary. **(3.2.1)**
Unfair Calling	Claim by the beneficiary under a demand guarantee without having any contractual reason to do so. **(3.3)**

UCP	UCP 500, Uniform Customs and Practice for Documentary Credits. ICC rules for Letters of Credit. **(Box 2.18)**
URC	URC 522, Uniform Rules for Collection, issued by ICC. **(Box 2.10)**
URCG	URCG, Uniform Rules for Contract Guarantees, issued by ICC. **(Box 3.7)**
URDG	URDG Uniform Rules for Demand Guarantees, issued by ICC. **(Box 3.7)**
Usance Bill (or usance Letter of Credit)	An expression sometimes used for a term Bill of Exchange or Letter of Credit with a future payment date, thereby, extending the buyer a specified period of credit. **(2.4.3)**
Validity period	The period under which a guarantee, a Letter of Credit or any other similar undertaking will be honoured by the Issuing Bank. **(2.5.1)**
Value date	The execution date for foreign exchange contracts.
Warranty Guarantee	Undertaking on behalf of the seller, covering any contractual maintenance or performance obligations during a period of time after delivery or installation. **(3.2.1)**
(The) World Bank	The 'World Bank' is the name that has come to be used for the International Bank for Reconstruction and Development (IBRD) and the International Development Association (IDA), two of the United Nations specialised agencies. These organizations provide low-interest loans, interest-free credit, and grants to developing countries.
With/Without recourse	See Recourse.

Can't find what you are looking for?

The author welcomes any comments or suggestions for additional words or abbreviations to be included in the glossary.

Email: glossary@nordia.co.uk

Index